Activating the
Art Museum

AMERICAN ALLIANCE OF MUSEUMS

The American Alliance of Museums has been bringing museums together since 1906, helping to develop standards and best practices, gathering and sharing knowledge, and providing advocacy on issues of concern to the entire museum community. Representing more than 35,000 individual museum professionals and volunteers, institutions, and corporate partners serving the museum field, the Alliance stands for the broad scope of the museum community.

The American Alliance of Museums' mission is to champion museums and nurture excellence in partnership with its members and allies.

Books published by AAM further the Alliance's mission to make standards and best practices for the broad museum community widely available.

Activating the Art Museum

Designing Experiences for the Health Professions

By Ruth Slavin, Ray Williams,
and Corinne Zimmermann

ROWMAN & LITTLEFIELD
Lanham • Boulder • New York • London

Published by Rowman & Littlefield
An imprint of The Rowman & Littlefield Publishing Group, Inc.
4501 Forbes Boulevard, Suite 200, Lanham, Maryland 20706
www.rowman.com

86-90 Paul Street, London EC2A 4NE

British Library Cataloguing in Publication Information Available

Library of Congress Cataloging-in-Publication Data

Names: Slavin, Ruth, author. | Williams, Max R. (Max Ray), author. | Zimmermann, Corinne, author. | American Alliance of Museums.
Title: Activating the art museum : designing experiences for the health professions / by Ruth Slavin, Ray Williams, and Corinne Zimmermann.
Description: Lanham : Rowman & Littlefield, 2023. | Includes bibliographical references and index.
Identifiers: LCCN 2022050889 (print) | LCCN 2022050890 (ebook) | ISBN 9781538158548 (paperback) | ISBN 9781538158555 (ebook)
Subjects: LCSH: Art museums—Educational aspects. | Medical personnel—Professional relationships. | Museum outreach programs.
Classification: LCC N435 .S59 2023 (print) | LCC N435 (ebook) | DDC 708—dc23/eng/20221121
LC record available at https://lccn.loc.gov/2022050889
LC ebook record available at https://lccn.loc.gov/2022050890

♾️™ The paper used in this publication meets the minimum requirements of American National Standard for Information Sciences—Permanence of Paper for Printed Library Materials, ANSI/NISO Z39.48-1992.

For our children: Arthur and Corinne, Will, Ryan, Clyde, and Evan

Contents

Contents

Figures

COLOR IMAGES

Figure 1

Gustave Moreau, *The Young Man and Death*, 1856–1865, oil on canvas, 85 × 48½ inches (123.2 × 215.9 centimeters). Harvard Art Museums/Fogg Museum. Gift of Grenville L. Winthrop, Class of 1886, Photo © President and Fellows of Harvard College, 1942.186

Figure 2

Felix Gonzalez-Torres, *"Untitled" (Portrait of Dad)*, 1991, white mint candies in clear wrappers, endless supply. Overall dimensions vary with installation. Ideal weight: 175 pounds. Photograph by Ruth Slavin/Installation view *Come as You Are: Art of the 1990s* at the University of Michigan Museum of Art, October 16, 2015, to January 13, 2016. © Estate of Felix Gonzalez-Torres/courtesy Felix Gonzalez-Torres Foundation

Figure 3

Dawoud Bey, in collaboration with Dan Collison and Elizabeth Meister, *Theresa, South Shore High School*, 2003. Chromogenic print 40 × 50 inches (101.6 × 127 centimeters) and audio recording. The David and Alfred Smart Museum of Art, The University of Chicago; Commission. © Dawoud Bey, Photograph © 2022 courtesy of The David and Alfred Smart Museum of Art, The University of Chicago and Sean Kelly, New York

Figure 4

Robert Colescott, *Emergency Room*, 1989. Synthetic polymer paint on canvas, 7' 6$^1/_8$" × 9' 6$^1/_8$" (229 × 289.8 centimeters). Jerry I. Speyer and the Millstream Funds, Digital Image © The Museum of Modern Art/Licensed by SCALA / Art Resource, New York, 70.1991 © 2022 The Robert H. Colescott Separate Property Trust / Artists Rights Society (ARS), New York

Figure 5

Unidentified artist Indian, Uttar Pradesh, Mathura, *Standing Buddha Offering Protection*, Gupta period, late fifth century, red sandstone, 33$^{11}/_{16}$ × 16¾ × 6½ inches (85.5 × 42.5 × 16.5 centimeters). The Metropolitan Museum of Art, Purchase, Enid A. Haupt Gift, 1979

Figure 6

Rogier van der Weyden, *The Crucifixion, with the Virgin and Saint John the Evangelist Mourning*, c. 1460, oil on panel, left panel overall 71 × 36 $5/16$ inches (180.3 × 92.2 centimeters), right panel overall 71 × 36 $7/16$ inches (180.3 × 92.5 centimeters). Philadelphia Museum of Art, John G. Johnson Collection, 1917

Figure 7

Mequitta Ahuja, *Parade*, 2007, enamel on canvas, two panels, 96 × 160 inches (243.8 × 406.4 centimeters). Blanton Museum of Art, The University of Texas at Austin, Gift of Melanie Lawson and John F. Guess, Jr., in honor of Jeanne and Michael Klein, 2010 © Mequitta Ahuja 2007

Figure 8

Joan Mitchell, *White Territory*, 1970, oil on canvas, 111$3/8$ × 88 inches (282.9 × 223.5 centimeters). University of Michigan Museum of Art, Purchase assisted by Friends of the Museum of Art and a grant from the National Endowment for the Arts. Photograph by Charlie Edwards © Estate of Joan Mitchell/courtesy Joan Mitchell Foundation

Acknowledgments

We are grateful to be part of the adventurous and generous field of art museum education. Our colleagues go about doing amazing work in the world, modestly, and without the recognition they deserve. When we think of museum professionals who have inspired and joined us in this work with the health professions, we think with warm appreciation of Barbara Bassett, Lorena Bradford, Elizabeth Benskin, Peggy Burchenal, Rika Burnham, Sara Egan, Brooke DiGiovanni Evans, Michelle Grohe, Linda Friedlaender, Francine Healy, Elizabeth Manekin, Siobhan McCusker, Carrie McGee, Hollis Mickey, Judy Murray, Bonnie Pitman, Sam Ramos, Pamela Reister, Francesca Rosenberg, Jessie Schlosser Smith, Hope Torrents, Grace Vandervliet, Akiko Yamagata, and Philip Yenawine.

We are deeply grateful to the healthcare colleagues who have given us entry into their world, and from whom we have learned so much. Our close colleagues and partners in the health professions include Nadaa Ali, Grace Huang Amadi, Swati Avashia, Kamna Balhara, Nan Barbas, Mary Blazek, Elizabeth Buzney, Christine Celio, Meg Chisolm, Ellen Clemence, Linda Delaporta, Paul DeSandre, Liz Gaufberg, Janet Gilsdorf, Cheryl Giscombe, Sharon Gold-Steinberg, Holly Gooding, Stephanie Hoffman, Joel Howell, Jennifer Huang, Clay Johnston, Joel Katz, Erin Kelleher, Mrinalini Kulkarni-Date, Julia Langley, Beth Miller, Sarah Mills, Alejandro Moreno, Patricia Moyer, Liz Powell, Mariah Quinn, Laura Rice-Oeschger, Anita Rubin-Meiller, Allie Ruff, Pooja Rutberg, Garth Strohbein, Mary Thorndike, Molly Tokaz, Greg Wallingford, Ricardo Wellisch, Lisa Wong, Clara Yang, Shira Yun, and Ali John Zarrabi. A special thanks to Chisolm, Gaufberg, and Jorgensen for feedback on drafts. We thank all the students, trainees, physicians, nurses, and health professions educators who have participated generously in workshops and gallery experiences with us over the past fifteen years. None of this would have been possible without you.

Generous readers of our drafts include Lisa Bessette, Kaywin Feldman, Neal Flynn, Dominique Harz Fresno, Ingrid Ganske, Dabney Hailey, Tyler Jorgensen, Amanda Millay Hughes, Nicole Mills, and Shari Tishman.

We are grateful for the editorial services provided by Emily Bowles, as well as the editorial team at Rowman & Littlefield.

We appreciate the patience and support from our families, who gave us the peace and quiet we needed to write: Stephen Brown, Hao Sheng, Clyde Da Sheng-Williams, and Paul Worthington.

We are profoundly grateful to all the health professions educators and museum educators who take the risk to work across disciplines and believe that art can make all the difference. We celebrate the perseverance and generous spirits of both communities. Thank you for keeping body and soul together; we hope you will find ways to flourish in the face of challenges. This book is our response to your life-giving work and a call for continuing to expand these conversations across disciplines.

Acknowledgments

Foreword

Lisa Howley, American Association of Medical Colleges

Success in today's dynamic and complex healthcare environment requires new skills that have traditionally not been taught or intentionally experienced in medical and other health professional schools. Skills such as imagination and curiosity, communication and empathy, critical thinking and social advocacy, adaptability and flexibility, inclusion, and contextual thinking require intentionally designed learning experiences. In this book, Ruth Slavin, Ray Williams, and Corinne Zimmermann demonstrate the valuable expertise and skills that museum educators bring to co-creating and facilitating these meaningful learning experiences. The insights and practical scenarios laid out in this text will allow readers to more easily envision creative approaches to integrating the visual arts into their local programs. We need this boost of creativity!

As an educational psychologist who has worked in medicine for over twenty-five years, I have seen the arts and humanities embraced in new and different ways over time. In 2017, I launched a new national initiative at the Association of American Medical Colleges called the Fundamental Role of the Arts and Humanities in Medical Education, with the goal of improving the education, practice, and well-being of physicians through deeper integrative experiences with the arts and humanities. In order to design and oversee the first phases of this initiative, I convened and charged a diverse arts and humanities integration committee, which fortunately included Ray Williams. I am indebted to Ray for his service to this initiative and for sharing his vast knowledge and expertise in museum-based medical education. In 2020, with the assistance of this integration committee, we released a report with several recommendations for the future of medical education, including further integration of the arts and humanities into competency-based education and greater collaboration among faculty, learners, patients, and arts and humanities partners in the process of curriculum design. *Activating the Art Museum: Designing Experiences for the Health Professions* is an excellent complement to this broader 2020 Fundamental Role of the Arts and Humanities in Medical Education monograph.

My own musical background has given me great joy. My love of the arts and humanities has helped me appreciate the unique value they play in deep and meaningful learning. Earlier in my career, I worked very collaboratively with museum educators and gained firsthand experiences and appreciation for the power of partnering with these experts to effect change in communication, teaming, and wellness. As this text vividly depicts, connecting through the experience of art allows us to engage in meaningful conversations and to share moments of joy, sorrow, frustration, and curiosity. The arts and humanities can serve as a healing salve for some of the sorrows and traumas experienced by those training and working in healthcare.

Like most in our field, I have spent my life being curious—about why some "smart" medical students have weak bedside manners; how the end of life can be both beautiful and horrific, and how simple acts in this context can make all the difference; how the arts can break down invisible divides between cultures, races, and hierarchies; how egos and poor communication skills can lead to errors; and how some can embrace ambiguity while others become stymied by the uncertainty and complexity of medicine. I am reminded daily that the traditional approach to medical education is insufficient for preparing physicians to practice in increasingly dynamic environments. The complex challenges of this century go well beyond the solutions that the biological sciences are able to provide. As the authors of this book artfully explain, we need pedagogical practices that weave the arts and humanities into the fabric of education. Thank you, Ruth, Ray, and Corinne, for your creativity and expertise on thoughtful design and skillful facilitation of museum-based educational experiences!

—Dr. Lisa Howley
Senior Director for Transforming Medical Education,
Association of American Medical Colleges

Preface

Your three authors see the creation of this slim volume as our "pandemic project." While our husbands cooked amazing dinners or went to the backyard to build a rabbit hutch or focused on political activism in our "battleground state," we compared notes, researched, dreamed, talked with colleagues, and argued. And we wrote!

We have known one another for many years. At times we have worked together within the same museum, and at other times we have found ourselves working along parallel lines of inquiry across great distances. With the emergence of Zoom, we fell into conversations about the book we might write together to share our experiences partnering with students and professionals in medicine—and, more broadly, in health care—within museum education work. Each of us has been seriously committed to this work for nearly fifteen years now and has met, both in person and online, with thousands of students and clinicians. Although we have pursued different paths and developed different activities in response to the stated (and unstated) needs of our partners in health care, our values are aligned.

The book we envisioned would provide vivid descriptions of the potential for art museum experiences—thoughtfully designed and skillfully facilitated—to support students and clinicians in their quest for both professional excellence and personal flourishing. We wanted to engage and inspire readers from both the museum world and the health professions, even the skeptics, by grounding our writing in medical literature and showing the relevance of interpretive conversations about art and a range of embodied or reflective activities designed for museum settings. We have drawn extensively on our ongoing conversations with students and professionals in the health fields to develop composite scenarios that distill and represent their perspectives for our readers, while respecting privacy concerns.

It was relatively easy to develop our list of chapters; the challenge was in negotiating who got to write on what topic! In the end, we all had extended conversations about every chapter, offering anecdotes, lesson plans, and pearls of wisdom to its designated author. We all gave each other feedback on chapter drafts, but final decisions rested with the individual writer. Our readers will notice shifts in style and tone that reveal the voices of three different individuals. At one point, we considered signing our chapters. In the end we opted to embrace a degree of inconsistency—or, to reframe, "variety"—that we hope our readers will enjoy.

LOOKING AHEAD

The chapters that follow present and illuminate some of the main themes that have emerged through our collaborations with health professions educators. Readers will find vivid descriptions and analyses of gallery activities, as well as advice about setting shared goals with a collaborator, selecting provocative images, and designing a gallery lesson with a clear trajectory. We present a selection of engaging activities, with voices from healthcare bringing their own insights into museum-based teaching as it relates to health professions education and professional development. Readers are encouraged to either proceed sequentially or choose a topic that seems most appropriate to their own circumstances.

Chapter 1: Why the Art Museum?

Experiences with original works of art in a museum setting can be designed to directly support students and clinicians in the health professions along multiple dimensions. Participants may look and wonder without the pressure of mastering information. An outline of a sample lesson provides moments for professional reflection, building community, and self-care.

Chapter 2: Thinking in the Art Museum

Responding to Dr. Jerome Groopman's seminal 2007 book, *How Doctors Think*, this chapter explores connections between thinking in art museums and thinking in medicine. Doctors need to observe closely, synthesize various types of information while noting anomalies, generate strategic questions, avoid premature closure, and synthesize various types of information. This chapter provides a rich description of a gallery session exploring two works of art that address loss and mortality.

Chapter 3: Cultivating Empathy

Physician and researcher Dr. Helen Riess links the practice of empathy to better patient outcomes and to a renewed sense of purpose among physicians. This chapter uses Riess's framework to demonstrate how experiences with works of art can cultivate empathic capacities. We provide museum-based strategies to foster perspective-taking and deep listening, cultivate emotional awareness, and practice nonverbal communication skills.

Chapter 4: The Power of Story

This chapter explores a range of approaches to sharing stories in museum settings. Stories that are embodied in a work of art can offer wisdom that enhances understanding across cultures. When telling personal stories, people gain insight into their own values, motivations, fears, and limitations. Clinical stories offer possibilities for professional reflection, affirmation, and affiliation with colleagues. A "commitment to story" requires skills that will enhance communication with patients and their families, as well as a stance toward work that may enhance feelings of gratitude and connection to core values.

Chapter 5: Strengthening Interprofessional Teams

This chapter offers a case study of museum-based work with interprofessional teams. Rooted in Professor Amy C. Edmondson's work on teaming and psychological safety, it provides a rich description of a workshop plan designed to build community and improve interprofessional communication and team dynamics. The complexity and richness of human experience—embodied in both the artworks and the team members—opens new possibilities for teaming.

Chapter 6: Confronting Bias

The practice of medicine has been, and continues to be, influenced by negative social forces, including racism and other forms of bias. There is a pressing need for authentic discussions of these difficult topics in order to build awareness and skills. This chapter features an interview with Dr. Kamna Balhara of Johns Hopkins Medical Center regarding a multi-layered intervention she co-developed to support BIPOC health professionals and improve patient care for all. The interview provides insights into how Balhara demonstrated proof of concept and secured administrative support. The chapter concludes with a gallery lesson co-designed with Balhara and one of the authors, illuminating how thoughtful discussions about works of art can help catalyze change.

Chapter 7: Caring for the Spirit

During the natural course of their work, health professionals in the United States find themselves interacting with patients from diverse cultural backgrounds during times of extreme joy, suffering, and loss. They are asked to pray and to attend to spiritual needs. How can clinicians prepare for this sensitive work so that each patient receives appropriate and affirming care, especially at the end of life? This chapter explores how works of art can support health professionals in learning about rituals and beliefs that might inform patient care.

Chapter 8: Nurturing Well-being

In the past five years, the authors have received an increasing number of requests for museum experiences that promote well-being. This chapter explores cultivating supportive relationships; fostering connection and community; reflecting on core values, meaning, and purpose; and building habits of joy and gratitude.

Chapter 9: Practicing Mindfulness

This chapter responds to Dr. Ronald Epstein's 2017 book *Attending: Medicine, Mindfulness and Humanity* and builds on Dr. Jon Kabat-Zinn's foundational work in mindfulness. After providing a useful synthesis of these medical perspectives, the author provides three mindfulness-centered gallery experiences that take advantage of the museum environment while focusing on using works of art.

Chapter 10: Building a Community of Practice

In this concluding chapter, the authors reflect on the importance of developing shared values and practices, briefly outlining key recent developments. The chapter includes an interview with Dr. Elizabeth Gaufberg, co-founder of the Harvard Macy Institute's Art Museum-based Health Professions Education Fellowship, the first of its kind—in which two of the authors serve as faculty alongside their medical peers. Finally, the authors offer practical tips for starting new partnerships and revisit "Why Art Museums" in terms of today's challenges to both museums and health care.

This book is timely. It is framed by a foreword by Lisa Howley, Senior Director for Transforming Medical Education, American Association of Medical Colleges, and an afterword by Kaywin Feldman, Director, National Gallery of Art, Washington, DC. Each offers their perspective as a leader and policy maker. In some ways, both art museums and the health professions are in a moment of crisis, forced to respond to pressures for change from both external and internal constituencies. Art museums are being challenged to become more inclusive, more flexible in their understanding of their social role, and more engaged with the "real world." The health professions are challenged by problematic systemic structures and administrative demands. Healthcare is facing an epidemic of moral injury and the urgent need to address issues of access and equity. The stories and examples offered in this book highlight how partnerships between art museums and the health professions demonstrate new ways for museums to be relevant, while addressing pressing issues in healthcare and nourishing the well-being of providers and educators.

1

Why the Art Museum?

We believe that art is fundamental—to human expression, as inspiration, and as a catalyst for reflecting on a diverse range of experiences. We believe in the potential of the art museum to be activated on behalf of both individual and societal needs. And we, the authors, have seen through our work in museum settings with several hundred groups of health professionals and students that the museum can be a uniquely effective site for the training and nourishment of health professionals.

For far too long, the vast majority of museum professionals have allowed the disciplinary values of art history to control how collections are presented and interpreted. They have focused on classifying and categorizing artworks, emphasized stylistic relationships and changes, and supported linear narratives of visual "development." Their work has often ignored minor trends and outlying artists—often women and people of color—in favor of an "authorized" version of art history. Perhaps unintentionally, museums have been set up to make visitors feel inadequate, to feel that they must know something about art in order to appreciate it. This raises questions about who really belongs, who deserves access to these rich repositories of compelling visual achievement. Many visitors dutifully follow the preordained path, reading explanatory labels and trying to connect this written information to what they see. But art is bigger than this, much bigger—too big to be contained by academic disciplinary boundaries.

Museum educators have been central to recent trends that empower visitors to make their own meaning(s), to use the museum as a resource in pursuing their own questions and in their own process of "becoming."[1] This book explores and shares what we—seasoned museum educators based in Ann Arbor, Austin, and Boston— have learned over the past twenty years of intense collaboration with medical educators and other health professionals. As the title of this book indicates, our goal is to promote understanding of how art museums can be activated on behalf of the needs of various health professionals—to promote clear thinking, respectful teamwork, culturally responsive practices, well-being, and empathy.

Our work builds upon foundations laid by Linda Friedlaender, the pioneering curator of education at the Yale Center for British Art, in partnership with dermatologist Dr. Irwin Braverman.[2] In 1997, Friedlaender and Braverman initiated a program they called "Enhancing Observational Skills" for medical students at Yale. Their program, now required of all first-year medical students, focuses on extended periods of close looking at and describing works of art, to build skills essential to medical diagnosis. The Yale program has had widespread influence. Art historian Amy Herman developed similar ideas while at the Frick Collection and now has an active practice focused on teaching observational skills to physicians, police officers, and others. A handful of recent publications in medical journals have attested to the effectiveness of art-based pedagogy, primarily assessing use of Visual Thinking Strategies (VTS) in developing observational skills in doctors.[3] One longtime course at Harvard Medical School, Training the Eye, uses VTS with medical students, and the newly established Harvard-Macy Institute's Art Museum-based Health Professions Education Fellowship introduces medical educators to the VTS method. A skillful VTS facilitator can engage a group in a lively exploration of an image to encourage multiple observations and interpretive comments grounded in visual evidence.

Observation skills are clearly critical to the work of health professionals, and they readily understand that the art museum is a logical setting in which to develop these skills. However, our own work has explored expansive new territory beyond this, usually in partnership with medical educators and with reference to an array of current concerns in the health professions. Our readers from the museum field will benefit from the extensive references to seminal works from the medical literature and beyond: Dr. Jerome Groopman on thinking, Dr. Helen Riess on empathy, Dr. Ronald Epstein on mindfulness, and Prof. Amy Edmondson on teaming, among others. We will demonstrate how familiar staples like interpretive conversations may be adapted to the needs of health professionals. We will introduce original activities that will expand educators' repertoires of teaching moves and inspire new thinking.

Educators from the health professions will benefit from our detailed descriptions of gallery teaching that give a sense of how a well-chosen work of art can catalyze professional reflection, how an engaging activity can build relevant skills, and how a skillfully conceived lesson plan develops a trajectory from framing to exploration, reflection, and synthesis. These teaching stories often include revelatory moments in which participants suggest some of the struggles in the healthcare sector that have damaged workers' morale and resulted in epidemic levels of burnout. When integrated into medical training and professional practice, skills and attitudes developed through thoughtfully designed museum experiences result in better treatment for patients, more compassionate communication with families, and greater possibilities for satisfaction—even joy—among health professionals.

The art museum environment offers respite from the charged hospital environment, with its high stakes and relentless demands for decisive action. Removed from professional competition and hierarchy, the art museum can serve as a place for medical students and professionals to build upon one another's ideas in a collaborative search for meaning and to share thoughts and feelings about their work. Surrounded by beauty and inspired by expressions of human experience from many times and places, they can reflect and recharge in this environment. The pedagogical approaches we have developed with the needs of health professionals in mind

Why the Art Museum?

rescue participants from the tyranny of expertise, the constant pressure to master information, and the need to maintain a certain high-powered mode of professional decorum. As facilitators, we do not assume that participants have any prior knowledge of art; all activities are accessible to the curious beginner.

To introduce the museum's unique qualities as a site for learning, and argue for the power of engaging in person with original works of art, we provide a rich description of one complex lesson plan designed as part of the "humanistic curriculum" offered by the Brigham and Women's Internal Medicine Residency Program. Although we will be describing many diverse activities and pedagogical moves in subsequent chapters, it is important to present at the outset a coherent design that will help readers envision the complete trajectory of a museum experience for healthcare professionals. Through this first example, we hope to suggest how the alchemy of evocative spaces, well-chosen works of art, and skillfully responsive facilitation might operate to catalyze and deepen a professionally relevant conversation among individuals who have devoted themselves to the art of healing.

A RESPONSIVE AND RELEVANT MUSEUM EXPERIENCE, BY DESIGN

Prelude

To develop a strong gallery lesson, the museum educator and the medical educator need to plan together—to share information about goals and expectations, logistics, and current group dynamics. In the initial consultation that led to the two-hour lesson plan described here, the mentor physician indicated that the session was part of a monthly series of evening meetings comprising a "humanistic curriculum." Other sessions in the series were devoted to discussions of poetry, short fiction, and film, with some attention given to the principles of narrative medicine.

"This internship year is intense," the mentor physician said during the planning meeting. "These interns work incredibly long hours, and for the first time in their training, they are heavily engaged in clinical work with patients that are suffering, even dying. It's such a great group of people, but they are often exhausted and stressed out." Their museum visit would be designed to support a sense of community among the interns, invite reflection on their professional challenges, and refresh their energy and sense of well-being. This hour-long consultation by two educators from very different professional backgrounds established a warm rapport and a shared vision for the session. Although the museum educator would be responsible for developing the detailed lesson plan and leading its facilitation, both partners would be actively engaged in supporting a wide-ranging, unscripted conversation with the interns about art and their own professional lives.

A Warm Welcome and Careful Framing (full group, 10 minutes)

The group of medical interns and their mentor arrive on time. Although a few of the interns look tired, there is a definite buzz of excitement. The interns cross the threshold into a different world; they stand up a little straighter, and even as they gather for the session, they are looking around and pointing out things that catch their eye in passing. The mentor greets me (Williams) warmly and introduces me to the group. She tells them that she and I have already met to think together about the sort of experiences that would be meaningful for this group, and that she is eager to share this time with them.

I welcome the group, tell them that I have been looking forward to meeting them and that I know they are in the midst of a very intense period of their professional development. I mention that I have developed a special interest in activating the art museum on behalf of health professionals over the past several years, focusing on empathic communication skills, resilience, and well-being, as well as interprofessional team dynamics.

Because health professionals and students are intelligent and driven to excel, it is important that a museum visit be framed with specific reference to its professional relevance. I simultaneously keep the tone warm, the pace brisk, and the framing of topics and expectations strategic and clear. After welcoming the group, my first move is to counter any expectations that they may have arrived with by stating,

> Remember that this is not a guided tour, but a workshop designed in partnership with your physician mentor. We will be looking at a broad range of works of art and reflecting on connections to clinical experiences and skills physicians need to exercise. No prior art expertise is expected—just be prepared to look closely and pursue questions and possible meanings. In the back of your mind, keep alive the question, "What does this have to do with being a physician?" We will reflect on this question at various points. Finally, this is not a test. The stakes are low! There will be no "art emergencies" or demands for heroic action in the next two hours. The groups that have the most fun just plunge in and make the most of the invitation to be together in this new space. Any questions or concerns? . . . Grab a folding stool, and let's go look at some art!

Interpretive Conversation (full group, 25 minutes)

We move from a brightly lit, modernist atrium with its high ceilings into a series of small galleries that display works of art from colonial America. I have chosen a painting by John Singleton Copley, *Watson and the Shark*, for an "interpretive conversation" intended to warm up the group and bring them together. The large painting—six feet tall and seven and a half feet wide—is dramatically lit. It is featured as the sole work of art on a free-standing, deep-blue-green wall with a bench directly in front—the museum's signal that this is one of its gems. The interns set up their gallery stools in a semi-circle in front of the large painting so that everyone can see it. This tight arrangement signals to other visitors that we are a group and diminishes distractions. The interns are now ready to focus intently for what will be a half hour of extended contemplation and discussion.

After one or two minutes of silent looking, I begin an activity in which everyone present participates. I ask everyone in the group to think of "one word that, for you, captures the overall feeling of this scene" and then move through the two rows of seats asking each person to share their word. As we move into exploring the imagery, I paraphrase comments offered by participants and encourage more look-ing, pursuit of more questions, and generation of additional theories. I encourage participants to back up their theories with visual evidence. The interns are actively engaged in working together to solve the interpretive problem before them. Perhaps they sense a resonance between this process of close looking, wondering, and generating theories with the clinical processes of examination and diagnosis. They are working as a team: proposing and entertaining various possibilities, looking for visual evidence, and asking questions to move toward understanding.

Questions about the painting's nude figure with long, almost silvery hair are central to the conversation. "Why is she in the water with the sharks? . . . Will the group on the boat be able to rescue him?" To our contemporary eyes, the figure's gender may be ambiguous; later, in reflecting on our wide-ranging conversation, this momentary confusion will lead to a point about how what we see may be culturally conditioned and the vital need for physicians to stay alive to the evidence, to remain open to the unexpected. There is also an extended consideration of the various roles the nine men in the boat are playing in this rescue at sea. Two men lean out of the boat, trying to grasp the imperiled swimmer; a third helps keep one of them from falling overboard; others man the oars. A dark-skinned man tosses a rope, and a standing figure with flying brown tresses tries to spear the attacking shark.

Copley's masterful composition, with its emotional intensity, convincingly naturalistic style, and epic scale, takes the group to another time and place. They are fully engaged and eager to know more. After a good fifteen minutes of noticing, wondering, and discussing, I provide some contextual information: the swimmer, Brook Watson, was a fourteen-year-old boy attacked by a shark in Havana Bay in 1749. He survived the attack, but lost part of one of his legs.[4] After going on to become Lord Mayor of London in middle age, he commissioned Copley to depict this life-changing event through conventions of painting that were typically used for mythological or biblical narratives. Thus, the painting provides a heroic explanation for the Lord Mayor's missing limb and presents him as physically strong and coura-geous, facing down death itself.

After a pause during which the group takes yet another look at the painting with this new information in mind, I venture, "So, what might our consideration of this painting have to tell us about being a physician?" In some ways, the connec-tions to be made with this "warm-up" image were relatively straightforward: the painting illustrates the importance of working as a team in which each individual has a well-defined role to play, the demand for courage in the face of danger, and the possibility of overcoming trauma and ultimately achieving success. The very processes inherent to interpretive conversations—examination, questioning, pos-iting theories, grounding theories in evidence, listening to alternative ideas, and moving toward a shared understanding—have direct parallels in clinical practices. Such conversations are so natural and immersive that participants are often unaware of the skills they are exercising, so it may be helpful for the clinical mentor or museum educator to point them out in order to reinforce the assertion that this time spent with works of art is strategically designed to support their professional development.

Metaphorical Connections (small groups, 20 minutes)

After this extended, focused consideration of a single work of art, the next planned activity is designed to engage small groups in a more relaxed, sociable conversation. As we move to our next stop, I ask the students to form four groups of four. I instruct each group to choose one of six modern sculptures I have indicated on a floor plan of the three galleries we are entering.

"Take about five minutes to look at the work from all sides and share your initial impressions and ideas," I say. "Then begin to explore the question, 'What might this work of art have to say about being a medical professional?' Of course, this is not the artist's primary interest, but you will be able to find metaphorical connections to your clinical experiences. In about ten minutes, we'll meet back at this first sculpture, look at each work of art together, and hear some of the connections you were able to make."

I give each group the annotated floor plan and a written recap of the directions, and indicate that I will be circulating among the groups to eavesdrop and support their process. The groups head off on their mission, chatting and pointing out interesting sights along the way to "their" sculptures. Once arrived, they seem to enjoy looking together and casually sharing first impressions. I prompt each group to take on the challenge of making a connection: "Try inventing a simile: This aspect of the sculpture is like . . . what aspect of medicine?" I circulate and reinforce a playful energy.

It is clear to me that these young professionals are skilled at synthesizing and presenting information, even if metaphorical thinking is like an atrophied muscle for some. Each group presents their sculpture and the connections they have made to their clinical experiences. The infinite repetition of an intricate, mirrored cube by Josiah McIlheny spoke to them of the endless line of patients seeking care and the sometimes-mechanistic routines of the hospital. The rotund, larger-than-life sculpture of a nude woman created in bronze by Fernando Botero stimulated thinking about patient anxiety during examinations, obesity, and the ways that physicians might protect a patient's modesty and sense of safety. Another work remained mysterious to its group, prompting questions about how to tolerate the ambiguity of a diagnosis that does not come easily, a process that requires maintaining an open-minded stance.

I signal that it is time to move on. "Thank you! I had wondered what connections you would be able to find among this very diverse group of sculptures, and it was so interesting to hear your ideas! Human beings are expert at making meaning, and you will be able to find whatever you are looking for in the art museum. We've got to cover a fair amount of territory to get to our next stop, so please stay together and move along—but keep your eyes wide open! I know you will want to come back on your own."

Professional Reflection (full group, 30 minutes)

Now in one of the less-frequented galleries of ancient art, the group gathers around an Etruscan sarcophagus from the third century BCE. We consider its depiction of a reclining couple, softly embracing and covered by a light sheet—all sensitively carved in stone. I offer some grounding information: "Etruscan women had greater autonomy and social influence than their Greek counterparts, and Etruscan artists did not follow the Greek example of depicting idealized human bodies." In the figures, we note the couple's loving familiarity, along with signs of late middle age—a receding hairline, a paunch. The artist has portrayed them as specific individuals sharing the intimacy of a bed and has helped realize their intention to be buried together for eternity.

I then ask, "Does this ancient work of art connect in any way to experiences you are having in your clinical work these days? Does it evoke any memories or associations?"

"Well, yes," one of the interns responds, after a brief silence. "Like, earlier this week, shortly after learning that his wife of fifty years is going to die of cancer, a man came rushing out of her hospital room with tears in his eyes. He ran into me in the hall. And he looked at me, waiting for me to say the right thing. . . . I felt so inadequate. I'm only twenty-six, but I was their physician. I was supposed to know what to say to this man."

This halting confession brings sympathetic murmurs and nods of understanding and affirmation from surrounding colleagues. The conversation continues for another twenty minutes, bringing forward similar stories, as well as words of advice and encouragement from the physician mentor. The hospital environment had failed to support these young physicians in their early encounters with terminally ill patients, both in coaching them on effective communication and in helping them process their own experiences of anxiety, depletion, and sorrow. A gentle invitation in the form of a question asked outside the hospital, grounded by the experience of a work of art from long ago, led to a trove of powerful, hidden stories; a stronger sense of community among these interns; and perhaps, insights and renewed energy for the work ahead.

Guided Relaxation (full group, led by physician mentor, 10 minutes)

After the intensity of these timely reflections on the stress of dealing with terminal illness and family grief, it feels good to move together through the Classical galleries, replete with funerary monuments, and into the galleries devoted to the arts of Asia. The physical procession and changing visual delights prepare our group for something completely different. In a darkened gallery designed to evoke the atmosphere of a Japanese Buddhist temple, I quietly signal the group to find a place facing any one of several images of the Buddha. Everyone falls naturally into a respectful, curious silence. With minimal introductory information to the gallery, I invite the group to put both feet squarely on the floor and to sit tall but relaxed in preparation for a guided relaxation exercise.

> Breath is central to Buddhist meditation, as it is to life. From your comfortable place, noticing that you are settled squarely on your seat and aware of both feet on the floor, take three deep breaths in your own time. As you attend to your breath, try to inhale through your nose, and exhale through your mouth . . .
> Now let's do the breaths together: Inhale . . . 2 . . . 3 . . . exhale all the way . . . 2 . . . 3 . . . 4.
> Good. Now just keep breathing, as you will, and listen to my voice, as I draw your caring attention to different parts of your body.

Over the course of ten minutes, we bring our attention to neck, shoulders, chest, stomach, seat, knees, calves, and feet. We tighten and relax. We notice and appreciate. We breathe. I quietly take my gallery stool and prepare to leave, suggesting they join me outside the gallery when they are ready.

Choice and Exploration (individual choice and sharing in pairs, 15 minutes)

Knowing that the deepest work of the session has been accomplished—and that some time for individual discoveries is always welcome—I suggest a playful, exploratory activity: "Let's play 'Off to See the Wizard!'" I offer business card-size images of the original illustrations in L. Frank Baum's book *The Wonderful Wizard of Oz* portraying the Scarecrow, Tin Woodman, and Cowardly Lion, who, I remind the group, were in search of a brain, a heart, and courage, respectively. Each participant selects a card to focus their wandering (and to keep as a souvenir): "You are ready for your quest, which you will complete in ten minutes of searching the nearby galleries. If you chose the Scarecrow, find a work of art that has something to say about *intellect*. For the Tin Woodman, find a work of art that has something to say about *feelings*. Those who chose the Lion will find a work that has something to tell you about *courage*. There will be many possibilities but try to land on a relevant work of art within about five minutes. Take another five minutes to enjoy looking and to think about the associations that come up for you. Then find a colleague nearby and share. Come back here at 7:45." I send them off into the galleries, so full of possibilities for connection. The varied prompts honor different ways in which work in medicine stretches these young clinicians, while the "pair share" may reveal shared or divergent experiences and invite participants to articulate core professional values.

Closing (full group, 10 minutes)

Our time together is ending. While the interns explore and share, I plan for some closing moments of synthesis and reflection. I had originally prepared a written prompt asking for reflections on the workshop, which would have provided useful feedback for the next iteration. But based on the energy level of the group and the need for a hard stop at 8:00 p.m., I opt for an alternative closing—one that invites participants to step out of the immersive experiences we had shared and to note resonant aspects.

The group reconvenes in small clusters, continuing conversations begun in the nearby galleries and teasing about being a "brain" or a "cowardly lion." I gesture and ask that we form a circle. "Let's take a few minutes to think back on the past couple of hours. What did we do? . . . We will go right around the circle and hear from everyone. Just a few words or phrases—not a paragraph—to recall something we did here that you found worthwhile."

What did we do? The group is thoughtful, looking inward. The observations start to come, stimulating nods of agreement and punctuated by appreciative chuckles.

We looked. And looked again.

We breathed together! (I never have five minutes just to breathe.)

We interpreted art.

We were vulnerable.

We were creative . . . we made connections.

We supported each other.

We listened . . . and spoke. Sometimes we disagreed.

We had strong feelings—and they were visible.

We struggled.

We appreciated this incredible museum! (I want to come back with my partner.)

We explored.

We made choices.

We relaxed.

We enjoyed being together in a new space.

We reflected on our clinical experiences . . . and other experiences, too.

The physician mentor says how impressed she was with the group's willingness to plunge into the experience and noted specifically the value of taking the risk to speak honestly about hard things. "Internship year is rough. Part of your preparation needs to be developing strategies for taking care of yourself. We need to continue talking in our group about the stresses of dealing with terminally ill patients—and finding meaning in our work."

I close by thanking the group for being fully engaged with the museum experience, as well as for their intense preparation for the demanding and vital work in caring for patients. "I hope you will remember the museum as a place of beauty and meaning, a destination to share with others, and a site for reflection and nourishment. Please share any feedback on this experience with your mentor, who will pass it on to me. We are always trying to refine the workshop plan to make it more relevant to your concerns. Take good care!"

WHAT'S GOING ON HERE?

This extended example of a custom-designed museum experience for young physicians demonstrates a wide range of the pedagogical moves that an experienced museum educator can draw upon. The lesson was carefully designed to welcome a group that might have very little experience looking seriously at art; to engage relevant skills of close looking, interpretation, reflection, and self-awareness; to build a sense of community; and to leave them feeling refreshed. The museum educator's depth of knowledge of art history and the specific collections of the museum informed the design of the activities and made it possible to respond flexibly to the participants' observations and interests. A variety of approaches—interpretive conversation, sharing personal stories, guided meditation, and play—established a changing rhythm and furthered a natural trajectory. Advance planning and negotiation of shared goals between the museum and medical educators was essential, as was the museum educator's understanding of medical culture and willingness to flex away from museum norms in response to this group's curricular and psychosocial needs.

The museum environment was a powerful force in the story, too, influencing thoughts and feelings, physical movements, and social relationships. The interns crossed a threshold into new terrain. They turned off their phones and pagers and prepared for the unexpected. Many of them were intrigued by the inclusion of a museum visit in their training. They carried themselves differently in this expansive space.

The lesson plan required a journey through many types of spaces. We responded to shifts in lighting, colors of walls, heights of ceilings, and activity levels within busy corridors and quiet, more intimate corners. Even the travel time between galleries allowed for processing intriguing glimpses, sharing responses, and the feeling of our bodies moving—individually and as a group—through space. We were aware that the galleries presented visual expressions from many cultures, even if we did not stop to savor what was on display. The facilitator provided comfortable seating to support both concentrated looking and physical relaxation. There were opportunities to work in small groups, to explore as individuals, and to share with a colleague.

Works of art have their own aura, a presence rooted in their moment of creation and encompassing all that they have meant to viewers over time. Their materiality speaks of human effort, natural resources, experimentation, and culture. Looking closely at the original object, we see indications of use and physical changes over time. Our body comes into relationship with the object. Scale matters; we may be drawn in close to notice the details on something small and delicate, or an expansive canvas might fill our range of vision and remind us of our own small place in the scheme of things. None of these exploratory movements, none of these nuanced, sensory operations are available to us through the use of digital reproductions. We cannot overstate our belief in the importance of inviting health professionals to step into the domain of art, with all of its history, mystery, and resonance.

Why the Art Museum?

NOTES

1. David Carr, *The Promise of Cultural Institutions* (Walnut Creek, CA: AltaMira Press, 2003), 10.
2. Jacqueline C. Dolev, Linda Krohner Friedlaender, and Irwin M. Braverman, "Use of Fine Art to Enhance Visual Diagnostic Skills," *Journal of the American Medical Association* 286, no. 9 (September 5, 2001): 1020–21.
3. Gauri G. Agarwal et al., "Impact of Visual Thinking Strategies (VTS) on the Analysis of Clinical Images: A Pre-Post Study of VTS in First-Year Medical Students," *Journal of Medical Humanities* 41 (August 21, 2020): 561–72; Joel T. Katz and Shahram Khoshbin, "Can Visual Arts Training Improve Physician Performance?" *Transactions of the American Clinical and Climatological Association* 125 (2014): 331–42.
4. John Singleton Copley, *Watson and the Shark*, 1778, oil on canvas, Museum of Fine Arts, Boston, https://collections.mfa.org/objects/30998/watson-and-the-shark.

2

Thinking in the Art Museum

This chapter explores why art is "good to think with" during medical education,[1] as well as in support of ongoing clinical practice. Participants in museum-based sessions encounter complex works of art representing human experiences. They practice inquiry, learn to look with purpose, and gain experience in thinking flexibly. In the museum, away from the demands for quick thinking and decisive action, participants work together to slow down, expand their thought processes, to develop and reconsider their interpretations. As participants develop interpretations and listen to those of others, they do so in a calm, often peaceful, and beautiful environment in which they are invited to reflect on thinking in its many dimensions and consequences.

In his book *How Doctors Think*, Dr. Jerome Groopman recounts his first night of residency. He arrived with a pocket full of index cards representing his carefully categorized store of knowledge. All too quickly, he was thrust into an emergent situation wherein a stable patient quickly became very ill. Fortunately, an experienced physician from another hospital happened to be on hand. In the book, he describes his feeling of gratitude as this doctor took over, and Groopman was able to watch the minute-to-minute thinking of his more experienced colleague, made visible in action. In those moments, a frightening gap appeared between his methodically obtained knowledge and his experience in clinical thinking, and he realized that, alongside differential diagnosis and Bayesian analysis, he would need other tools for clinical thinking.[2] Many decades later, now a senior physician, and prompted by his sense that his students were failing to "question cogently, or listen carefully or observe keenly," he began to pose a repeated question to his seasoned colleagues: "How should doctors think?"[3]

Groopman organizes his book around case studies based on results from his examination of this question. Through storytelling about specific cases, he connects the narratives with relevant research on cognitive errors, personal attributes, and habits of mind that lead to medical "misses." He writes:

> Every physician, even the most brilliant, makes a misdiagnosis or chooses the wrong therapy. This is not a matter of medical mistakes. . . . Misdiagnosis is different. It is a window into the medical mind. It reveals why doctors fail to

question their assumptions, why their thinking is sometimes closed or skewed, why they overlook the gaps in their knowledge.[4]

Groopman's stories illuminate the complex connections between observing and interpreting, and between thinking, feeling, and decision-making. He also examines, through specific stories of experienced physicians and their patients, the human side of medicine, offering examples of how values and personal attributes affect habits of thinking.

As studies from across myriad disciplines have shown, the human mind is highly vulnerable to thinking errors. Some may be intrinsic to human thought, while other biases are learned, explicitly or implicitly.[5] Table 2.1 briefly identifies common types of known thinking problems in medicine, noting situational or dispositional contributors.[6]

Table 2.1

Narrow cognitive frame	Thinking is predetermined, too narrowly focused, may fail to elicit all relevant information (less likely to use open-ended questions)
Anchoring	Thinking becomes "anchored" to one or more salient features which dominate further thinking
Confirmation	Search only for information that will confirm rather than challenge diagnosis
Availability	Relying on what comes easily to mind, the familiar
Satisfaction of search	Stop "looking" once something fits, may miss other issues, failing to recognize multiple diagnoses (multiple things can be true)
"Order" effects	Primacy (identified or heard first) and recency often occur in transfer of information from one health professional to another
Commission/Omission	Tendency toward action or its opposite, may be personality-based or due to experience (or lack of experience)
Overconfidence	When combined with commission bias may result in quick action on incomplete information
Attribution	Negative stereotyping—can be related to implicit bias, also to assumption or presence of drug use, alcoholism, psychiatric diagnosis, obesity; additional diagnoses are missed or discounted
Liking/disliking patients	Both positive and negative feelings may affect decision-making, limit investigative thinking or patient contact
Visceral bias	Immediate strong automatic or triggering reactions including culturally learned and implicit biases

While the issues are presented here individually for clarity, in practice, one "thinking problem" often leads to, overlaps with, or results from another. The relationship between emotions and thinking are evident in some issues such as visceral bias, and those arising in positive or negative emotions. In addition, a recent research literature review singled out low tolerance for ambiguity as an important contributing factor across many thinking dispositions.[7] Dr. Patrick Croskerry, who has written extensively on these topics, refers to these categories as "cognitive dispositions to respond," arguing that this more neutral term acknowledges human fallibility, while encouraging physicians to become more self-aware and to seek insights into their own thinking.[8]

Recent research and writing on thinking dispositions, associated personality traits, and situational factors point to their ongoing relevance in medicine. A 2016 literature review synthesized twenty studies on medical thinking, noting the frequency of anchoring, availability, and other "framing" issues, and investigating how personal attributes might play a role in overconfidence and low tolerance for ambiguity. Time pressures, fatigue, interruptions, incomplete information, initial framing information (and the source of the information), and the context for encountering patients have all been cited as factors affecting thinking in healthcare settings.[9] It is also well recognized that the introduction of computers into the exam room has created new sets of situational pressures and cognitive challenges.

In response to these concerns, some physicians have written about strategies to monitor and support clinical thinking. Drs. Pat Croskerry, Geeta Singhal, and Silvia Mamedes have written about situations that increase the risk of physician error. They encourage physicians to consider their immediate work context and to assess their cognitive overload, fatigue level, emotional states, and reactions when making decisions.[10] Justin Morgenstern has contributed to and built on these publications with a series of articles on cognitive bias—in theory and in action—in the context of emergency medicine where risk of error is high due to the complexity and urgency of decision-making. Morgenstern and other researchers advocate systemic change to reduce the situational risks factors. He also describes steps physicians can take themselves such as making a practice of regular "cognitive stops" for the explicit purpose of reconsidering and challenging their own diagnostic thinking.[11]

In the process of sharing the stories in How Doctors Think, Groopman also provides a positive road map for thinking practices that are helpful in clinical reasoning. In the introductory chapter and subsequent narratives, he returns repeatedly to the fundamental importance of questioning, listening, and observing, and urges a self-aware and reflective approach to thinking. He stresses the value of holding room for doubt—not as an emotional state, but as a thinking practice—arguing that physicians who practice doubt and study their mistakes are most likely to achieve clinical excellence.[12] He also notes that bedside manner—meaning effective and empathic communication—and excellence in clinical work usually travel together, not separately as the common stereotype suggests.[13] Finally, his last chapter underscores a humanistic philosophy regarding the importance of collaboration between physicians and patients. He advocates for creating ongoing dialogue between patient and doctor and suggests key questions. What are we missing? What else could this be? What serious possibilities are we overlooking? Listening, observing, and questioning are crucial for patients and their families too, empowering them to actively participate in order to ensure they receive the best possible care.[14]

Groopman's stories explore the human context of medicine for both the physician and patient, emphasizing the search for correct understanding and action, but also the need for connection and meaning within clinical practice. The rest of this chapter explores two art museum dialogues related to human mortality and loss. Each invites participants to discover relationships between thinking about art and thinking about clinical practice.

GETTING STARTED: OBSERVING AND INTERPRETING

Physicians often begin considering a patient's condition and story within a frame of reference that may include the patient's previous medical history, significant symptoms, test results, and, perhaps, a working diagnosis. In the extended example discussed in the following sections, medical-student participants at the art museum are given information at the beginning of their museum session that will shape their observations, and ultimately, their interpretations of two works of art that address human mortality and death. By design, the experience asks that the medical students explore the limits of observation, the power of information, and the value of tolerating ambiguity and uncertainty.

The museum educator introduces the frame of human mortality as an overall theme for that day's experiences, then gathers the group in front of the first work of art, a nineteenth-century oil painting (figure 1), inviting them to take time to look at it closely. After a few minutes, she asks them to share their initial thoughts. The figures and objects in this detailed painting have stimulated their curiosity, and people begin to share what they have noticed with few breaks in the flow of conversation. Following her plan to responsively layer in information following the group's thought process and direction, the educator shares the painting's title, *The Young Man and Death*, and notes that it was painted by Gustave Moreau in Paris during the mid-nineteenth century. She adds that the work's original title also carries a dedication: "*A la Memoire de Théodore Chasseriau.*"[15]

LOOKING WITH PURPOSE

In this first phase of looking, participants are invited to form some first impressions of the artwork. Physicians are trained in systematic protocols for examination and diagnosis. However, typically, a physician's initial impressions occur in a natural flow combining sensory information, visual observations, and thoughts of all kinds (associations, readying oneself for interaction, inner sensations such as hunger and fatigue, etc.). Groopman notes that in the exam room, "the physical examination begins with the first visual impressions . . . and with the tactile feedback gained by shaking a person's hand. Hypotheses about the diagnosis come to the doctor's mind before a word has been spoken."[16]

There are discussions elsewhere in this book—particularly in chapter 3: Cultivating Empathy—that describe practices used to disentangle observations from interpretations, or which investigate the impact of feelings on clinical decision-making. However, in the two examples in this chapter, participants are encouraged to begin with whatever combination of looking and thinking comes naturally to them in response to the art. After that stage, just as the physician or medical student might then begin a more systematic or purposeful questioning or inventory with a patient, the educator moves the group in that direction with three prompts for looking and analysis.

To maximize the students' participation and deepen discussion, the educator asks that each person choose one area of focus and join a small group for its discussion. She presents the three choices:

- Look closely at the three main figures, examining their relationship and noting details. What might we infer from the way their bodies are positioned?
- Look for objects that might be symbols and think about what messages these objects might be intended to convey.
- Look at the work as a whole and find things in this highly detailed painting that are strange, puzzling, or don't seem to fit.

Because the participants work in teams—to discover, but, also, to discard ideas—this structure for looking mitigates against individual overconfidence and, also, confirmation bias.

Over the next ten minutes, the small groups ebb toward and away from the painting back to their home circles. Their physical movements suggest their weaving together of direct visual observation, thinking, and dialogue as they refine their responses. As group discussions quiet, the educator invites everyone back together to share in the larger group.

Members of the group who were asked to look at the three main figures describe how their thinking has grown more detailed and focused, but also more speculative. They offer possible interpretations and request more information as they test other ideas. Though unfamiliar with this representation, they agree that the young female figure represents death. There is some debate, and different ideas about why the artist has included the baby in the form of a cherub in the foreground—perhaps to emphasize youth and the harshness of death at a young age, or life's opportunities cut short. One person suggests that the warmth of the baby's skin tones was chosen to contrast with the relative pallor of the other two figures, with the young man painted in tones midway between those of death and the cherub's warm, rosy coloring. While the description of the figures and their relationship is laid out convincingly, they conclude with two questions generated by their observations: "Who is Théodore Chasseriau?" and "Why is death portrayed in such a languorous form, floating behind the young man?" While not all observations are equally important or on point, the facilitator offers verbal support for their open-ended thinking, trusting the group to examine and discard ideas in their search for the most potent ones, and remarking that, as in medicine, more information may narrow or widen the search for answers.

The second group, which looked for symbols, notes the sword and the hourglass carried by the female figure (Death) and many additional elements that allude to time or decay, such as the sputtering torch held by the child and the flowers and their petals scattered on the ground. They note that both the female figure and the young man have wreaths, and question why the youth is holding his wreath, which appears to be made of golden leaves, above his head. They think that the bird in flight might be a symbol—but do not know of what. And they note that in contrast to the flowers with their scattered petals on the ground, the young man holds fresh flowers upright in his right hand.

The last group, tasked with exploring puzzles and contradictions in the painting, has been listening intently. They have focused most on the image as a whole and have identified some of the same questions as the other groups. They offer their remaining questions, putting all the elements together as they work toward interpretation. Echoing previously shared thoughts, a spokesperson says that some in the group are puzzled by the representation of the young man, who is pale but also vigorous, in contrast to the floating figure of death. Death holds a sword, yet the figure doesn't seem active as might be implied by the sword. They also wonder aloud about where this whole scene is taking place, and question why the young man is walking down steps. Is he going toward the afterlife or underworld? Why is death so passive and placed behind him? Building on the work of their colleagues, they wonder if the artist is depicting the actual moment of transition between life and death.

They agree with the observations of the group that was looking for symbols and have the same question about the bird, but they have focused particularly on the wreath and the cut flowers held by the youth. One participant, who majored in classics as an undergraduate, talks about the "wreath of Apollo," depicted as golden laurel leaves such as that held by the young man. Such wreaths were commonly used to symbolize victory, including for athletes at competitions. He notes that Apollo was associated with poetry and also healing (his son was Asclepius, god of medicine in ancient Greek religion and stories). Lastly, in response to the painting's dedication, the group wonders if this work depicts Théodore Chasseriau himself.

At this point, the larger group has generated many more observations, ideas, and questions; their thinking has grown richer, more divergent, and speculative. While the participants worked together thoughtfully and with energy, the educator has stepped back from leading, but now decides this is another inflection point where more information about the artwork will stimulate further thinking. She tells the group that Théodore Chasseriau was himself an artist who was a friend and mentor to Gustave Moreau and that Chasseriau died in 1856, at the age of thirty-seven, when Moreau was thirty. The creation date on the label is given as a range: "1856–1865."

Although the painting was begun the year Chasseriau died, it was not exhibited publicly until 1865, in Paris. We don't know to whether Moreau actively worked on it during those nine years, or he just kept it in his studio. As far as scholars have determined, this is not a representation of Chasseriau.[17] Moreau was very interested in symbols and their use. Here, the bird might be invoking a visual tradition in which a bird represents the soul in flight. The cut flowers held by the young man are likely intended to restate the idea of a young life cut short.[18]

Taken together, this information might support the intriguing idea discussed by the group, that for storytelling purposes the artist might have chosen to include these items to heighten the sense of immediacy, of a specific moment, in which we, also, are present.

THINKING ABOUT THINKING WITH *THE YOUNG MAN AND DEATH*

Now that the group has shared observations and considered ideas, questions, and puzzles, the educator's next move is to invite personal responses and reflections as well as connections to the overall theme of human mortality. She says, "Thinking about your initial thoughts, and what you heard in our discussion, how do you make sense of and interpret the artist's choices, including the wreath of golden leaves you were still puzzling over? What message about human mortality is the artist conveying? How does it land with you?" A dialogue among group members begins:

I think the artist is lifting up his friend—even though it is not a portrait—and saying that he is the victor.

For me the fact that the young man who died is holding the wreath in his own hands feels very moving. I can't explain exactly why.

He is in control . . .

I like the idea that the artist is painting the transitional moment. In the hospital that moment can be slow or fast, but here the artist makes you pay attention to it.

But what are we paying attention to? This guy does not look dead, and death is just floating passively behind him. Maybe he is not dead yet—hasn't even reached that moment. His foot is just on the top step . . .

We are paying attention to his moment of death, we are stopping to consider it, think about it.

The youth himself seems to be the fulcrum between different aspects of death: the cut flowers are the loss, mortality, but the wreath seems to say he has won. And Death isn't asserting herself at all in this! (Laughter)

I am having trouble with what seems to be a heroic depiction of a young person's death. For the people left behind—the family, friends—there is so much suffering.

I think it might be important that it was dedicated to his friend, even though it is not a portrait.

Yes, I agree with that—and the idea that he is lifting up his friend, the memory of his friend, as present with him.

We are seeing him as his friend, the artist, remembered him, or wanted
him to be remembered

Regarding victory, I want to add that cultural values can make a difference
too.

In my religious tradition, there is an afterlife—so this life is not it, not all
there is.

There is an afterlife in mine also, but I still dread the first time someone
I am taking care of as a physician dies, especially a child or someone my age.

As the discussion of the work concludes, the educator tells the group that she
would like to share a quote from the Christian Bible in response to the themes of
loss and mortality as well as, perhaps, suggestions about the golden wreath held by
the youth. "When this perishable will have put on the imperishable, and this mortal
will have put on immortality, then will come about the saying that is written, Death
is swallowed up in victory. O Death, where is your victory, O Death where is your
sting?"[19] To provide context for the quote, she observes that Moreau often based
his paintings on religious and mythological stories. Although he lived and worked
in France—a predominantly Catholic country—he was not a believer himself. The
participants are quiet, each reflecting.

Before they move on, the educator summarizes the thought processes they
have used, noting that the subject of human mortality was their overall frame for
their looking and thinking. After a period of self-directed looking, they shared their
initial observations. After that, they focused their attention on specific goals, testing
the idea of human mortality against the artist's specific choices, and identifying
contradictions and things that raised questions. The educator functioned as both
a leader, through creating a structure for looking and offering information, and a
follower, following the group's lead by listening carefully and adapting her plan and
information to their contributions and direction.[20]

As in medicine, participants dealt with ambiguity and missing information as
they continued to generate questions and interpretations. They listened thoughtfully to each other and revised their thinking, by considering what they might have
missed initially. They considered connections to their own experiences in life and
in medicine. The educator shares appreciation for their skills in moving between
different types of thinking and keeping space open for different views and invites
them to relax and enjoy the walk to the other end of the museum for part two of
the session.

ENCOUNTERING THE UNEXPECTED

While still focusing on the theme of human mortality, the educator has planned to
use a slightly different process for the second artwork. A work of contemporary art,
it offers limited recognizable elements to analyze and, therefore, their initial observations are likely to rely on their immediate associations and previous experiences.
Works of art such as this one provide the opportunity to explore thought processes,

feelings, and associations while tackling a novel thinking task, initially with little information or context.

The educator plans to provide context and information as part of the development of the dialogue, distributing selected information about the work by group, rather than giving everyone the same information simultaneously. In doing so, she intends to bring attention to how different information and the availability of information, or lack of it, shapes their thinking, particularly with respect to an ambiguous work.

Arriving in a very large gallery filled with contemporary art, the educator stops before a pile of gold-foil-wrapped candies massed into a pyramid shape in a corner[21] (figure 2). The candy shines against the charcoal gray walls, lit from above. A small sign near the candy says, "Please take only one." The participants respond in varying ways—with laughter, puzzlement, or quiet—as the educator invites them to spend a few minutes just looking at the work of art in this space. After three or four minutes, the educator opens the conversation to first impressions and immediate questions, which include the following:

> I really didn't expect to be looking at something like this in an art museum. It's very strange to walk around the corner and see this pile of golden candy glinting under the spotlights.
> Is this even art? Did the artist make the candy?
> The sign says, "Please take only one" . . . Is that for real? Are we supposed to take a candy?

The educator responds, "Yes, help yourselves, but please do take only one." Laughter follows, then quiet. Several participants approach the work, lean down, and take a piece of candy. Some eat the candy, while some just turn it over in their hand or tuck it into a pocket.

> Normally you aren't allowed to touch anything in a museum—or eat anything. It's strange to pick up and eat a piece of candy in a museum.
> So . . . wait. If people are eating the candy, the size of the pile is going to change over time.
> My first impression was that this work is much simpler than the first one, much less to look at, but maybe harder to understand.
> You said both works today dealt with mortality?

Hearing this, the educator asks for first thoughts about that connection.

> As someone said, the candy will be disappearing, if, in fact, people do take some. It looks very plentiful today. My reaction [to taking candy] might be different if there wasn't much left.

Okay, the work has this unexpected [for an art museum] element of change. But I hate work like this. There is very little to work with. It's frustrating.

Well, I am just enjoying looking at this big pile of golden candy. I know I don't understand it, but I like it. I feel drawn to it.

The educator thanks the group for sharing their initial thoughts, and notes that some people sound curious, some amused, and some frustrated. Acknowledging that this work might have fewer specific reference points to start from, the educator offers some information. The artwork was made in 1991 by American artist Felix Gonzalez-Torres. The artist was born in Cuba, raised in Puerto Rico, and came to New York City at the age of twenty-two to study photography.[22] Gonzalez-Torres often made works of art using ordinary objects that could easily be purchased in a store: clocks, light bulbs, and, in this case, candy. He titled most of his works "Untitled", but some include additional parenthetical information, such as this one, which is "Untitled" (Portrait of Dad). Many of them have participatory elements requiring decisions or actions by the exhibitor and/or the visitor.[23]

The museum educator asks the participants to form three groups and find a spot to sit where they can see the work. She tells them that they will receive more information with which to continue thinking about the work.

INFORMATION AND COMPLEXITY

The educator hands one person per group a yellow envelope, each labeled with a number from one to three. Each envelope contains one of the following narratives. Groups are asked to read, discuss, and prepare to share the information in their envelope, along with their responses and questions about the work.

Envelope 1

Gonzalez-Torres created twenty candy works; only six included the name of a person in parentheses after "Untitled". This work is "Untitled" (Portrait of Dad). Included in the envelope is an image of "Untitled" (Portrait of Ross in L.A.), also dated 1991. In real life, the artist's father and the artist's life partner, Ross Laycock died within a few weeks of each other. However, the artist puts this additional information in parentheses because he wanted the work to be accessible to everyone's life experience.

Each candy work includes a caption which describes the work and guides exhibitors of the work. The caption for "Untitled" (Portrait of Dad) specifies white candies wrapped in cellophane, while the caption for "Untitled" (Portrait of Ross in L.A.) specifies that the candies be in variously colored wrappers. Each work's caption states "endless supply" and each states an ideal weight of 175 pounds of candy. Although this information offers guidance, in fact many elements are left up to the exhibitor—such as the format (pile, rectangle, ribbon, etc.) as well as whether and when to replenish the "endless supply." Thus, some elements of the work are affected by the artist's parameters, some by those people exhibiting the work, and, subsequently, also by visitors.

Thinking in the Art Museum

Depending on the size of the groups and how the discussion is going the educator decides when to call everyone back together. She invites the group that had the first envelope to begin sharing.

We don't know for sure that the title means this work is about his father, or that the weight of 175 pounds described his father either. But the idea that this may have been made with a specific person in mind, and—perhaps to memorialize them—resonated with us.

We got a photograph of another candy work—also from 1991—which may reference the artist's partner, called *"Untitled" (Portrait of Ross in L.A.)*— that one listed the ideal weight of 175 pounds of candies too.

This got us questioning the concept of ideal weight in relationship to a person, real or imagined? Are these works about these two human beings?

Learning that [the artwork] might be for or about his father was very poignant. We wonder if the artist's partner also died.

We talked quite a bit about why visitors are taking pieces away. What does "endless supply" mean in this context? We are still thinking about that. Is endless supply just about the candy?

The museum educator knows that, as in the earlier session, more information and greater context will open up new ideas and questions for the group.

Envelope 2

In 1988, Gonzalez-Torres began making work related to the AIDS epidemic, such as a set of twenty-one graph-paper drawings derived from test results of T cell (a type of white blood cell) counts that are measured to track weakening of the immune system due to HIV/AIDS. The work, *"Untitled" (21 Days of Bloodwork—Steady Decline)* explores themes of decline and diminishment as both a metaphor for and a real phenomenon experienced by individuals and communities within the larger context of the AIDS pandemic.[24]

In 1990 Gonzalez-Torres's partner Ross Laycock became very ill. The rigors of this illness that his partner went through can be felt in the artist's words that as Ross became less and less of a person, he loved him more.[25] In 1991, Ross died of complications of HIV/AIDS at the age of thirty-two. In his will, Ross asked that his ashes be distributed in one hundred yellow envelopes. Three weeks after Ross's death, the artist's father also died.[26]

We got some much more specific information about the artist's work in relation to the AIDS pandemic in the late 1980s and into the 1990s.

If the artist were our patient, we might be thinking about how much loss he experienced in a short time.

We were also trying to recall what we know about the disease before today's treatments. We spent some time discussing the "wasting" nature of HIV/AIDS at that time: people would become very debilitated and weak. The artist made a work about declining T cells as a progression marker in the disease.

As we discussed the uncertainty around the replenishing of the candy, that uncertainty entered our discussion. If the piles of candy might be slowly disappearing, the work felt more somber despite the candy—even ominous, and sad to us—as we imagined its gradual transformation.

We learned that the artist said that as his partner became sicker and weaker, the artist said he loved his partner more deeply. We got the sense of a very loving relationship in the face of death.

Our reactions were a bit all over the place. It was a lot to absorb—emotional—and at the same time I guess our group was struggling with placing these works in history and history of medicine also, and the magnitude of the epidemic. . . . And looking at all this sweet, bright candy.

Envelope 3

Many of Gonzalez-Torres's works of art incorporate elements of participation and transformation. The candy works exist as a set of instructions that are then manifested by the exhibitor. Visitors may take a piece of candy—it is their choice, and the works may change as a result. Similarly, exhibitors know the caption descriptions stated "endless supply." However, some candy works may be constantly replenished by the exhibitor, while others might be allowed to dwindle.

Today, many of Felix Gonzalez Torres's works are dependent on the actions of others who have outlived the artist himself. He died of complications from HIV/AIDS in 1996 at the age of thirty-eight.

The group who received the third set of information shares their thoughts:

We grappled with the aspect of participation and transformation. We discussed why we choose to take or not take the candy. What does it mean? Why all these instructions when at the same time really, they were flexible parameters?

I guess the most significant thing we learned was . . . well . . . everything [about the work] looked a bit different after we learned the artist died himself in 1996—he was thirty-eight.

Someone in our group said maybe these works have "instructions" because he already knew when he made them that he wouldn't be around.

Honestly that changed everything, but I don't think we can summarize the depth of our discussion.

THINKING ABOUT THINKING WITH "UNTITLED" (PORTRAIT OF DAD)

As with *The Young Man and Death*, the educator invites participants to reflect on the evolution of their thinking process, as well as to make connections to medicine.

Well, I was in the first group, and I feel like in terms of understanding the potential meaning of the work, we got much less additional information.

Yes, that was kind of frustrating to experience. There was information given to other groups—such as about AIDS—that really was quite thought-provoking. There are a lot of layers here.

Well, I like this process, because I could track myself taking in each new set of information when we did the group share. But then I could go back to what I originally knew . . . I felt it was like a puzzle and more interesting that way.

If I am honest, it felt like rounds [in the hospital], where one piece of information—maybe the one I am missing—transforms the thinking—and then you feel, oh, I was looking in the wrong direction, looking at the wrong thing.

The museum educator acknowledges that there can be frustration in having partial or misleading information and points out that this can be a common experience in medical training and beyond, as physicians both take care of people individually and also work in teams. For example, handoff information or a behavioral health note might significantly shape one's thinking. The educator goes back to the group to ask what they are thinking about at this point.

I think it is unusual that we are allowed to help ourselves but limited in what we can take. When does that happen in real life?

Halloween. (Laughter)

Sharing dinner growing up. . . . I have three brothers.

Communion. It is a symbolic meal, so everyone gets a little bread and a little wine.

I am still on the idea of memory—of keeping and sharing some kind of memory of a person—in connection to the candy,

The educator asks if anyone has thoughts they will take away relating to being a physician in training.

Even within our small group discussion, it became clear that people have had different experiences with death, either in their personal life or in the clerkships.

I had a hard time [with death] the first time—no one on the team really seemed to talk about it much. We didn't know much about the patient.

I haven't had a patient die yet. I am not sure I know how to be ready for that.

People want there to be meaning in death; both these artworks show that. But we think about that very differently depending on our connection to the person and our personal beliefs.

For me, the most moving thing was learning about the artists' personal connections to these people. I recently had an experience which made me very aware of how the family and even people who were on the care team were very affected by a death.

The educator expresses the hope that the day's discussions provided the participants with an opportunity to look closely, observe, question, and revise their own thought processes—ones they likely use every day in medical school—here, in an environment that is very different from the hospital. And that making time to take in and think about how they consider the interpretations of others—whether those of artists, colleagues, or their patients—about human mortality, loss, and memory may resonate beyond today.

THINKING IN THE ART MUSEUM

Museum-based sessions offer medical students and their mentors a unique thinking experience, one that is shared with others and in which time for looking, sensing, feeling, and thinking is expansive. Together, participants create immediate, layered experiences around significant works of art that have connections to human experience, and which can foster a rich and meaningful discussion with relevance to medicine—here, loss and death. In this example, each experience with the work of art begins with first-impression thinking followed by reflection, and then progresses through sequences of guided thinking. Infusions of information are combined with explicit invitations to reframe and rethink. As always, participants bring their own values, cultural beliefs, and experiences; since participants play a strong shaping role, no two sessions are alike. The educator has thought deeply and prepared carefully, usually in partnership with medical colleagues, to think through the territory and goals for the session, but does not rigidly predetermine any specific path to understanding once the dialogue begins.

Gallery activities are shaped around thinking tasks that are relevant to the complexity of thinking processes in medicine. Guided at times by the educator's structure, participants practice "problem-finding" (such as considering "puzzles" and things that don't fit). They generate their own questions as a key part of the process. Purposeful sequencing, slowing down the pace of thought processes, allows people to notice and integrate first impressions, observations, analysis, and interpretations.

In these sessions, participants were told that both artworks dealt with human mortality. The two works were chosen to offer different types of thinking opportunities. *The Young Man and Death* rewards close looking due to its representation of many objects that carry well-known symbolic connotations. This familiarity builds confidence and encourages students to notice what does and does not fit their emerging interpretations. Questions and gaps in information also become apparent. As in medicine, more information may lead to more questions—an active invitation to look at thinking as a testing process rather than just a search for a result. The invitation to notice what is lacking, hidden, or puzzling emulates clinical practices for guarding against errors rooted in confirmation and search satisfaction.

In the discussion of *The Young Man and Death* there were no large or unexpected curves or obstacles to derail the group. The experience was one of "unfolding"—an easy gentle road with some changes of view along the way. It feels like a shared experience which establishes common ground while making room for the groups' opinions and personal associations to take the conversation on divergent paths.

Working with artworks such as "Untitled" (Portrait of Dad) offers a different thinking opportunity, one in which observation processes are fruitful for experiencing how one confronts ambiguity or low-information situations in medicine. Some thinking errors arise in medicine as doctors narrow their frame, fail to see all that is present, and confirm their conclusions by anchoring them in early impressions. In the museum setting, an artwork that gives few clues as to how to interpret it may help bypass thinking issues related to narrow cognitive framing. The viewer cannot really establish that frame and, by design, is slowed down. One move that the participant can make in response to ambiguity is to like or dislike the work. Such a strategy—to close off and decide "there is nothing more to see here"—too has parallels in medicine. The museum educator's job is to interest participants in taking time with an artwork, to fully experience it and become curious about it. When it is unlikely that any participant is familiar or knowledgeable about the work, this creates a level field of play in which there is less desire to "go it alone." In the museum, where stakes are low, this parity can also promote interest in collaborative interpretation, mitigating individual's tendencies toward overconfidence or premature closure. Medical educators working collaboratively with a museum educator may choose to make these connections more explicit in debriefing the experience.

The processes of identifying what you think you know and forming hypotheses are much more straightforward midway through the experience with The Young Man and Death than with "Untitled" (Portrait of Dad). Distributing information to the smaller groups rather than to the whole group at the same time is intended to foreground how issues of context and lack of context influence interpretation. As the smaller groups take in, apply, and then share out the information they have received, there is a startling expansion of knowledge. Working from different types of information—artistic, historical, medical, personal—the participants become aware of how context affects understanding. This is relevant to many situations in medicine when information is lacking, ambiguous, or differentially distributed across a healthcare team.

"Medicine has always been an uncertain science," Jerome Groopman writes in How Doctors Think.[27] Art museum sessions provoke insights achieved through complex thinking practices, even as they address human values in medicine. They engage participants in observing, wondering, interpreting, and knowing. Art museums offer a valuable place to encounter one's own patterns of thinking. The ability to entertain novelty and sustain doubt—not as an emotional state but as a cognitive practice—is deeply tied to a practitioner's conscious development of an intentional, ongoing commitment to observe, listen, and question. Student clinicians learn early on how important it is to know the right answer and take the right action; this may be essential and ethically necessary to produce well-trained clinicians. Yet, in these intense and formative years, trainees will also encounter highly complex, novel, and ambiguous problems. Then, and throughout their careers as physicians, they will encounter human beings facing illness and pain, loss, and death. Art is good for thinking, in part because it insists on the intrinsic value of human experience in all its diversity. Ultimately, the art museum can offer a place to confront "not knowing" while maintaining engagement and curiosity and to practice embracing with humanity the uncertainty and ambiguity that is inevitably part of clinical medicine.[28]

NOTES

1. Claude Lévi-Strauss, *Totemism* (Boston: Beacon Press, 1963), 89. This is my translation of *bon a penser* which has been variously translated as "good to think," "good to think with," and other translations.
2. Jerome Groopman, *How Doctors Think* (Boston: Mariner Books, 2008), 27–33.
3. Groopman, *How Doctors Think*, 4–6.
4. Groopman, *How Doctors Think*, 24.
5. Pat Croskerry, Greta Singha, and Silvia Mamede, "Cognitive Debiasing 1: Origins of Bias and Theory of Debiasing," *BMJ Quality & Safety* 22 (2013): ii58–ii64.
6. Table 2.1 draws on Croskerry et al., "Cognitive Debiasing 1"; Mark Graber, Ruthanna Gordon, and Nancy Franklin, "Reducing Diagnostic Errors in Medicine," *Academic Medicine* 77, no. 10 (2002): 981–92; Pat Croskerry, "The Importance of Cognitive Errors in Diagnosis and Strategies to Minimize Them," *Academic Medicine* 78, no. 8 (2003): 775–80; Jerome Groopman, *How Doctors Think*: 22–26, 34–58, 64–69, 74–76, 124–28, 149–55, 169–75, 179–80, 184–87, 239; and Justin Morgenstern, "Cognitive Errors in Medicine: The Common Errors," First10EM, updated September 22, 2019, https://first10em.com/cognitive-errors/.
Note: I (Slavin) worked comparatively across these sources to understand the most common or important cognitive dispositions, as an aid to museum educators, in particular.
7. Gustavo Saposnik, Donald Redelmeier, Christian C. Ruff, and Philippe N. Tobler, "Cognitive Biases Associated with Medical Decisions: A Systematic Review," *BMC Medical Informatics and Decision Making* 16, 138 (2016).
8. Pat Croskerry, "The Importance of Cognitive Errors in Diagnosis and Strategies to Minimize Them," *Academic Medicine* 78, no. 8 (2003): 775–80.
9. Saposnik et al., "Cognitive Biases"; and Croskerry, "The Importance of Cognitive Errors."
10. Croskerry et al., "Cognitive Debiasing 1."
11. Morgenstern, "Cognitive Errors in Medicine."
12. Groopman, *How Doctors Think*, 8, 151–55.
13. Groopman, *How Doctors Think*, 17. Here, Groopman draws on the research of Judith Hall and Debra Roter regarding doctor-patient communication.
14. Groopman, *How Doctors Think*, 175, 260–69.
15. Gustave Moreau, *The Young Man and Death*, oil on canvas, 1856–65, Harvard Art Museums/Fogg Museum, Gift of Grenville L. Winthrop, Class of 1886, 1942.186, https://hvrd.art/o/230409.
16. Groopman, *How Doctors Think*, 12.
17. *The Young Man and Death*, Harvard Art Museums, https://hvrd.art/o/230409.
18. Zuhre Indirkas, "The Presence of Death in Gustave Moreau's Paintings," *Synergies Turquie* 3 (2010): 69–78.

19. 1 Cor. 15:53–55, New Testament, ASV.
20. Rika Burnham and Elliot Kai Kee, *Teaching in the Art Museum: Interpretation as Experience* (Los Angeles: Getty Publications, 2011), 79–93. This example is closest to dialogue, as described by the authors, in having an "open, improvisatory" quality, yet, also, specific purposes.
21. This description details the installation of *"Untitled" (Portrait of Dad)*, 1991, at the University of Michigan Museum of Art, in the exhibition *Come As You Are: Art of the 1990s*. At University of Michigan Museum of Art, the candy was white candy in gold wrappers. The official information about this specific work of conceptual art is available on the Felix Gonzalez-Torres Foundation website: https://www.felixgonzalez-torresfoundation.org/works/untitled-portrait-of-dad. All candy works, their official descriptions, and photographs of the work are accessible at https://www.felixgonzalez-torresfoundation.org/works/c/candy-works.
22. Julie Ault, "Chronology," Felix Gonzalez-Torres Foundation, accessed June 2, 2022, https://felixgonzalez-torresfoundation.org/attachment/en/5b844b306aa72cea5f8b4567/DownloadableItem/5ebff7ff2bab2c1a7505f817.
23. Sources consulted include Robert Storr, "When This You See, Remember Me," in *Felix Gonzalez-Torres*, edited by Julie Ault (Gottingen, Germany: Steidldangin, 2006), 5–37; Julie Ault, "Chronology," Felix Gonzalez-Torres Foundation, accessed June 2, 2022, https://felixgonzalez-torresfoundation.org/attachment/en/5b844b306aa72cea5f8b4567/DownloadableItem/5ebff7ff2bab2c1a7505f817; "Felix Gonzalez-Torres," Guggenheim Museum Collection Online, accessed June 3, 2022, https://www.guggenheim.org/artwork/artist/felix-gonzalez-torres; "Felix Gonzalez-Torres Bio," Queer Cultural Center, accessed June 3, 2022, https://queerculturalcenter.org/felix-gonzalez-torres-2/; "Felix Gonzalez-Torres," The Art Story, accessed, June 2, 2022, https://www.theartstory.org/artist/gonzalez-torres-felix/; Andrea Rosen, "'Untitled'" (Neverending Portrait), in *Felix Gonzalez-Torres Catalogue Raisonne*, edited by Dietmar Elger (Ostfildern-Ruit, Germany: Hatje Cantz Verlag, 1997), 44–59; Charlotte Maratta, "Unending Sweetness: Identity and Loss" in *"Untitled" (Portrait of Dad)*, *Colby Echo*, March 1, 2018, https://medium.com/@colbyecho/unending-sweetness-loss-and-identity-in-untitled-portrait-of-dad-825a37d43de0. See also "Candy Works," Felix Gonzalez-Torres Foundation, https://www.felixgonzalez-torresfoundation.org/works/c/candy-works.
24. FGT website.
25. Julie Ault, "Chronology"; Ross Bleckner, "Felix Gonzalez-Torres," *Bomb* 51 (April 5, 1995), https://bombmagazine.org/articles/felix-gonzalez-torres/.
26. Julie Ault, "Chronology."
27. Groopman, *How Doctors Think*, 7.
28. Physician and historian Dr. Joel Howell has been an invaluable thinking and teaching partner regarding the complex dynamics of uncertainty and ambiguity in medicine since 2009.

3

Cultivating Empathy

Art museums, replete with objects and stories from different cultures, historical periods, and perspectives, are environments well suited to cultivate empathy. As described throughout this book, they are places where we can come together in community to develop skills and share observations, feelings, thoughts, and stories. In this chapter, we offer perspectives, ideas, and designs supporting the cultivation of empathy. We provide extended examples of strategies to foster perspective taking and deep listening, to notice one's own emotional responses and patterns of thinking, and to heighten awareness of nonverbal communication. We engage participants in creative play, reflective writing, and interpretive conversations, including the widely used Visual Thinking Strategies (VTS) method of teaching. Although each of us has been working with healthcare partners on empathy in the art museum for nearly fifteen years, we draw on the recent work of physician and empathy researcher Helen Riess and its practical, research-tested application in healthcare to frame the chapter's narrative.

In her 2018 book, *The Empathy Effect: Seven Neuroscience-Based Keys for Transforming the Way We Live, Love, Work, and Connect Across Differences*, Riess writes,

> When people show empathy for others, they are usually good at *perceiving* what others feel, able to *process the information*, and able to *respond effectively*. So, it is important to broaden the definition [of empathy] as a capacity that encompasses the entire loop from perception *of*, to response *to* someone else's experience, and, finally, to check with that person for accuracy, if there is any doubt. This last part of the loop is called empathic accuracy.[1]

Drawing on research in neuroscience, Riess stresses that empathic capacity requires both emotion and cognition.[2] As outlined earlier, her model stresses the importance of action, as well as direct feedback, to check interpretations and assumptions.

Today, there is growing consensus that empathy is important to excellent patient care. Riess writes that patients "are more likely to trust their doctors, stick to medical recommendations, and have better health outcomes," if their doctors are perceived as empathetic.[3] At the same time, empathy's definition, purpose, and practice in medicine continue to be debated, as well as whether it can be increased or "taught." These questions are pressing ones. Research has identified increased stress and burnout among not only medical students, but also interns and residents, early career physicians, and senior physicians.[4] Regarding physicians in her training sessions and research studies, Riess writes, "they reported that by learning to sit down and notice the whole person before them, and not just the illness or injured body part, they felt more connected to their patients and their profession."[5]

The fact that empathy also benefits physicians—that it enables them to feel strongly connected to their purpose and their patients, and more satisfied with their work—is more important than ever. Far from the hectic demands of the hospital or clinic, art museums can also offer healthcare providers a unique space to process emotions and share stories with one another. While the stories in our initial example demonstrate the trainees' empathic capacity, they also illuminate challenges to empathy, as well as questions about how physicians can best practice empathic connections to patients while maintaining their own equilibrium and well-being.

CLERKSHIP STORIES: BECOMING A DOCTOR

Every doctor first encounters the hands-on practice of medicine by taking care of patients during clinical rotations or "clerkships." Significant experiences during their training years stay with physicians and shape their professional identities and practices. At the University of Michigan, as part of an elective course two hundred medical students have created a personal "clerkship story." Each has chosen a work of art and used it to reflect on their clerkship experiences. Students share their story with a group that includes peers, mentoring physicians, and a museum educator. Their stories enable us to see how each student uses specific details of the work of art to reflect upon their clerkship experiences, as well as to gain new perspective.

The following stories illuminate students' efforts to care for patients while mastering the balancing act of being a young physician trainee. Here are two students' stories in response to the painting *Bauhaus Stairway* by Oscar Schlemmer.[6]

In *Bauhaus Stairway* (1932), eight figures, each only partially in the frame, are seen at various stations on an angular staircase set against large windows with gridded panes. . . . I couldn't stop thinking about Schlemmer's stairway as a hospital stairwell. It is the stairwell that I cried in after a particularly demoralizing standardized patient experience. It's the one that I escaped to so I could briefly glance at my phone and scroll through my family chat to see if I'd missed anything important during the past fourteen hours I'd spent between the operating room and the floor. This time, Schlemmer's figures stood out to me for their solitude. Stairways are places of transition. They may be crowded, but they are no one's destination.

This student continued to explore her themes of loneliness—even while surrounded by people—and the need for empathy as she recounts watching a patient being prepared for a procedure. It wasn't going smoothly, and the patient's face showed that they were in pain from the repeated attempts.

> The patient kept wincing in pain, and in doing so moving slightly, which in turn made it more difficult to complete the procedure. I couldn't think of a more important time for someone to not be alone. I went around the bed and without thinking, I held this person's hand. I told them to squeeze my hand like a stress ball; I rubbed their arm.
> There are a million interpersonal dynamics that seem to go on in hospitals, dynamics that can feel like land mines to medical students. It can be exhausting to recognize these dynamics and try to "perform" without encroaching, overstepping, detonating. At that moment, though, I completely forgot about them. This man's loneliness, or at least, aloneness, was so overwhelming that it drowned out all of the other noise in the pre-op bay. As a medical student, I may have overstepped. I am still figuring out where lines are when it comes to physical contact with patients, when an empathetic touch on the arm is appropriate and when it is discomfiting. But at that moment, it felt like my only choice. My human brain overtook my medical-student brain. My only goal was to ease the aloneness and the pain.[7]

Another student told of witnessing a patient being informed of a serious complication that would delay their further treatment. The message was delivered by the attending physician in a brief and straightforward way during rounds with a group of residents, medical students, and fellows. The patient began to cry in front of the assembled group, who left very soon after. The patient later found them in the hallway and pleaded with the physician to reconsider delaying the treatment.

> In our rush to continue with rounds, we moved away quickly and did not adequately address the situation. As we walked towards our next patient's room, I trailed behind the group and quietly shed a few tears. In this memory, we as providers were the figures in the painting, moving urgently away from the discomfort and the feelings that we neglected to embrace, and keeping our heads down to avoid eye contact. I believe that we left this patient with the feeling of desolation that I experienced as a viewer of this painting. I imagine him as the viewer, watching our emotionless faces and our backs turn, as we left him to cry by himself. I wish I had had the courage to stay behind. I would have let him know that I was there with him, and that we were not abandoning him. I will carry this memory with me for a long time. Human connection holds incredible power. As I am learning the art and the practice of medicine, I want to continue to remind myself to slow down and look up—to connect with my patients and understand and embrace their experiences.[8]

After students share their clerkship stories, each hears a heartfelt "thank you for sharing your story." Sometimes the assembled listeners respond actively, and sometimes they remain quiet. In this case, one of the senior physician mentors responded, "Your story touches me. The reflective moments we take to consider our clinical experiences, I think, enable us to 'stay behind'—or at least return later to connect with patients, and simultaneously take care of ourselves."[9]

The Moon, by Brazilian artist Tarsila do Amaral, is an abstract night scene of a rolling landscape painted in deep blues and greens and with a large yellow crescent moon.[10] Medical students frequently choose this work for their clerkship stories, as they often begin and end their shifts in darkness. The themes they explore through this work are varied; among them are solitude, longing, mission, and human connection. One student used specific elements of this painting to tell a story of human connection with a patient, his family, and their care team, as the patient prepared to end a long hospital stay and enter hospice.

> In *The Moon* I see a dying man facing his death with acceptance, courage, and grace. I see a semi-circle of caregivers—some who cared for him for years, others who came into his life only a few days before—offering silent comfort and collectively honoring a beautiful soul while he told stories from his life. I see the curve of the earth fade into an inky, uncertain horizon. Above the abyss, however, I see ethereal promise lying in wait. During my first month of clinical work, I had the true privilege of caring for a dying man.
>
> I marveled at stories of his life's great adventures, collecting snippets of his wisdom to enrich my own journeys yet to come. The dying man and his wife embraced me as a member of their care team and welcomed me into their lives during a time of raw vulnerability. In return, I was rewarded with the opportunity to bear witness to a beautiful love story. In caring for this couple, I experienced a profound sense of purpose. I left the hospital each day knowing I had made a positive impact in the lives of others and felt deeply valued for the comfort I offered. At several critical points in my journey towards becoming a physician I have wondered whether it was all worth it. As I reflect on my experience caring for this elderly couple, I am met with a sense of peace and relief. I am more sure than ever that no matter the hardships I encounter along the way, my journey towards becoming a physician and my pursuit of a career of service to others is well worth the costs.[11]

Responses and evaluations from these story-sharing sessions express how much medical students value these opportunities to integrate their perceptions, feelings, and thoughts from clinical rotations with their evolving values and identities. We who listen find resonance in the experiences described and connect to our shared humanity. In the students' stories we see the difference that empathy and human connection can make to their sense of self and of vocation during these first years of clinical work. Together, we reflect on the complexities of learning to be a doctor.

CARING FOR THE LIVES OF OTHERS

Physicians develop their professional identities in a medical culture in which excellence, competitiveness, decisiveness, and action are valued, and emotions may often be devalued. As physician Ronald Epstein writes, trainees often receive little explicit guidance to deal with their empathic responses.[12] Compassionate care does not require that healthcare professionals feel what their patients are feeling. Especially for trainees, emotional responses can lead to overidentification, automatic responses, or withdrawal, any of which may reduce empathic capacity or interfere with gaining an accurate understanding of the patient and their illness. Further into their careers, doctors work under demanding, often stressful conditions where the stakes are high and mistakes can have significant consequences. Long past the training years, difficult emotions are an inevitable part of medicine, especially for all who care most directly for patients.[13] Yet opportunities to process emotions or sort through them for clinical information can be hard to come by in medicine.

As described, empathy is based in human capacities including both cognition and emotion.[14] Cognition plays a fundamental role in perspective-taking, diagnostic thinking, and checking for accuracy in the empathy loop, but what about emotion? Dr. Jodi Halpern's 2001 book, *From Detached Concern to Empathy: Humanizing Medical Practice*, details how detached concern was considered instrumental to clinical objectivity and emotional equilibrium. In advocating for alternatives to detached concern, Halpern uses the term "emotional reasoning" to describe the way in which physicians employ emotions as data in order to pursue an accurate and holistic clinical understanding. She argues that a physician's attention to body language, facial expressions, moods, distinctive words, and associations (and discrepancies among these) are clinical data, as are the physician's intuition and gut feelings.[15]

Halpern also argues that attunement to the patient—understanding when to listen, and when and how to talk or pose questions—is essential, as these skills establish trust and good communication in the doctor-patient relationship, and are fundamental to the accurate clinical understanding necessary for excellent medical care.[16] Needless to say, attunement must be complemented by analytic thinking on the part of the caregiver in order to assess meaning, accuracy, and reliability. The physician relies on both cognitive and emotional reasoning. Because the empathy cycle is a dynamic one, Halpern, like Riess, argues that it is critical for doctors to define and develop specific skills, rather than simply exhorting them to "have compassion." She notes that some types of observations have been devalued and urges doctors to make use of "what they already notice but have learned not to pay attention to."[17]

Self-awareness and self-acceptance help doctors stay alert to the need to modulate their own emotions. Visceral feelings, automatic thoughts, and gut reactions can offer insight, but may also signal cognition errors originating in feelings. The inability to detect one's own automatic thoughts and reactions makes it harder to check one's bias. Indeed, such internal awareness is essential to successful "perspective taking." The ability to maintain healthy boundaries within a compassionate response supports a physician's effectiveness and protects their well-being. Feeling and thinking work together to achieve better self-regulation which, in turn, supports the physician's ability to practice medicine with empathy toward each and every patient.

Riess writes, "By definition, empathy . . . requires an intimate comprehension of the others' inner lives, the context in which they live, and their resulting actions."[18] Yet, even as we try to fully imagine the lives of others, there are barriers to empathy. Most people are more empathetic toward, and can more easily take the point of view of, those whom they perceive as similar to themselves.[19] Stereotypes and bias—conscious and unconscious—can impede our attempt to perceive and process accurately and respond compassionately.[20] Challenges found in both life and medicine—among them high-stress situations, time pressures, burnout, and mental health issues—can powerfully affect our human ability to marshal empathic capacity when responding to others, as well as toward our own needs. Amid the many inputs of modern medicine—for example, entering information into an electronic medical record on a computer, or quickly reviewing medications, tests, and treatment protocols—it may be easy to lose sight of the patient as a unique and autonomous person whose life has its own meaning separate from the medical context.[21] Therefore, the commitment to practicing empathy across differences is not achievable through a superficial universalism, but through repeated attempts to understand, imagine, and respect lives and experiences different from our own.

EDUCATING FOR EMPATHY

Despite the benefits of empathy for both patient care and physicians' well-being, there have traditionally been few opportunities in formal medical training to explicitly learn skills that support empathic communication and inquiry. In 2009, Dr. Mohammadreza Hojat et al. published a landmark study suggesting that medical training might even contribute to *declines* in empathy among students as they complete clinical rotations.[22] Hojat's study and others persuasively argue for including formal training to build empathic skills within undergraduate and graduate medical education. In a 2018 article about physician training, "Kindness in the Curriculum," Hojat asserts that "empathy is the "the backbone of the patient-physician relationship."[23]

Through an iterative cycle of research and training, Riess has developed the seven keys of E.M.P.A.T.H.Y.®[24] to provide a clear model for training health professionals and others in the skills of empathic communication. It addresses both cognitive and emotional aspects of empathy, the importance of paying attention to nonverbal communication, and the necessity for developing reflective self-awareness.

E.M.P.A.T.H.Y.® stands for the following:

- Eye contact: Making eye contact, even briefly, can help one feel seen and promote a sense of trust. Eyes hold emotion.
- Muscles of facial expression: Layers of meaning can be discerned through various aspects of facial expression, including those of the mouth, the eyes, and the lines on one's face.
- Posture: Reading the body language of patients can offer insights, as we often hold emotions visibly in our bodies. Riess also recommends providers pay attention to their own bodies; sometimes we mirror the body language of others, and at other times our embodied responses can clue us into our own emotional states.
- Affect: One gains clarity by naming the emotions perceived in others, as well as paying attention to one's own emotional responses. Reiss writes, "Emotions are at the core of all challenging conversations. Without naming the affect [emotion] you cannot be fully conscious about why a conversation is challenging."[25]
- Tone of voice: Listening beneath the words being spoken to the tone of voice being used can help one understand someone else more deeply. Being aware of the impact of our tone of voice when speaking can help us communicate effectively.
- Hearing the whole person: Being fully present when someone is speaking requires attunement and listening with openness, compassion, and without judgment. When one hears the whole person, they are attending to the interplay of words, facial expression, body language, tone of voice, and emotion, and considering them in the larger context of the person's life narrative.
- Your response: Riess argues that to be empathic communicators we must develop awareness of our own emotional responses. Noticing our own emotions allows us to modulate them as necessary.

It is important to note that E.M.P.A.T.H.Y.® includes elements which can be enacted in a visible manner. One can "perform" empathetic actions, saying what we think are the right words and demonstrating other tangible signs of empathy such as softening and lowering the tone of voice. We all adjust in order to communicate—there is nothing wrong with intentionally checking and adapting these elements. However, Riess clearly indicates by including "hearing the whole person" and "your response" that empathy requires being present with the patient and with oneself.

E.M.P.A.T.H.Y.® AT THE ART MUSEUM

In this next section we describe ways Riess's E.M.P.A.T.H.Y.® can be practiced and enacted in the art museum setting. Riess writes, "When art is at its best . . . there is nothing more powerful to move society toward a more empathic stance."[26] An interprofessional group of experienced health-professions educators, including physicians and nurses, gathers at an art museum for a session focused on empathy.

As educators, they are dedicated to helping their students cultivate skills that will enable them to be more empathic with their patients and with themselves; the educators have come to the museum to learn some strategies to incorporate in their teaching. The following examples describe ways Riess's E.M.P.A.T.H.Y.® can be practiced and enacted in the art museum setting.

After a warm welcome and an introduction to what the E.M.P.A.T.H.Y.® acronym encompasses, a museum educator invites the group to stroll around the gallery, as she offers a series of prompts. "As you pass someone, acknowledge them with a gesture." Some people wave, others nod their heads. One person curtsies while their partner bows. The group continues walking. "Now acknowledge the person you are passing with a facial expression." Most people smile. On the third prompt, the group is invited to make eye contact as they continue mingling around the space. On the fourth and final prompt, everyone slows down as they are asked to stop, turn to the person next to them and to acknowledge each other by offering their hands and looking into one another's eyes (some people gently rest their palms together while others choose to hold their hands in a hovering position). "As you exchange gazes," the educator continues, "notice your partner's eye color."

Upon reflection, the group notices that despite a bit of discomfort, the activity fostered a sense of connection and even a sense of intimacy. There is a vulnerability that can occur when exchanging gazes in an openhearted way. (For some participants, the activity also provoked an awareness of possible power dynamics that might be part of the medical gaze—who has permission to look at whom?—leading to reflections on how they might subvert that.) Perhaps, the group mused, making reciprocal eye contact is something that doesn't happen frequently enough. While acknowledging that in some cultures direct eye contact might be considered intrusive, Riess suggests that training oneself to subtly notice eye color when first meeting a patient can be a helpful strategy toward seeing someone as an individual. She writes, "Studies suggest that people who rate higher on emotional empathic capacity scales spend more time fixated on eyes, even when the person they are observing is on video."[27]

Riess advocates for more emphasis on nonverbal communication training and practice, reminding us that missing the many ways patients communicate and express emotions nonverbally has a cost in terms of health outcomes and patient satisfaction. William Laughey et al. agree, arguing that too great a focus on empathy as verbal communication skills, can contribute to "empathy as . . . . artifice."[28] Furthermore, Riess reminds us that as patient populations become more culturally diverse, reading such clues is imperative:

An urgent need exists to teach nonverbal aspects of communication, as medical practices must be reoriented to the increasing cultural diversity represented by patients presenting for care. Where language proficiency may be limited, nonverbal communication becomes more crucial for understanding patients' communications. Furthermore, even in the absence of cultural differences, many patients are reluctant to disagree with their clinicians, and subtle nonverbal clues may be the critical entry point for discussions leading to shared medical decisions.[29]

Honing these skills is increasingly important, as several recent studies note generational declines in empathy, particularly in the ability to interpret facial expressions and body language.[30]

Portraits and images of people make ideal stimuli for learning to read nonverbal subtleties of body language, facial expression, mood, and emotion. In this example, a group of interns and residents explore Dawoud Bey's large-scale photograph *Theresa, South Shore High School* (2003), from *Class Pictures*, a 1992–2006 series portraying high school students (figure 3). In *Seeing Deeply*, Bey states he sought to give young people opportunities for self-expression and to challenge common stereotypes of teens "as socially problematic or as engines for a certain consumerism."[31] Before the artist photographs each student, he asks them to write a personal statement. Bey's work encourages the viewer "to see deeply"—to pay attention to and to celebrate the everyday lives of Black Americans and others who have not historically been represented in cultural spaces. It is fundamentally empathetic in its purpose.

In the photograph, Theresa looks directly out from the frame. Several people in the group are immediately drawn to the figure's gaze, and a range of observations and thoughts are offered. For some, the photograph's directness conveys a sense of connection, while for others, feelings of sadness, apprehension, confrontation, and waiting are elicited. The group continues to tease out their interpretations, considering nuances of Theresa's facial muscles, the set of her lips, and her body language. One person remarks that her direct gaze makes him feel he is being observed rather than being the observer. The stillness of her face contrasts with the energy of her hands causing another participant to state "those hands seem to contain a whole world of meaning." The positioning of the hands, in particular, sparks investigation. Theresa is seated at a table or desk with her elbows on the wooden surface. Her left arm is upright, resting in a vertical position, while the right is angled diagonally across the desk. The fingers of both hands are intertwined. Activating a form of embodied inquiry, many in the group try to approximate the positioning of Theresa's hands using their own, wondering if they might hold clues to her emotional state. Is the position a defensive one? Is she using them as a subtle protective barrier?

With a slight tilt, Theresa's head rests on her entwined hands, and her body subtly leans forward. Noticing this, participants add the possibilities of contemplation and vulnerability to the dialogue. Some ponder what can be learned from clothing and hairstyle. For many, Theresa appears a bit guarded. As they imagine encountering Theresa in a clinical setting, the group wonders about her story and how they might begin to establish trust. Building on the direction of the group's comments, the museum educator continues to guide participants through the empathy loop of "perceiving, processing, and moving towards action" by inviting them to brainstorm strategies they might use to begin building a relationship and establishing trust.[32] The possibility that the group's multiple interpretations could simultaneously be true highlights the complexity of lived experience. A resident offers she would respectfully approach Theresa by pausing and waiting for an invitation to proceed. Another suggests asking Theresa, "As your care provider, what would you like me to know?"

Intertwining cognitive perspective-taking and emotional reasoning, the group has used the language of emotions, and looked for visual evidence as they built interpretations. Shari Tishman, a researcher studying emotion at Project Zero, proposes that "Emotions are interpretations waiting to be explored. When we use them as starting points to look further and dig deeper, it helps us learn more."[33] Multiple perspectives surfaced throughout the discussion of *Theresa*, and the group's thinking evolved, reminding us of the humility that is called for when we try to understand another person.

As a final part of the experience, the museum educator shares a recording of Theresa reading her personal statement:

> I watch *60 Minutes* with my father, and so I hear about different things around the world, and I also listen to Andy Rooney. Yeah . . . he seems sort of funny . . . 'Cause, uh, I remember one thing he was talking about—opening medicine. He was saying that, um, trying to open a medicine, he said that it's children proof, but it's adult proof too because it's hard to open the capsule. And the reason that I'm saying this is because it's hard for a female to open up on what they'll be, or what they are. And for me, for what *I* am, it's sort of hard because I face, like, you face discrimination. . . . They see . . . males see you, um, they see you weaker than they are. And they say, you can't do this, you can't do that, and I know . . . I can *overcome* that because I believe in myself. And nobody can put me down.[34]

To conclude the discussion, the museum educator shares a quote from artist Dawoud Bey: "Through close engagement with other human beings, there is the potential to learn not only about that person you are looking at, but ideally to learn something about oneself."[35] She invites the group to reflect on the arc of their museum experience of looking closely, and to share what they learned about Theresa and themselves. After listening to Theresa's words, people begin to offer personal stories. Several discuss the various forms of racism and bias they have encountered in their professional lives; others remember what it was like to be a teenager—being simultaneously bold and insecure, or feeling anxious and yearning for connection. The sharing of stories, and vulnerabilities, helps the group recognize their common humanity. One member concludes that the process of attentive engagement with the photograph helped her move from a position of distance to a feeling of openheartedness, leading to a desire to know more about Theresa, as well as more about her own colleagues.

Perspective-taking is a core aspect of cognitive empathy. It helps us "appreciate . . . that another person has thoughts/feelings separate from our own."[36] In designing experiences that focus on empathy, we recommend that educators carefully choose artworks that reflect diverse situations and emotional states. Listening to the thoughts, associations, and emotional responses of others can enhance and expand one's perspective. When a group engages in an open-ended, interpretive conversation, participants often express surprise at how a single object of shared focus can provoke so many different responses. Such encounters invite reflection on how lived experiences and individual lenses inform observations and meaning making. With reflection, assumptions and blind spots may also become visible.

EMPATHIC IMAGINATION AND PERSPECTIVE-TAKING

Riess and Halpern posit that in addition to genuine curiosity and presentness, seeing the world from someone else's perspective requires activating one's imagination. As Riess writes, "Imagination is the first step in building empathy: how can I develop empathy for you if I can't imagine what it's like to be you?"[37] The rich holdings of museums offer myriad opportunities for activating our empathic imaginations through creative approaches to perspective-taking. A flexible strategy often used in museum-based education for healthcare professionals is the group poem. With a carefully chosen prompt, group poems can help foster empathic capacity by inviting participants to imagine the stories, thoughts, and feelings of another person. In a space of rehearsal, group poems can also help prepare new practitioners for leading potentially sensitive conversations. In the following example, a group of twelve interns carefully observes a seventeenth-century portrait of Spanish poet and monk *Fray Hortensio Félix Paravicino*, by El Greco at the Museum of Fine Arts, Boston.[38] The museum educator divides the interns into two groups of six. Distributing strips of paper, she invites everyone to write one line in response to the following prompt: "Imagine you are an adult sibling of this person. What would you say to his health team to help them better understand their patient?" After reading their individual responses aloud in their small groups, each team collaboratively arranges their lines in an agreed upon sequence and performs their poetic creation for their colleagues, as in the following example:

> He is the serious sort
> He helps the poor and the sick, and wears a Peter Pan collar
> My brother didn't play outside much as a child
> Please make sure he gets some sunlight
> I'm trying to decide whether to apologize or not
> He sings like an angel in the choir

After both teams present, the museum educator asks the group, "What did the activity ask of you?" Participants describe how they used observation skills and their own emotions and imaginations to envisage what might matter to the person portrayed and to a caregiver sibling. They pondered the larger context of someone's life and the qualities that make up an individual. And they notice that each of them offered a different lens into the imagined temperament, history, accomplishments, and behaviors of this person—perhaps informed by their own experiences. In making resonant connections to their professional roles, they identified the importance of gaining insight into the larger context of a patient's life. The group concludes by acknowledging a sense of responsibility for holding patients' stories; and they also consider their relationship to patients' family members.

Empathic inquiry invites different entry points into understanding the experiences of others. Our own emotions, memories, knowledge, reflections, and associations can potentially be resources as we work to interpret and understand another's story. They offer points of departure for further inquiry and deeper listening. We must use them, though, with humility and with the recognition that while insights might exist, our experience is not someone else's. Leslie Jamison, author of *The Empathy Exams*, writes, "Empathy requires inquiry as much as imagination."[39] Our own experiences can never fully approximate the singular experiences of another. As Reiss reminds us, part of the empathy loop in a clinical encounter is making sure to check for accuracy.[40]

IMAGINING AND OBSERVING: EXPLORING DUAL PERSPECTIVES

Medical training emphasizes systematic thinking and observation. The following activity uses photographs of people—alone or with others, from portraits to street scenes—to explore observing and imagining, and to inquire into the value of these perspectives in clinical care. Museum and medical educators guide participants through an exploration of associated issues. Students differentiate observing and imagining, reflecting on their values and priorities as physicians.

When welcoming the group into an intimate museum study space, the museum educator lets them know that the fourteen photographs before them have been brought out of storage for them. The chosen photographs are works that have ample details for observation and which can spark imaginative engagement.

1. Perspective-Taking and the Empathic Imagination (ten minutes)
   A. Students are given free time to look at all the photographs and choose an image that draws them in. They are invited to focus on one figure in the photograph and to use their imagination to write from that person's perspective, using the first-person voice ("I"). The museum educator encourages students to look closely for clues and ideas, and to draw upon their own emotions and bodily senses as sources of possible insight.
   B. When everyone is done, each person stands beside their selected photograph. A partner who has written about a different work joins them.
2. Observing (five minutes to write, ten minutes to share)

A. Next, students are asked to focus on the person in their partner's chosen photograph, and to write from an empirical perspective. The goal is to describe their observations in as concrete and factual a manner as possible.

B. Partners read aloud their writing beginning with the first-person narrative, then the objective perspective. They repeat this process with the second photograph.

3. What Did We Do? Examining the Dual Perspectives (fifteen minutes)

A. The museum and healthcare educator offer some questions for consideration as they circulate among the students to check in.

- What are the similarities and differences in the two narratives? Is there common ground between them? How did the tone and language differ?
- How was the experience of writing the second narrative different from the first?

B. The educators reconvene the group and invite at least two pairs to share their photographs and paired writings, followed by reflection.

- What was the experience like? Any aha moments? Surprises? What did they learn about themselves?

Typically, students relate how much they enjoyed using their imagination to connect while also realizing they were creating a story. Others may comment they liked the challenge of sticking to the physical facts. They may notice they used more sensory and "feeling" words in taking the perspective of another person.

4. Making Connections to Medicine

The educators ask the students:

- What connections can you make to your work as a physician in training?
- What can the attempt to understand a person's subjective experience add to your experience and effectiveness?

Students frequently comment that in the clinical setting they lack the luxury of quiet and a single focus when making detailed observations. Overall, they are typically struck by the "common ground" revealed, including observations of how body language, expression, gaze, mood, clothing, and setting informed both sets of writing. Taking each perspective separately sparks reflections about being a good observer, while also connecting with patients.

Students discover how hard it is to stop short of interpreting when describing—students ruefully note how automatically that leap takes place. Some students wonder if "imagining" might support healthy interest and curiosity when applied in the clinical setting, but also worry that they might be influenced by their own stereotypes and biases.

The museum educator and physician co-leader respond to issues that come up and offer thoughts about the benefits and limitations of this activity. The physician mentor validates the usefulness of both perspectives. He emphasizes that when in the clinic it is important to question one's own ideas, and to offer multiple opportunities for the patient to describe their experience and correct any physician misunderstandings.

5. Deepening the Discussion
   Facilitators may offer additional questions, or follow threads raised by the group.
   - Let's examine the oft-used phrase "putting yourself in someone's shoes." Can we really accomplish that?
   - When we imagine the lives of others, we can get things very wrong. Consider any stereotypes you might have resorted to, or any you consciously avoided in this activity.[41]
   - What strategies might you use to check your ideas directly with the patient? What language might you use?

The student-participants have extended their imagination toward another human being; they have taken notice of the connections and differences between observing and imagining. A study by social scientists Adam Galinsky and Gordon Moskowitz found that "perspective-takers"—those who were asked to imagine inhabiting another person's perspective—had more positive comments, connections, and attitudes toward that person than those in a comparison control group, who were asked to try and actively suppress stereotypes.[42] Throughout this chapter we have emphasized how important it is to pursue accurate understanding through direct communication. While we cannot check the accuracy of our understanding of a person through looking at a photograph of them, the act of imagining in the "first person" may increase our sense of shared humanity and our interest in learning more about someone. It may be worth checking on our sense of human connection, even as we also rigorously check our assumptions and biases. In the clinical setting, this may help us see the human before us and activate our caring curiosity. Medical practitioners may become more aware that a doctor's visit has a place and meaning in a patient's life and begin to more astutely recognize their potential role in that story.

AMBIGUITY, UNCERTAINTY, AND EMPATHY

Much of the current literature on clinical empathy details patient encounters that challenge a provider's capacity for empathy. The reasons are myriad; encounters may be situational and influenced by provider fatigue, burnout, and/or their reluctance to care for a patient who is considered challenging for some reason. For those experiencing difficult clinical encounters, Riess argues that we first need to recognize our own emotional responses in order to provide effective care. She offers the ABC acronym:

A: Acknowledge: Recognize and name the feelings in the room, including one's own feelings and physical sensations.

B: Breathe: Breathing helps us pause, allowing us to find the space to modulate our own responses.

C: Curiosity: Engaging curiosity, paired with nonjudgment, helps us continue interacting from a position of openness.[43]

By explicitly inviting participants to recognize, name, and explore feelings of discomfort or antipathy during encounters with works of art, museum facilitators create opportunities for self-awareness.

The following activities proceed from the belief that space and time away from the hospital in which to practice moving through challenging encounters and reflect on who one is and how one responds in the face of difficulty is valuable. Both the examples offered allow for authentic discomfort while also practicing delaying judgment and staying engaged. In the first activity, participants are invited to seek out works of art that are difficult for them to relate to; the stakes are low, and discovery and self-awareness are more manageable. In the second activity we highlight the VTS method, a widely used museum-based pedagogy in healthcare, in an extended example of how interpretive challenges can support the development of empathic capacities and explore parallels between the method and clinical practice.

EXPLORING AMBIGUITY

Halfway through their clerkships, a dozen medical students arrive at the art museum with a clinical mentor, an internal medicine physician. Shortly after a welcome and introductions, the students spread out across several galleries of modern and contemporary art. Their first task is to find a work of art that they actively dislike, find boring, or would otherwise prefer to "walk right by." Coming directly from their clerkship rotations, it is easy to observe the students relax into this very different environment, some laughing and chatting about this surprising opening request. When each identifies the artwork that fits the task, they place a small green construction paper triangle on the floor in front of it. The museum educator and physician note which works have accumulated several triangles and use their location to plot the group's route through the galleries so that the exercise will end by looking at the artworks with the most markers. The leaders gather the group and begin the tour of the choices. The museum educator asks that each person describe what aspects of their chosen work they reacted to, inviting their thoughts, visceral responses, and associations.

Eventually, the museum educator guides the group to the last two works of art, which happen to be across the gallery from each other. "Several of you picked one of these, so let's change things up a bit." She invites those who picked one of these works to gather in front of it, share their "whys," and look even more closely at the work so that they can give an expanded description. The remaining seven students are invited to also choose one of these two works and to think together about this question: "What strategies can you come up with—questions, actions, information—to stimulate those who would otherwise walk right by this piece to stay with this work and consider it more closely?" Everyone is given five minutes before regrouping.

The leaders gather everyone before a six-foot-by-eight-foot gray canvas with a pocked and marked surface. Only a few very thin brush marks of color run down the front edges of the work. The students who did not like or connect with the work mention emptiness, ambiguity—both *what* it is and *why* it is—and a perceived lack of content as their initial points of disconnect. The "how to engage" team offers strategies that include looking at what appears to be a uniform field more closely to see the variations that exist, speculating how this "field of gray" was created—there are no brushstrokes!—and relating this work to a patient experience in the clerkships. The physician co-teacher and museum educator have planned together in advance to offer certain ideas at the right moment. They exchange glances, and the physician steps forward. "Anybody have a patient they don't like? How about a case that you just can't find a way 'into'? Or a person you can't—or maybe don't really want to—get to know?"[44] The students are intently focused on this senior medical educator's face as he advises that they will each be faced with all of these situations at some point, and with more consequential versions of today's activity: How will you react in these situations? How will you engage further, and ultimately, who will you be as a physician under these circumstances, in those moments?

The senior physician has posed important questions, ones we imagine medical students might return to at various points in their work as healthcare providers. Through tone and body language, the physician encourages students to prepare to make choices about challenges, and to shape their future selves with intention.

VTS: A TOOL FOR EMPATHY?

VTS, co-developed by museum educator Philip Yenawine and cognitive psychologist Abigail Housen,[45] is one of the most widely used museum-based pedagogies in healthcare.[46] Initially, VTS was used to help medical students hone their observation skills.[47] More recently, it is being explored as a method to support clinical reasoning, tolerance of ambiguity, and empathy.[48] In 2017, a research study showed that medical students who engaged with complex artworks using VTS reported an increased tolerance for ambiguity, defined as the capacity to hold multiple possibilities simultaneously. Furthermore, the study suggested a correlation between tolerance for ambiguity and empathy:

> Empathy necessitates the ability to see "the world" from the other person's viewpoint, while keeping well-drawn boundaries between self and other. Yet such ability is contingent upon acknowledging that there can be other views of the world or multiple interpretations of it, namely that we are able to tolerate ambiguities. Therefore, from this perspective, empathy and tolerance of ambiguity are closely related.[49]

In the following VTS conversation, a group of medical students observes a complex work of art for an extended period of time and works together to understand it, with the guidance of a trained VTS facilitator. While the method is participant-centered, the role of the facilitator is an active one. In stewarding the structured conversation, she is responsible for including as many voices as possible, weaving together emerging thoughts and ideas, and making choices about what to prioritize when asking for evidence or elaboration. It's important for VTS facilitators to recognize the authority they carry, and to guide a discussion in a manner that supports a group as they endeavor to understand a work of art and their responses to it.

Since this is a session focused on empathy, the museum educator has selected an image that many people find uncomfortable, even challenging. The educator informs the group they do not need experience with art to participate and does not share any information about the artwork. She introduces Reiss's definition of empathic capacities and the E.M.P.A.T.H.Y.® acronym and asks the group to consider how they might be manifested in the following conversation. A group of participants intently observe Sarah Lucas's photograph *Self Portrait with Fried Eggs* (1996),[50] which presents a seated figure, dressed in torn jeans and a T-shirt, with what looks like two fried eggs on their chest. The person gazes directly at the viewer, their arms resting on the chair's arms and their legs spread open.

Becoming attuned to patients' emotions as well as your own is an essential component of empathy; the educator asks students to write down one word to capture their emotional response to Lucas's photograph, and to notice where in their body that feeling is located. She continues, asking them, "What's going on in this image?" "I'm feeling hostility," one student offers. "I can't find any warmth." The group describes the figure as defensive, confrontational, unwelcoming, unapologetic, challenging, and defiant. With the goal of understanding, the facilitator paraphrases each comment and asks students to support their interpretive ideas with visual evidence ("What do you see that makes you say that?"). In response, participants decode nuances of the subject's facial expression, debate the meaning of the gaze, and dig into body language clues. They speculate about gender. After further examining physical evidence, they offer that perhaps this is a woman—noting the person's small frame, tapered waist, outline of breasts, and narrow ankles—while acknowledging possible gender stereotypes. The educator paraphrases, "So, based on visual evidence, you think this person could be biologically female," leaving open the idea that the person might choose to identify otherwise.

Throughout the discussion, the facilitator keeps the group in a process of inquiry by asking "What more can we find?" The group is both captivated and disturbed by the presence of the fried eggs. Perhaps they are meant to be comic, or to offer social commentary on the frequent association of breasts with food? One participant notes that the detail causes him extreme discomfort. "What I am hearing," paraphrases the facilitator, "is that, for you, the fried eggs are shocking. Did I get that right?" "Not really shocking," replies the student, "but perhaps surprising and disturbing."

The more the group looks, the more they uncover contradictions. "The initial vibe I get from this person is 'I don't care,' but the more I look, the more I think they care a lot." This particular comment motivates the group to look for evidence of intentionality and leads to a discussion about ways individuals—and patients—might carefully craft a self-image. The wide-open positioning of the subject's legs is identified as stereotypically male, reminding some of "manspreading" and its association with an entitled way to take up space. Some women in the group remember being admonished when they were young "to sit with my legs together." "I love this image!" a female student spontaneously declares. For her, it is transforming from an image of hostility into an image of power—of someone in control of their own image humorously defying conventional stereotypes. "She owns her image," someone else agrees, "and challenges us to do the same."

"Who is this person, really?" the group wonders, and they turn their attention to the setting for more clues. Details such as a painting leaning against a wall, an ashtray filled with cigarettes, and a case of beer in the background are identified. New interpretive possibilities and narratives emerge. Perhaps this is a studio, and this person is an artist? Are the cigarettes and beer evidence of a life that might contain stresses and struggles? Perspectives begin to shift. Perhaps the gaze is not challenging and directed at the viewer; maybe this is a tired artist appraising their work at the end of a day. The group continues pondering. From initial impressions of confrontation and the perception of an inability to connect with this person, they have become more curious. They have moved beyond first impressions and responses, to wonder about motivations and life circumstances. Some find inspiration for their own lives. They have practiced how closely attending to another person and staying in a mode of inquiry can spark curiosity and appreciation for a fellow human being.

After the conversation, the group reflects on the activity's clinical relevance and connections to the principles of E.M.P.A.T.H.Y.® Many participants mention the importance of going beyond first impressions and acknowledge how easy it is to jump to a conclusion given the time pressures they all experience. One student shares their intention to try to better understand "the why" rather than immediately responding with "paternalism," frustration, or blame when a patient presents as "quote unquote difficult." The process of evidence-based, reflective self-awareness generated by the question "What do you see that makes you say that?" inspires agreement about the necessity of checking in both with oneself and with patients. The participants also felt that this activity helped them understand their colleagues' thinking. An aha moment for many VTS participants is the experience of hearing a range of perspectives and ideas in response to a shared image, which offers a good reminder that others see and experience the world differently than we may.

Most VTS research studies focus on the experience of the participants. Yet to be studied is the possibility that learning to facilitate VTS offers a useful set of techniques for developing empathic capacities.[51] It cultivates a stance of being fully present to and curious about the experiences, thoughts, and feelings of individual

The Visual Thinking Strategies (VTS) Method

A VTS discussion begins with silent looking and is structured around three open-ended questions:

1. *What's going on in this painting (text, patient, etc.)?*
2. *What do I see that makes me say that?*
3. *What more can we find?*

The first question is used only once to open the conversation. The facilitator then moves back and forth between the next two questions.

Throughout the experience, the facilitator paraphrases comments and links ideas. The discussion concludes with an expression of appreciation for the group's observations and insights.

participants and the group as a whole. The approach has direct and valuable parallels to conversations in the clinic.

Let's consider how each of the VTS techniques might support empathy in clinical practice. Beginning in silence is an invitation to pause, start with attentiveness, and give the process of observing and thinking time: it underscores the importance of creating space for each patient. The VTS questions, which may seem simple, are extremely precise and intentional in their wording. They are useful for participants and the facilitator. "What's going on?" is open-ended and invites a variety of responses; it signals that there can be many paths to understanding. The VTS method does not presume any one way of beginning. Responding to a VTS question, people start where they are or with what matters most to them. A question like "What do you see (or experience) that makes you say that?" can help a clinician understand what might be behind a patient's statement. Parallel to this is Riess's call to healthcare providers to "move beyond the chief complaints . . . to valuing . . . chief concerns."[52] Asking oneself, "What more can we find?" enables one to move beyond initial ideas and uncover more layers of possible meaning or valuable information.

The three VTS questions are useful techniques for clinical reasoning.[53] With modifications, they can be applied with patients or with oneself. One can imagine a provider meeting a patient, taking a few moments of silence, and asking oneself, "What's going on with this patient (or in this hospital room, with this family, etc.)?" and noting their own initial impressions, which they then scan for evidence by asking themselves the follow-up question, "What do I see that makes me think that?" The third question, "What more can we find?" encourages a mindset of openness and continued exploration. Dr. Joel Katz, a clinician with whom we work, describes how even if he feels sure of his diagnosis, he asks himself, "What more can I find?" because it helps him check his thinking and see his patient as a whole person.[54] Viewed as a whole, we see that the VTS process can help health practitioners move between what Daniel Kahneman calls "fast thinking" (cognitive shortcuts) and "slow thinking" (done with deliberation, self-awareness, etc.).[55] The three questions can help support a way of being that is characterized by openness, rigor, humility, and curiosity.

A core skill for VTS facilitators and health providers is the ability to listen and paraphrase. Facilitating VTS is a highly skilled process, requiring more than just asking the questions. The effective facilitator puts aside their own thoughts and emotions in order to listen with full attention and without judging. There is a strong parallel with Reiss's description of empathic listening. She writes, "The basic principle behind empathic listening is to first try to understand the other person's perspective and then try to have your own point of view understood. . . . It means setting aside your own emotions and listening with openness."[56] Deep, reflective listening means attending to the meaning and/or emotion beneath the speaker's words. It is a full-body experience—we listen with our ears and our eyes, and we signal attention, acceptance, and presence through our body language and tone of voice. Paraphrasing means trying to hear what's important to the speaker and offering it back with nonjudgmental/appreciative language that conveys understanding. The language used is conditional ("could be . . ." "my understanding is . . .") in order to keep the conversation open. The process requires choosing words carefully in order to honor the integrity of someone's thinking and feelings. When necessary, we check for understanding ("Do I have that right?"), signaling our desire to understand correctly. We are appreciative when someone feels comfortable clarifying, as in the previous example. All of these choices can help individuals feel heard.

Listening also includes linking ideas across the span of a conversation, which requires an engaged presence in order to remember and hold a number of ideas simultaneously. New facilitators remark how difficult this process can be. Deep-focused listening requires stamina and practice. Taking time to listen attentively, to reflect back, and to pull together diverse thoughts and ideas is a way of both developing and demonstrating care. VTS conversations take time, and so does empathy. How often does a patient get ready to leave an appointment, and then says, "Oh, by the way . . .," and then shares a vital piece of information? Used during a patient encounter, VTS offers a structure for slowing down, creating space, and listening carefully so that critical observations, information, insights, and stories can emerge.

"YOUR RESPONSE" AND BARRIERS TO EMPATHY

While the benefits of empathy for patients and healthcare providers are well recognized, conditions in the field of medicine that act as barriers to empathy exist during both the training years and well beyond them. In the training years, future physicians are not only learning the knowledge and skills of medicine, but also grappling with how to be a physician to patients with diverse lives and illnesses. Feelings of guilt and shame are common, and self-compassion may be lacking. During these years, medical students look for role models for how to offer excellent care. How their teachers and clinical mentors respond to the clinical environment and the challenges of medicine (often referred to as the "hidden curriculum") shapes medical students' and residents' professional socialization. Espoused values may not always be made visible in practice, and disparaged practices may go unchecked.

Empathy fatigue has also been identified as an occupational hazard within the field of medicine, extending far beyond the training years. Stanford researcher Dr. Jamil Zaki notes that challenges to practicing empathy can be pervasive, particularly with the evolution of managed care. Electronic records, increased workloads, and ever-increasing time constraints are contributing to "a dangerous cycle of empathy exhaustion, and callousness in medicine, and it's accelerating."[57] Multiple studies have demonstrated that physicians, in particular, suffer high rates of burnout and moral injury. The final letter in Riess's E.M.P.A.T.H.Y.® acronym is "Y" for "Your Response." As we have noted throughout this chapter, developing self-awareness and emotional attunement are essential for the practice of empathy. According to Zaki, "Physicians who ignore their feelings make less accurate diagnoses and are more likely to take their frustration out on patients," and studies show that "people who could pinpoint their feelings had an easier time controlling them and bouncing back from hardships."[58] Recognizing one's own reactions in response to another's situation helps one engage with empathic concern rather than empathic distress.[59] Reflective self-awareness can also make a difference in times of challenge and fatigue, which are frequent in clinical medicine. Because self-reflection takes time and practice, the intense demands and time constraints of clinical work often make it difficult.

Physician Rick Wellisch has been bringing interns and residents to art museums since 2010 with the express purpose to provide reflection time for the integration of thoughts and feelings about key events in their practice of medicine. In response to the emphasis on thinking in medical training, and in recognition that there are many ways of knowing, one of his overarching goals for museum visits is to give students the opportunity to process emotions and a space to "think less, feel more."[60] When we design sessions that focus on empathy, we leverage the museum's rich and varied holdings and beautiful spaces. We design them with purpose, creating opportunities for groups to slow down, process what they are looking at, and reflect with colleagues on shared experiences and deeply felt moments, ones that can include difficult situations and emotions. Using artworks as catalysts for reflection and meaning making, we bring groups into a shared community of intimacy and fellowship.

In closing, we offer two final examples of the value and depth of museum-based work around empathy and "Your Response." In the first, we see how *Field Day*

(*Crowd #4*), a black-and-white photograph by Matt Saunders,[61] generates empathic perspective-taking as well as reflection on feelings of depersonalization, and even dehumanization. In the foreground of the image, a human figure stands with arms crossed. Fanning out behind, in a triangular shape, are six other bodies. Each of the figures is blurred; their faces are impossible to read, and the black-and-white color scheme conveys a sense of sameness. For one person in the group the image provokes thoughts about the patient experience, including what it might be like to be lying in a bed with a blurred phalanx of figures dressed in white coats standing over you. For another student, the image offers the opportunity to talk about the feelings of depersonalization she was beginning to experience with her patients. She entered medicine to practice care, to connect with patients and improve their lives. The image resonated with her concern that she was losing her capacity to see her patients as individuals. A third student expresses his concern that his own individuality—his humanity—was being subsumed by his role.

The second example comes from a personal response activity. At the museum, members of an interdisciplinary team respond to the prompt "find a work of art that has something to say about grief." A medical student selects Walter Hancock's large-scale model for the Pennsylvania Railroad War Memorial.[62] The monument depicts a winged figure lifting the dead body of a young man upward. The weight and plasticity of the figure's muscular body suggests we are observing the moment immediately after passing. To this young man, the sculpture is beautiful in its evocation of loving care in the moment of death. His team had lost a patient that day, and he shares that it was his first experience with death. In the pressured environment of the hospital, there had been no time for him to process the experience and his feelings, to fully honor the moment of transition. He wonders out loud about the team's responsibility to the patient's family, who had been left grieving. As he speaks, tears well up in the eyes of other team members. The group pauses and silently stands together in a moment of shared vulnerability and acknowledgment. After a few moments, a senior member of the team expresses his gratitude to the young medical student.

Museums are designed to make us pay attention. Throughout them one can find beauty—in the physical spaces, the artworks, the light streaming into a room. We have argued in this chapter that museums can also support the cultivation of empathy in numerous ways: as places to activate our imaginations; to process and share ideas, experiences, and emotions; to model and practice empathic skills of active listening and perspective taking; and to hone habits of self-reflection and awareness. When carefully crafted with intention and care, museum experiences can be transformative, enabling us to connect with ourselves and others.

NOTES

1. Helen Riess with Liz Neporent, *The Empathy Effect: Seven Neuroscience-Based Keys for Transforming the Way We Live, Love, Work and Connect Across Differences* (Boulder: Sounds True, 2018), 10 (italics in original).

2. Helen Riess, "The Science of Empathy," *The Journal of Patient Experience* 4, no. 2 (June 4, 2017): 674-77; Helen Riess, "Empathy in Medicine: A Neurobiological Perspective," *The Journal of the American Medical Association* 304 (2010): 1604-5.

3. Mohammadreza Hojat, Daniel Z. Louis, Fred W. Markham, Richard Wender, et al., "Physician's Empathy and Clinical Outcomes for Diabetic Patients," *Academic Medicine* 86, no. 3 (March 2011): 359-64.

4. Liselotte N. Dyrbye, Colin P. West, Daniel Satele, Sonja Boone, et al., "Burnout Among U.S. Medical Students, Residents and Early Career Physicians Relative to the General U.S. Population," *Academic Medicine* 89, no. 3 (March 2014): 443-51; Tait D. Shanfelt, Colin P. West, Christine Sinsky, Mickey Trockel et al., "Changes in Burnout and Satisfaction with Work-Life Integration in Physicians and the General U.S. Working Populations between 2011 and 2017," Mayo Clinic Proceedings/Elsevier 94, no. 9 (2019): 1681-94; Pamela Hartzband and Jerome Groopman, "Physician Burnout, Interrupted," *New England Journal of Medicine* 382 (June 25, 2020): 2485-87.

5. Riess, *The Empathy Effect*, 4; Helen Riess, John M. Kelly, Robert W. Bailey, and Emily J. Dunn, "Empathy Training for Resident Physician: A Randomized Controlled Trial of a Neuroscience-Informed Curriculum," *General Journal of Internal Medicine* 27 (October 2012): 1280-86.

6. Oscar Schlemmer, *Bauhaus Stairway*, 1932, New York: Museum of Modern Art, https://www.moma.org/collection/works/80049. The vast majority of clerkship stories sessions occurred in University of Michigan Museum of Art's Modern and Contemporary galleries. During the pandemic, we opted to use the rich online collection of the Museum of Modern Art, New York.

7. Personal communication, Dr. Emma Claire Bethel, Michigan Medicine, Class of 2022, May 13, 2022.

8. Personal communication, Dr. Cory Dodson, Michigan Medicine, Class of 2022, May 13, 2022.

9. Personal communication, Dr. Nan Barbas, Michigan Medicine, June 9, 2022.

10. Tarsila do Amaral, *The Moon (A Lua)*, 1928, Museum of Modern Art, https://www.moma.org/collection/works/199984.

11. Personal communication, Dr. Sloane Brazina, Michigan Medicine, Class of 2020, May 13, 2022.

12. Ronald Epstein, *Attending: Medicine, Mindfulness and Humanity* (New York: Scribner, 2017), 7.

13. Danielle Offri, *What Doctors Feel, How Emotions Affect the Practice of Medicine* (Boston: Beacon Press, 2014).

14. Riess, "The Science of Empathy," 74-77.

15. Jodi Halpern, *From Detached Concern to Empathy: Humanizing Medical Practice* (New York: Oxford University Press, 2001).

16. Jodi Halpern, "What is Clinical Empathy?" *Journal of General Internal Medicine* 18, no. 8 (2003): 670-74.

17. Halpern, "What is Clinical Empathy," 670-74.

18 Riess, *The Empathy Effect*, 13-15.

19. Riess, *The Empathy Effect*, 32-33.

20. Riess, *The Empathy Effect*, 32-41, 61-71.

21. Dr. Mary Blazek reminds students that as physicians they will see patients at a particular moment in that person's complex life. Personal communication, April 21, 2022.
22. Mohammadreza Hojat, Michael J. Vergare, Kaye Maxwell, George Brainard, et al., "The Devil Is in the Third Year: A Longitudinal Study of Erosion of Empathy in Medical School," *Academic Medicine* 84, no. 9 (September 2009): 1182–91.
23. Beth Howard, "Kindness in the Curriculum," AAMC News/Healthcare and Education, September 18, 2018, https://www.aamc.org/news-insights/kindness-curriculum.
24. Riess, *The Empathy Effect*, 43–60. The trademark E.M.P.A.T.H.Y.® is a registered trademark of, and under exclusive license from, Massachusetts General Hospital to Empathetics, Inc.
25 Riess, *The Empathy Effect*, 53.
26. Reiss, *The Empathy Effect*, 46.
27. Riess, *The Empathy Effect*, 46.
28. William F. Laughey, Megan E. L. Brown, Angelique N. Dueñas, Rebecca Archer, et al., "How Medical School Alters Empathy: Student Love and Break Up Letters to Empathy for Patients," *Medical Education* 55 (October 2020): 396–97.
29. Helen Riess and Gordon Todd-Kraft, "E.M.P.A.T.H.Y.®: A Tool to Enhance Nonverbal Communication Between Clinicians and their Patients," *Academic Medicine* 89, no. 8 (August 2014): 1108.
30. Riess, *The Empathy Effect*, 117.
31. Dawoud Bey quoted in Jacqueline Terrassa, "What is the Work?" in Dawoud Bey, *Seeing Deeply* (Austin: University of Texas Press, 2018), 195.
32. Riess, *The Empathy Effect*, 10.
33. Shari Tishman, "The Power of Art: Pathways to Critical Thinking and Social-Emotional Learning," presentation at the National Gallery of Art in conjunction with "National Gallery of Art Summer Institute for Educators," Washington, DC, July 13, 2021.
34. © Dawoud Bey, *Theresa, South Shore High School*, 2003, Courtesy Sean Kelly, New York, https://smartmuseum.uchicago.edu/chicagoproject/portrait_theresa.shtml.
35. Bey quoted in Terassa, "What is the Work?" 195.
36. Riess, *The Empathy Effect*, 22.
37. Riess, *The Empathy Effect*, 130.
38. El Greco, *Fray Hortensio Félix Paravicino*, 1609, oil on canvas, Museum of Fine Arts, Boston, https://collections.mfa.org/objects/31236/fray-hortensio-felix-paravicino.
39. Leslie Jamison, *The Empathy Exams* (Minneapolis: Greywolf Press, 2014), 5.
40. Riess, *The Empathy Effect*, 10.
41. Diana Burgess, Michelle van Ryn, John Dovidio, and Somnath Sah, "Reducing Racial Bias Among Health Care Providers: Lessons from Social Cognitive Psychology," *Journal of General Internal Medicine* 22, no. 6 (June 2007): 882–87. Thanks to Grace Huang Amadi for the addition of the "stereotypes avoided/not avoided" questions.
42. Adam Galinsky and Gordon Moskowitz, "Perspective-taking: Decreasing Stereotype Expression, Stereotype Accessibility, and In-group Favoritism," *Journal of Personality and Social Psychology* 78, no. 4 (2000): 708–24.
43. Reiss, *The Empathy Effect*, 11.

44. Physician and historian Dr. Joel Howell has enriched my (Slavin's) understanding of the impact of ambiguity and uncertainty in clinical medicine during our fourteen-year teaching partnership (2009 to the present).

45. Philip Yenawine, *Visual Thinking Strategies: Using Art to Deepen Learning Across School Disciplines* (Cambridge: Harvard Education Press, 2013).

46. Margaret S. Chisolm, Margot Kelly-Hedrick, Mark B. Stephens, and Flora Smyth Zahra, "Transformative Learning in the Art Museum: A Methods Review," *Family Medicine* 52, no. 10 (2020): 739.

47. Gauri Agarwal, Meaghan McNulty, Katerina Santiago, Hope Torrents, and Alberto J. Caban-Martinez, "Impact of Visual Thinking Strategies (VTS) on the Analysis of Clinical Images: A Pre-Post Study of VTS in First-Year Medical Students," *Journal of Medical Humanities* 41, no. 4 (2020): 561–72.

48. Prince, G., R. Osipov, A. J. Mazzella, and P. R. Chelminski, "Linking the Humanities with Clinical Reasoning: Proposing an Integrative Conceptual Model for a Graduate Medical Education Humanities Curriculum." *Acad Med* 97 (2022): 1151–57.

49. Miriam Ethel Bentwich and Peter Gilbey, "More than Visual Literacy: Art and the Enhancement of Tolerance for Ambiguity and Empathy," *BMC Medical Education* 17, no. 200 (2017): 7.

50. https://www.tate.org.uk/art/artworks/lucas-self-portrait-with-fried-eggs-p78447.

51. https://medium.com/@dabney_hailey/what-more-can-we-find-how-visual-thinking-strategies-unlocks-innovation-in-a-complex-world-46b541378cb6. Anecdotally, business leaders who are trained how to facilitate VTS value VTS as tool for empathic communication and psychological safety.

52. Helen Riess, "Empathy in Times of Crisis," The Beryl Institute, March 17, 2020, https://www.theberylinstitute.org/blogpost/947424/342524/Empathy-in-Times-of-Crisis.

53. Margaret S. Chisolm, Margot Kelly-Hedrick, and Scott M. Wright, "How Visual Arts-Based Education Can Promote Clinical Excellence," *Academic Medicine* 96, no. 8 (2020): 1101–2.

54. Dr. Joel Katz, personal communication, October 15, 2020.

55. Daniel Kahneman, *Thinking, Fast and Slow* (New York: Farrar, Straus and Giroux, 2013).

56. Riess, *The Empathy Effect*, 55.

57. Jamil Zaki, *The War for Kindness: Building Empathy in a Fractured World* (New York, Crown Publishing Company 2019), 104.

58. Zaki, *War for Kindness*, 112

59. Zaki. *War for Kindness*, 113.

60. Dr. Rick Wellisch, personal communication, October 6, 2021.

61. Matt Saunders, *Field Day (Crowd #4)*, 2010–2011, photograph, Museum of Fine Arts, Boston, https://collections.mfa.org/objects/556468/field-day-crowd-4.

62. Walter Hancock, *Scale-model for Pennsylvania Railroad War Memorial*, 1949–1952, https://collections.mfa.org/objects/321599.

4

The Power of Story

Human beings are all, innately, both makers and eager consumers of story. Stories are used to pass on wisdom. Stories help us look at and process our own experiences and allow us a glimpse into the experiences of others. Let's remember, for example, the moving story in this book's introduction, told in a museum in front of an ancient Etruscan sarcophagus by a young intern who felt inadequate in his communications with the family of his dying cancer patient. Through sharing his story, he was able to connect with peers who had had similar experiences and receive support. The story also gave him an aesthetic distance on the event, allowing him to consider the circumstances and his role as a "character." Telling his story helped him, and perhaps his listeners, process concerns about how to engage with the inevitable proximity to death and loss that work in healthcare will bring. There may even be an element of rehearsal in such stories, an opportunity to imagine how the character we hope to become would behave, what they might say in a similar encounter. And this small story of a particular moment becomes part of an ongoing, larger narrative that both documents and nourishes this young physician's professional identity development and values.

In this chapter we will consider various uses of storytelling, inspired by works of art, in the development and sustenance of health professionals. Art museums with culturally diverse collections offer opportunities to learn about various religious beliefs and worldviews that may ultimately inform patient care. We will outline a complex gallery lesson that features both cultural and personal stories and includes detailed instructions for a playful activity designed to build skills in both telling and generous listening, skills that will improve communication with patients and their families. We will consider how an image and its related story can catalyze and support our consideration of difficult topics, such as sexual violence and suicide. Finally, we will consider the value of adopting a stance in which we look for stories in our daily lives—and how sharing personal stories builds relationships both at work and at home.

First, as always, we invite you to look. This tenth-century sandstone sculpture from central India represents a Hindu god, Ganesha. Originally, it would have been placed on the exterior of a large temple, probably near the entrance, as Ganesha is sometimes called the "lord of beginnings" and "remover of obstacles." Elephants

Figure 4.1. Unidentified artist, Indian, possibly Madhya Pradesh, *Dancing Ganesha*, mid-tenth to mid-eleventh century, Sandstone, 23^{1}/$_{16}$ × 13^{11}/$_{16}$ × 7¼ inches (58.5 × 34.8 × 18.4 centimeters). Ackland Art Museum, University of North Carolina at Chapel Hill. Gift of Clara T. and Gilbert J. Yager in honor of Dr. Charles Morrow and his wife, Mary Morrow, for their many contributions to the University and to the Ackland Art Museum during his term as Provost, 85.2.1

have the power to remove obstacles, and Ganesha's animal vehicle, the rat, is able to chew through or squeeze between them. Many Hindu people today pray to Ganesha before embarking on a new enterprise—marriage, a course of study, a journey—asking for success in the face of obstacles.

What do you notice, or wonder about, when you consider this image of Ganesha? Did you notice that he (originally) had six arms? Some have been broken, as has his right tusk. These signs of damage are evidence that the physical object itself has a story to tell. "Extra" arms are often used in images of deities to indicate an extraordinary, divine being. Ganesha's elephant head, joined so naturally to a plump, dancing human body, also signals divine strength and intelligence, even as it raises questions for those outside of the Hindu tradition.

There are culturally sanctioned stories available to us that respond to many of our questions about Ganesha. Depending on the goals of the museum visit, the gallery teacher may tell the story of "How Ganesha Got his Elephant Head," "How Ganesha Won a Race Around the World," or "Why the Moon is Shaped Like an Elephant's Tusk."[1] Hindu people in the group may be delighted by the familiarity of these stories and the choice of an object that speaks of Indian cultural achievements. These stories also offer insights relevant to the care of some patients from India; at the very least, healthcare providers who learn about Ganesha will recognize the "remover of obstacles" when his image appears at a hospital bedside. In any case, the entire group will enjoy settling into the familiar experience of listening to a story.

Moving away from the usual back-and-forth of an interpretive conversation, the gallery teacher signals a different mode of communication. Magic words like "Let me tell you a story about . . ." or "Once, long ago and far away . . ." immediately invoke a story space. As the teller leans in, so does the group. Everyone understands that the story is beginning, and our attentive listening and imagination will bring it to life. To prepare for a dramatic telling, the gallery teacher has done some research, strategic thinking . . . and has *practiced*! (We recommend that you practice aloud, without notes, from start to finish, at least five times before using the story with a group.) The teller will have developed vivid imagery and dialogue that helps listeners visualize the setting, differentiate the characters, and follow a clearly articulated plot. The teller will know (through practice!) how long the story will take, and why it was chosen as meaningful for this particular group. Emotions will be conveyed through voice, gesture, and rhythm. (Never underestimate the value of a dramatic pause.) Finally, the teller will also signal, through tone of voice or a change in posture, when the group will move out of the timeless space that the story holds and resume ordinary communication in the here and now. The gallery teacher may then reiterate a particularly relevant point from the story and provide a transition back to the larger discussion. We look again at the work of art, with fresh eyes and deeper understanding.

This compelling encounter with Ganesha, with an emphasis on the god's role as the remover of obstacles, might be followed by an invitation for participants to share personal stories about the obstacles they face in their own work. Such stories may not be considered appropriate in the healthcare setting, but the choice of this sculpture and its traditional story has opened the possibility for reflection on the very real problems and barriers to flourishing that health professionals experience. Sharing these personal experiences with colleagues offers opportunities for affirmation, support, and perhaps even new strategies and solutions to problems.

Let's look at an annotated outline of a two-hour museum session that asks participants to consider ideas about "story" from several different angles. It will give a sense of how the Ganesha story might be used in a larger context; describe a collaborative, improvisatory activity that introduces the skills that go into telling a story; and encourage participants to share personal stories grounded in their own professional experiences and values.

ANNOTATED OUTLINE OF GALLERY LESSON ON STORY

1. Welcome, introductions, framing
   A. Today we will be looking at works of art that provide opportunities for storytelling.
   B. Let's start by crafting a six-word autobiography.
      "This is a narrative arc in six words, to introduce yourself. I'll share my own, by way of example: 'Appalachian childhood. Encountered art. Passionate teacher.'"
      (four minutes to write, eight minutes for all to share)
2. Ganesha sculpture
   A. Look together. Share story. (fifteen minutes)
      "I'm going to tell you a story that directly relates to this work of art. It's a religious story, from the Hindu tradition. There are many regional variations of this story, so you may have heard a slightly different version. I'm going to share it the way I learned it, but with my own storytelling style . . ."
   B. Reflect on the experience of "story space" and what can be learned. (five minutes)
      "How could you tell when the story began . . . ended? What was it like to be invited just to listen to a story? What did you learn about communication from the experience of listening to this story? What did you learn from the story itself?"

Thirty minutes into the workshop, the intellectual frame has been set, and the group has come together through a pleasurable, shared experience. They are being prepared for deeper explorations. The next move will build on this beginning through a creative, collaborative activity that engages participants with imagery, language, listening, and responding.

3. Improvisational storytelling: Bringing a "bare bones" plot to life
   A. Small group activity
   Divide into two groups of six. Position each of the small groups in front of a work of art you have chosen because of its connection to a meaningful theme such as courage, compassion, or calling (images of Hercules, the Buddha, David and Goliath, Cleopatra, and other well-known figures are often represented in museum collections). Each individual will be given a numbered slip of paper with a brief plot point they are expected to elaborate on using description, empathy, dialogue, etc., to indicate context and develop character. (eight minutes)

   Next, the groups of six will circle up and prepare to tell the story from beginning to end; the numbers on the individual slips indicate the sequence. Nobody has seen the overall narrative, although the stories chosen from religious, mythological, or historical traditions may be familiar to some.

   "The challenge of this game is to listen carefully to the preceding speakers, and to adapt your own expression to carry the plot forward seamlessly. Take seven or eight minutes to do a first run-through. Then, quickly check the original, simpler version to make sure you have not departed too far from the essentials of the original story. Please remember to respect the original context and tone of these stories, even as you bring them to new life. Develop consensus on any changes to your practice run in preparation for presenting your story to the other group." (ten minutes)

   Gallery teacher sets up the performance with reference to the related works of art. Two groups perform for each other. (twenty minutes)
   B. Reflection
   "What did we do? . . . What do the skills involved in this activity have to do with your profession?" (five minutes)

This activity, inspired by works of art embedded in a rich narrative milieu, asks that participants look for contextual clues, activate their empathic imaginations, craft expressive language that will help others understand a character's feelings and actions, listen and adapt to the choices made by previous speakers, and use body and voice to carry the action forward. Participants rely on their understanding of narrative conventions—gained from a lifetime of sharing stories—to present their story in an engaging, coherent form to an audience of peers.

In considering the professional resonance of the activity, participants say things like:

"This was a good opportunity for me to learn about an unfamiliar tradition."
"I often find myself in situations that I need to listen carefully to a patient or family member, while thinking about how to adapt my message so that it responds naturally to their primary concerns."

"We need to be able to think on our feet—and convey our message in a direct and memorable way that reaches our listener."

"I think I can be more intentional about my body language and tone of voice."

This improvisatory activity works well in team-building sessions and wellness retreats, even when the focus is broader than storytelling. The shared laughter and collaborative strategizing are side benefits.

TEXTBOX 4.1.

Resources for Improvisational Storytelling Activity

The following are some sample "skeletal plots" for stories frequently depicted in art. Each story conveys a theme that can lead to personal storytelling, if desired. Of course, the stories available will depend on your museum's collection—these are just examples. The main trick in setting up this activity is to write each fragment as *blandly* as possible, so the teller can make it sing. You can adjust the number of plot fragments to the size of your group; if you have an extra person, invite them to "direct" and offer some coaching after the practice run. The facilitator will want to choose works of art that are in fairly close proximity. Once the small groups start their process, the facilitator can move back and forth, helping the groups manage time and responding to any questions or concerns.

Be sure to remind the groups that the goal is to recreate a traditional story, remaining true to the original tone and purpose. This framing serves to prevent outlandish or inappropriately humorous renditions of culturally significant stories sometimes triggered by the idea of "improv." Especially when engaging with religious stories from the text-based Abrahamic traditions of Judaism, Christianity, or Islam, the facilitator will want to avoid stories that are central to the most sacred beliefs—stories about the crucifixion or resurrection of Jesus, the life of the prophet Mohammed, or the revelation of the Qur'an, for example. Traditions that are less committed to specific texts may be open to various versions of a story and offer more freedom of expression in the telling, but the tone should always convey respect. If a group does get carried away, it is the responsibility of the facilitator to remind the group members of the diversity of the patients they are serving and the need to maintain an inclusive, respectful tone.

Herakles and the Nemean Lion *(courage)*

1. The oracle determined that Herakles could be cleansed of past actions by using his strength to perform twelve miraculous "labors."

2. His cousin, King Eurystheus, was to assign impossible tasks to Herakles. The first labor was to bring back the skin of a lion that had been bothering people who lived in the hills of Nemea.
3. Herakles accepted the challenge and began his journey. He heard that this lion's skin could not be pierced by any weapon.
4. Herakles began tracking the lion through the hills of Nemea. His arrows were useless.
5. Taking his club and cornering the lion, Herakles killed the lion. He skinned the lion with its own claw and took the skin away.
6. Surprised by news of Herakles's return, King Eurystheus hid inside a bronze urn. A servant told Herakles to leave the lion skin at the gate.

David and Goliath *(courage)*

1. David was a shepherd, the youngest of his father's sons. His older brothers had joined other Israelites combatting the Philistines under the command of King Saul.
2. David was sent to the battlefront to give his brothers supplies and to return home with news. The armies were at a standoff.
3. David watched as an enormous warrior came out from the ranks of Philistines. The giant Goliath challenged the Israelites to send a champion for hand-to-hand combat.
4. No Israelite accepted Goliath's challenge, so David volunteered. King Saul noted David's youth but allowed the shepherd to take on the giant.
5. Certain that God would protect the Israelites, David approached the giant armed with a slingshot.
6. Hit by a stone, Goliath fell. David cut off the giant's head. The Philistines fled.

Siddhartha Pursues His Path *(calling)*

1. Siddhartha was born a prince in a small kingdom in northern India in the sixth century BCE. A dream before Siddhartha's birth foretold that he would become either a powerful ruler or a great spiritual teacher.
2. Queen Maya gave birth while traveling to spend time with her parents. The birth was accompanied by miraculous signs. Her newborn son took seven steps and spoke. Queen Maya died soon after.
3. King Suddhodana wanted his son to become a ruler and so educated him accordingly. Siddhartha grew up surrounded by luxury.
4. In his late teens, Siddhartha wanted to see the world outside the palace. He called for Channa, his charioteer, against his father's wishes.

5. Channa took Siddhartha out four times, once in each cardinal direction. Although the king sent orders that only beautiful, healthy people should be visible to his son, the young prince saw sickness, old age, and death for the first time.
6. Troubled by his new knowledge, Siddhartha decided to leave the palace and begin a new life in search of an understanding that would end suffering for all.

Cleopatra Gains Marc Antony's Allegiance *(presenting oneself with purpose)*

1. Cleopatra was intelligent—she knew seven languages and had maneuvered in a tricky political environment to gain control of Egypt and its enormous wealth. Still, Egypt was vulnerable to Rome.
2. Marc Antony, whom Cleopatra had met during the time she had lived in Rome as Julius Caesar's consort, was stationed with his Roman soldiers in Tarsus, near the coast of Turkey. Cleopatra decided to visit him before the army moved on to Egypt.
3. Cleopatra's barge was luxurious. Cleopatra dressed as Venus.
4. Cleopatra invited Marc Antony to a banquet, intending to impress him with Egypt's wealth and refinement. She gave away lavish gifts.
5. At the banquet table, Cleopatra removed a huge pearl earring, dissolved it in wine, and drank it.
6. Marc Antony was impressed. He spent the next year at Cleopatra's side in Alexandria, to the consternation of other leaders back in Rome. Although Marc Antony returned to Rome and made a political marriage, he was back in Alexandria a few years later, joining forces with Cleopatra until Egypt was finally invaded by Rome.

Having enjoyed the chance to immerse themselves in a diverse group of traditional stories and bring them new life through a creative, social experience, participants are ready to develop and share thematically related stories rooted in their own professional experiences. The richness and complexity of story will become even more evident in the next section of the workshop, as individuals are asked to remember and reflect, to develop language and resonant images, to speak and to listen. As Dr. Rachel Naomi Remen reminds us, "when we listen, we offer with our attention an opportunity for wholeness."[2] Sharing a personal story with a peer helps build a sense of connection and provides an opportunity for affirmation and support.

4. Sharing personal stories
   A. Guided imagery (five minutes)
   B. Free writing (five minutes)
   C. Share in pairs (twelve minutes)
   D. Two or three volunteers share their stories with the larger group (twenty minutes)

We begin by referring to the major themes in the stories that the groups have just presented: courage, calling, etc.

These traditional stories have survived through the ages; they come to us as examples of human responses to great challenges. I'd like to suggest that each of you has similar stories to tell—about your calling to the work of caring for the sick, about your courage in the face of fear, your strategies for overcoming obstacles. Sometimes these stories are entangled with so many other events and contextual details, that they need a bit of unraveling before they can be knit into a serviceable, narrative fabric.

We're going to take a few minutes to relax, using a brief guided imagery prompt to identify a professional experience that required courage. You will have time to make some notes and bring form to the story, before sharing it with one other person in the group, who will just listen generously, without questions or comments.

First, get your body into a comfortable, relaxed position—both feet on the floor, back straight, shoulders relaxed. Scan your body, intentionally tightening and then releasing your muscles, from head to feet.

Now, with your eyes lightly closed or a soft, downward gaze, scan your memory for a time at work when you felt anxious or threatened. . . . You may have flashes of several different moments. Just review this inventory, until you come across an incident that feels charged with interest.

See yourself in this situation from the past. . . . How old are you? . . . How do you wear your hair? . . . Who else is in the story? . . . Where are you? Take time to explore the environment.

Now just visualize, in your mind's eye, what happened. . . . Notice your thoughts and feelings. . . . What do you do, or say, in this situation? . . . How do others respond?

When you are ready, come back to the here, the now. . . . Use the paper and pencil to capture in words or images the main thread of this story. Reflect on the situation that gave rise to fear or anxiety, and how you faced the situation. What does this past experience have to tell you that might be useful or meaningful today? In the next five minutes, prepare to share your story with a partner, who will simply listen with generous interest, before reciprocating with their own story of courage.

The work of healers requires real courage, but clinical experiences are seldom discussed in terms that acknowledge the demands on the character and psychological strength of caregivers. Stories of courage—which always involve acknowl-edging fear—are rarely shared in the professional domain, but they are readily called to mind. In remembering, crafting, and sharing these stories, participants become more aware of their own strengths—and closer to one another. Individuals may even feel celebrated for a moment, or more certain of their ability to take on the next scary monster that comes their way. Calling up memories and *noticing* our own capacities teaches us to have confidence in them. We start to develop a stance toward our own lived experience, one that lets us see ourselves as a character in a story worth sharing, a character that is growing and changing in response to the twists and turns of the plot we are navigating. As theologian Sharon Daloz Parks has said, "The stories we live and tell provide coherence and meaning and orient our sense of purpose."[3] This grasp of meaning and a sense of purpose is essential to human flourishing, especially in the face of unrelenting stress such as that which permeates clinical work.

1. Closing (fifteen to twenty minutes)
   A. Mentors comment and/or share stories from clinical work
   B. From closing circle, individuals voice one powerful image of the day

The closing circle recalls circles created everywhere when people gather around a flame to share stories; it provides a last moment for our participants to look into one another's faces. We have taken the risk of being known in a deeper way, surprising one another with stories that were suppressed in the clinical setting. We see one another with deeper appreciation, an awareness of how our stories are intertwined, and a foreshadowing of future challenges. We are connected.

This detailed outline of one gallery lesson shows how a range of activities may be sequenced to develop a rich and varied workshop based on hearing and sharing stories. Designing any gallery experience demands the discipline of an editor. We must resign ourselves to the fact that one session cannot do everything—and yet, over time we accrue a broad repertoire of activities from which to draw. Our choices will be grounded in knowing how long an activity will take; what materials we will need to provide; what works of art or galleries are most resonant for the group; and whether to use an activity to pique interest, to deepen understanding, or to stimulate reflection and synthesis. Each activity should be prompted with clear and concise directions and launched with a seamless distribution of any necessary ma-terials. Finally, the gallery teacher must always have a rationale for using an activity and should be prepared to answer questions regarding its relevance to the group's professional development.

A SAMPLER OF ACTIVITIES

We would now like to share a handful of additional activities related to storytelling, in hopes that they fuel creative adaptations and inventions. Some of them have been widely used for years, and their origins are uncertain. We provide this annotated list for the convenience of our readers, acknowledging with appreciation the enormous creativity and willingness to share ideas demonstrated by so many museum educators.

The Story of Your Name—Good for introductions at the beginning of a session, as it helps the gallery teacher learn names and adds a layer of interest to colleagues who already know someone's name, but not the story behind it. Does not require much advance preparation, although a facilitator or mentor may want to go first, as a model (e.g., "Fun fact: Corinne Zimmermann is the fifth in a matriarchal line of 'Corinnes.' You can probably guess what she named her daughter.") This nonthreatening activity includes everyone and signals an element of personal sharing that will continue throughout the lesson. Allow about one minute per person. Keep the activity moving without interrupting, if possible.

Living Pictures—Inspired by a Victorian-era parlor game, a team of individuals works to recreate a complex, figural painting's composition. Look closely at the artist's use of gesture, facial expressions, and spatial relationships. A "director" may be useful in guiding the group. Take a photo to document the moment. This activity is fun for small groups to prepare separately, then present to the whole group. An extension might be for the individuals to continue embodying the same characters and show what happens next—how the scene might develop in the next fifteen seconds. This activity is playful, social, sometimes competitive. It highlights how we convey meaning through body language and facial expressions. See chapter 5 for an extended example. (ten to fifteen minutes)

Reflective Writing—After sharing a story depicted in a work of art, invite participants to do some quick writing that makes connections to their own experience. This affirms the expectation that individuals should always be looking for relevance and meaning in the museum experience. (four minutes)

Off to See the Wizard—This choice activity allows for some focused individual exploration of several galleries, before the group reconvenes to share findings. Start by reminding (or informing) the group of the three friends who accompanied Dorothy to see the Wizard of Oz in L. Frank Baum's children's classic. The Scarecrow was in search of a brain, the Tin Woodman needed a heart, and the Cowardly Lion wanted a boost of courage. Invite participants to find a work in nearby galleries that, for them, has something to say about the role of intellect, heart, or courage in their professional experience. (ten minutes to choose; three minutes each for sharing brief stories and reflections)

Fifty-five-word Stories—Turn an incident that happened at work into a short story! The trick here is that the stories individuals write must be exactly fifty-five words. This constraint requires attention to word choices, the relationship between contextual information and plot, and the notion of crafting a story to achieve a desired effect. The length is not daunting to those who dislike writing, and the experiences suggested by so few words may be quite revealing. Themes may vary according to the goals for the visit. (five minutes to write; five minutes for three to four volunteers to share)

The sample gallery lesson and activities listed manifest core values that resonate strongly with current trends in medical education. In part because of growing concern about levels of burnout among health professionals, medical educators have begun to prioritize skills and attitudes that will help sustain caregivers throughout their careers; foster a sense of community and interprofessional respect; encourage clinicians to hold on to the story of their calling; explicitly recognize the emotional demands of healthcare work; and pursue practices of mindfulness and gratitude. All of these are integral to the experience of finding, crafting, and sharing stories.

Leaders in medical education such as Dr. Rachel Naomi Remen of the University of California San Francisco, who developed the widely used "Healer's Art" course, and Dr. Rita Charon, who established Columbia University's influential program in narrative medicine, have written eloquently about the power of stories and the two-way healing power of listening. Their work, and that of many other writer-physicians, honors the telling and hearing of a story as a fundamental human need.

While narrative medicine is grounded in written expression, we have seen that works of visual art, too, readily support the emergence of stories. We have already considered how the visual features of works of art specifically created to convey a religious or historical narrative pique curiosity and comment. After a close examination of the work of art and the familiar experience of hearing a story, our group is more relaxed and open to the possibility of finding and sharing a personal connection to the theme. The invitation to share feels natural at this point. Some participants may even feel connected to a story's tradition—to ancestors and artists who also struggled to make meaning, forge bonds, and persevere in the face of mystery and adversity.

DISCUSSING DIFFICULT STORIES

The open stance created by looking in silence before hearing the story behind the art may be especially useful in engaging a difficult topic such as suffering and loss, loneliness, poverty, racial bias, addiction, or sexual assault. Medical settings are replete with such challenges, yet the frank discussions needed to inform responsive care may be elusive. Discussions catalyzed by works of art can provide a useful model for important conversations around difficult topics. Addressing such topics, whether in the museum or in a clinical setting, requires that we look, feel, and think together about these aspects of human experience. We benefit from the aesthetic distance proffered by the work of art, finding a rare opportunity to develop our ideas and rehearse our words in a safe, low-stakes setting.

One experience that clearly highlighted the museum's value in raising such charged issues occurred quite spontaneously during a session for a team of family medicine students, residents, and attending physicians. The residency director commented on a waiflike, contemporary image of Cinderella: "This makes me think about sexual trafficking—which spikes in our city with every home football game. She looks like some of the patients I see in clinic." This led to a brief conversation about how to recognize a victim of trafficking, what questions to ask during an examination, and what is the legal protocol for healthcare providers who suspect sexual abuse. There were indications of surprise, mild discomfort, and serious interest among the group. The collaborating medical and museum educators agreed to plan together, with more intention, future opportunities to introduce such charged, important topics.

Let's consider what a session designed to explore issues of sexual assault and its aftermath might look like. The museum educator could use a work like this large sixteenth-century painting by Luca Cambiaso, *The Suicide of Lucretia*, and invite a group of health professionals to find contemporary relevance in the image and the legend that inspired it. The painting confronts viewers with a female nude in a slightly awkward position—her feet are at different levels and her upper body is leaning on a high bed with pillows. The overall effect is not erotic for most viewers—perhaps because of the woman's distressed facial expression and the fact that she is plunging a knife into her torso, just below her right breast. When invited to wonder about the image, viewers want to know what events led up to this act of suicide. Tradition has passed down a story surrounding Lucretia, a Roman matron said to have died by suicide in about 510 BCE:

> As you can tell from the painting, the story is not a pretty one. I must ask you to prepare yourself for a story of sexual assault, suicide, vengeance, and war. You may well encounter some combination of these experiences in your work with patients, so discussing an ancient story through looking together at this sixteenth-century Italian painting may be useful to you.
>
> Lucretia's story has its origins in ancient Rome. It has inspired many great painters through the centuries—here, Luca Cambiaso, and also Botticelli, Artemisia Gentileschi, Rembrandt, Titian. . . . Historically, Lucretia has been presented as an exemplar of courage and honor, though our contemporary perspective may find this emphasis problematic.

With this introduction, the gallery teacher has signaled the group to maintain an aesthetic distance, perhaps even a skeptical stance, as they listen to the story that was crafted and disseminated approximately five hundred years after the events in question. In the end, Lucretia's traumatic personal experience was coopted to offer a justification for the overthrow of a tyrannical monarchy and the establishment of the Roman Republic.

The Roman historian Livy tells the tragic story of Lucretia, who was said to have lived and died almost five hundred years before his own time, in the sixth

Figure 4.2 Luca Cambiaso, *Suicide of Lucretia*, circa 1565, oil on canvas, 166.4 cm × 90.2 centimeters (65½ in. × 35½ inches). Blanton Museum of Art, The University of Texas at Austin, The Suida-Manning Collection, 2017

century BCE, when an Etruscan king ruled Rome. Lucretia was the daughter of a magistrate and the wife of an aristocrat in military service. She was known for her modesty, beauty, and embodiment of Roman values.

One night, a group of well-born Roman soldiers, having besieged a rival city, were sitting around the campfire feeling restless. The men started boasting of the virtues of their wives. They decided to make surprise visits to several homes, to test which wife was most virtuous. Most of the women were caught socializing and indulging in trivial pursuits. But Lucretia, who had married Collatinus, was with her handmaidens, engaged in the domestic duty of spinning wool.

Collatinus had won the bet, but he had also introduced his wife to one of the king's sons, Tarquin. Tarquin paid a second visit to Lucretia's household some days later and was received with appropriate hospitality. During the night, carefully stepping around sleeping guards and servants, Tarquin entered Lucretia's bedchamber and pressed her to have sex with him. When she refused his advances, Tarquin threatened to kill her and one of her slaves, and tell the world that he had found the two of them in the act of adultery. Under coercion, Lucretia gave in to his demands.

The next morning when Tarquin had gone, Lucretia sent messengers to summon her father and husband. She told them of the rape and asked them to take vengeance on her behalf. The men told her that she bore no blame or dishonor, agreeing that "where there is no consent, there is no guilt." In spite of her family's pleas, Lucretia plunged a dagger into her own heart. She died in her father's arms. The communal outrage at Lucretia's death led to an uprising among the Romans, the overthrow of the Etruscan dynasty, and the establishment of the Roman Republic.

After hearing the story and seeing the visual representation of Lucretia's suicide, the group is prepared to move into a consideration of current societal and clinical understandings of rape and suicidal ideation. The collaborating health professions educator might take the lead at this point, suggesting questions for discussion, such as:

- Why did Lucretia take her own life?
- What social attitudes put some individuals at risk of sexual assault?
- What constitutes consent in sexual relationships?
- Why is sexual assault endemic on college campuses today?
- What are some of the physical, mental, and social consequences of sexual assault and rape? Think about a range of different people who might be affected.
- What can we do to support and care for people who have experienced sexual assault or rape?

These questions, while directly relevant to caring for patients who have survived a sexual assault, are seldom considered at length among professional teams or included in the professional preparation in some medical specialties. The work of art, along with the story it conveys, functions as a catalyst for an important conversation about consent and sexual violence, trauma, societal pressures, suicide—and healing. Perhaps understanding Lucretia's story as one of trauma and loss—rather than as an example of virtuous behavior—could contribute to another, much-needed social revolution today.

PERSONAL STORIES FOR INSIGHT AND CONNECTION

Works of art often stimulate memories and associations. In considering the resonances we find when we look at art with an eye for personal meaning, we sometimes gain new insights into our own circumstances, feelings, and behaviors. The "Personal Response Tour," developed by Ray Williams in the mid-1990s, is now widely used in medical education. Briefly, the approach begins by providing each participant with an evocative prompt with which to explore a series of galleries:

> Find a work of art that reminds you of something in your past. Think about the connections.
> Find a work of art that reminds you of a value you hold dear.
> Find a work of art you might choose to share with a depressed friend.
> Find a work of art that reminds you, in some way, of a memorable patient.

(Group leaders may make up other prompts, according to the territory they want their group to explore.) Individuals wander, select a resonant work, and reflect on the connections they can make. The group then reconvenes and moves through the museum, stopping when a participant indicates "their" work of art. This activity asks that we craft language to share our insights and experiences with others—and listen deeply, without questions or comments. It offers a rare invitation to share something personal—maybe something emotional or spiritual or troubling—with professional colleagues. Through shared looking and the ancient power of story, relationships grow in their authenticity and depth.

A specific example of one physician's experience of the Personal Response Tour, shared via email correspondence in her own words, may be helpful. Dr. Pooja Rutberg had randomly drawn the prompt, "Find a work of art that your grandmother might have chosen for her own home. Think about the reasons for your choice, enjoying any memories that come up." Considering her grandmother's lack of exposure to art and museums, Rutberg was initially daunted by the prompt, but within a few minutes, she had landed on a complicated, modern piece of wooden furniture with a surprising mix of shelves, slots, and doors of various shapes and sizes and orientations.

> As I started walking around the gallery, I noticed a piece of furniture in one corner. "What is this thing?" I wondered. The label said it was a "skyscraper desk/bookcase" from 1928. I was drawn initially to its practicality and solidness. And I was relieved to have found something that resonated with my

The Power of Story

question. As I spent time with the piece, it came to life, bringing up memories both old and recent.

Recalling the experience two years later, Rutberg says that it still holds great personal meaning.

> The exercise gave a physical representation to my deep relationship with my grandmother, something tangible to hold on to, even as time changes the relationship in ways that I have limited control over. It has helped me understand her aging as an extension of the powerful force she had been, and to hold the sorrow of her aging in the same breath as the joy of the vibrant life she has shared with me.

Dr. Rutberg goes on, remembering the story she shared:

> My grandmother was one of six sisters; together they were the matriarchs of the family. There was no problem that they could not solve. For every achievement, small or big, they were there to cheer us on. And for every disappointment, they were there with advice and perspective.
>
> I picture this piece of furniture located centrally in my grandmother's house, with a telephone on one end that connected her to her sisters, as they collectively solved the problems of the family and the world. I picture her "storing" solutions and advice for different problems in the different drawers and slots, reaching in to one drawer to give advice about teenage angst, another to help with career decisions, and on and on . . .
>
> And now, she is eighty-seven; my cousins and I are grown with families of our own. Now I picture these drawers and slots still full, but messier. I picture her reaching for solutions to help us continue to figure out life, but without the same surety, without always being able to find what she is looking for. Now, she sometimes looks to us for help.

The group listened attentively, readily seeing how the various elements of this object could provide a metaphorical storage system for solutions to life's challenges, trying to imagine this powerful woman in India and what she meant to their colleague, perhaps remembering the grandmothers in their own lives or thinking about the diminished capacities that so often accompany aging. We were moved by the intimacy and the universality of these reflections, and open to the exchanges yet to come.

STORIES IN THE EVERYDAY

The Personal Response Tour demonstrates our wonderful capacity as human beings to make connections and find meaning. The stories, hidden sparks of experience brought to light, help us both to know ourselves and to build community. What if we began to look for stories in our daily lives—the stories that require an active, expectant stance in order to be seen and crafted? Dr. Remen says that "our present vulnerability to burnout may be caused more by the way in which we have come to see ourselves and our work than by the nature of the work itself."[4] Perhaps adopting a story-seeking stance would change the way health professionals see and experience their work lives, mitigating tendencies to burn out. By intentionally diminishing the tedium and humdrum of daily routines and becoming more alive to meaningful moments with patients, families, and colleagues—by turning these sparkling moments into stories that can be shared and savored—clinicians may find more satisfaction in their epic battles against human suffering. They begin to see themselves as a character in a story, and this awareness might influence how they choose to behave. The healers must then engage with patients and families knowing that those visitors to the clinical setting will be crafting their own stories, to come to terms with their experience of illness and the healthcare system in which their caregivers play major roles. How would any of them hope to appear as a character in such narratives? This awareness, this stance, helps clinicians remain alive to the particularities of each patient's situation and mindful of their own high aspirations for compassionate care. Finally, as a nurse or physician notices and amplifies moments that speak to their core values and commitments, they are affirmed in their calling. When they finally get home from a long shift, they can share a story of their time at work that engages their partner and family with the intense challenges and rewards that demand and develop their best self.

CLOSING

Life in medicine can be chaotic, often depleting. Learning to look for the storyline in the chaos, for connections, can bring order. Thinking of oneself as a character with the necessary skills and agency to help others may reduce feelings of being overwhelmed, and enable caregivers to activate their best selves. A story-seeking stance will minimize the tedium and amplify the beautiful and dramatic human connections that occur in the effort to relieve suffering. Caregivers become more cognizant of the ways they are making a difference through their work, more likely to remember past successes in moments of doubt. They also see beyond the immediate circumstance of an ailing patient, considering that individual's life in the larger world. Stories provide a helpful aesthetic distance on experience and invite us to consider diverse perspectives. Stories give us comfort, insight, and connection.

Developing the skills of noticing, crafting, and telling a story that speaks to its audience—the intentional use of voice, rhythm, posture, facial expression, word choice—will improve communication between health professionals, patients, and families. In becoming storytellers, we must think deeply about both speaking and listening. Listening with full attention will call forth clinically relevant information that might otherwise go unspoken. Listening to colleagues with empathy and understanding will strengthen the work of a team. Stories activate our senses; they carry traditional wisdom and primal power. Like works of art, they are of the body, the imagination, and the heart. Like our own lives, the art museum is brimful with the wisdom and transformative possibilities—the power—of story.

NOTES

1. For a source of stories about the Hindu god Ganesha, see Uma Krishnaswami, *The Broken Tusk: Stories of the Hindu God Ganesha* (North Haven: The Shoe String Press, Inc., 1996).
2. Rachel Naomi Remen, *Kitchen Table Wisdom: Stories that Heal* (New York: Riverhead Trade, 1996), 220.
3. Sharon Daloz Parks, "Foreword," in Robert J. Nash and Michele C. Murray, *Helping College Students Find Purpose: The Campus Guide to Meaning-Making* (San Francisco: John Wiley & Sons, Inc., 2010), vii.
4. To learn more about Dr. Remen's course, "The Healer's Art," go to www.rachel remen.com/learn/medical-education-work/the-healers-art/.

5

Strengthening Interprofessional Teams

The museum-based team-building workshop provides an opportunity to reflect upon my experiences and talk to others about them. It makes me a better provider and person.

—Healthcare provider, Brigham and Women's Hospital

It's 8:00 a.m. on a tenth-floor ward of a major teaching hospital in Boston. Nurses are moving in and out of patients' rooms, breakfast trays are being removed, and several people are typing away at computers. There is an active hum, punctuated with the sound of human voices and the intrusive beeping of machines. Slowly, a group of ten or so gathers in the crowded space between the large administrative desk and patients' rooms. The group is part of the Brigham and Women's Hospital's Integrated Teaching Unit (ITU), an interprofessional team of healthcare providers. For the next two to four weeks, they will work together to care for a shared group of patients. It is time for the morning rounds, when individual patient cases are discussed. A museum educator has joined them to observe their team dynamics and communication patterns at the hospital. Things the educator will note include how the group physically organizes itself as a team, in the hallways and at the patient bedside; who speaks and when; who listens to whom and responds to whom; and the role of nonverbal communication. The museum educator will also pay attention to themes or issues related to patient care that arise. Later in the week, the team will meet the educator at an art museum for a two-hour evening workshop designed to promote effective teamwork and communication.

The practice of medicine is changing. Increasingly, healthcare professionals are required to work on interprofessional teams. Research shows that good teamwork has a wide range of positive impacts including better patient care and outcomes, less testing, greater work satisfaction, reduction in burnout, and improved communication with patients and their families.[1] Conversely, the pitfalls of poor teamwork are notable. A total of 70 to 80 percent of medical errors are attributed to failures in teamwork such as poor communication.[2] Other adverse outcomes include increased rates of burnout, declines in patient and provider satisfaction, staff turnover, and higher costs.[3] Yet, within healthcare, the challenges to collaboration and teamwork are significant. Hospitals are traditionally hierarchical institutions. The perspectives of senior physicians are often privileged over those of other team members, including nurses, which can lead to feelings of disempowerment and a reluctance to speak up. Silence on teams can also result from a fear of being wrong and resulting negative consequences. In light of the compelling need for effective teamwork, medical training is incorporating teaching the inter- and intra-professional skills that support collaboration and teamwork. Focusing primarily on Brigham and Women's Hospital's ITU museum program, this chapter illuminates how a wide array of museum-based practices, grounded in Dr. Amy Edmondson's research on teamwork, can support interprofessional communication and help to cultivate positive team dynamics.

A key component of medical training is participating in a hospital residency program. Brigham and Women's Hospital's Internal Medicine program is highly respected. A large urban institution, the hospital has a national and international reputation for the quality of its services and for its leadership as an academic teaching center. Yet academic residency programs are often challenged by a dual mandate, manifesting in "a tension between service and education."[4] Interns and residents literally do not have enough time in the day to do it all, a situation which Arthur Feldman and Kenneth Ludmerer argue can result in a lack of thoroughness in patient care.[5] Furthermore, feelings of being overwhelmed can contribute to high levels of burnout among residents, a phenomenon well documented in the medical literature.[6] Around 2008, the Brigham revamped the structure of its residency program and created the ITU to mitigate these problems. Interprofessional teamwork is a foundational feature of the redesign.

The ITU model is considered an innovation within the field of graduate medical education.[7] It is a multidisciplinary team that includes two chief residents, four interns, two nurses, two medical students, and two attending physicians—a generalist and a specialist chosen for their clinical and teaching skills.[8] Patient caseloads are reduced, enabling more time for teaching and learning during rounds. The residents lead the team meetings, coaching the interns and medical students, while the attending physicians primarily play a teaching role on topics including patient care approaches, physical exam findings, and insights into their own specialties. They also serve as coaches for the lead residents. While transitioning to a multidisciplinary team structure at the Brigham has many benefits, it also exposed "physicians' poorly developed collaborative abilities."[9] Dr. Joel Katz, who helped create the ITU, notes that "prioritizing a physician's own point of view over that of other team members jeopardizes quality and value gains possible through 'accountable care.'"[10]

In her seminal book *Teaming*, Dr. Amy Edmondson, a professor at Harvard Business School, describes different ways of working together that resonate with the experience of ITU teams. She argues that in many industries, including healthcare, the notion of "team" as a noun has been replaced by "teaming" as a verb. Teaming, she writes, is "teamwork on the fly. It involves coordinating and collaborating without the benefit of stable team structures. Many operations, such as hospitals . . . require a level of staffing flexibility that makes stable team compositions rare."[11] In the fast-paced and complex world of healthcare, teams are constantly shifting, as interprofessional healthcare professionals move from team to team as schedules demand. At the Brigham, ITU teams share a patient caseload for a month, but the attendings may change halfway through the rotation. Nurses can play a role on several teams.

Within the dynamic environment of teaming, participants must cultivate certain mindsets and practices—such as recognizing and valuing team interdependence, and building trust and shared understanding—relatively quickly. Edmondson argues that people need to learn to team. She offers a set of principles, the first of which is that teaming requires an organizational mindset focused on active learning. Organizational environments defined by complex bodies of knowledge, rapidly changing information and technologies, and climates of uncertainty require flexibility and the ability to adapt in real time. She writes that leadership committed to an ongoing organizational process of learning, "supports the collaboration needed to solicit employees' knowledge, apply it to new situations or challenges, and to analyze outcomes."[12] Edmondson's research shows that successful teams with strong interpersonal relationships, interestingly, have higher reported rates of error than other teams, leading her to conclude that the most effective teams acknowledge, discuss, and learn from mistakes.[13] This has implications for the culture of medicine, where errors can be costly and are often accompanied by feelings of shame. To cultivate a teaming environment of engaged learning, Edmondson proposes the "Four Pillars of Effective Teaming": speaking up, collaboration, experimentation, and reflection.[14] As she suggests, though, there can be social, cognitive, and emotional obstacles to effective teaming, ranging from workplace hierarchies, lack of trust, a sense of interpersonal risk, and lack of skill in negotiating disagreements.

The essential foundation to authentically activating the four pillars is a team environment of "psychological safety," a term embraced by Edmondson that is now a widely explored concept in research on successful teamwork. She writes, "It describes a team climate characterized by interpersonal trust and mutual respect in which people are comfortable being themselves."[15] It is one "in which people feel free to express relevant thoughts and feelings."[16] In 2012, Google launched Project Aristotle which analyzed 180 of the company's teams to better understand what makes an effective team.[17] They examined various team configurations, taking into account personality types, education, and bodies of knowledge, and found no discernable patterns among them. Ultimately, they, too, discovered that the secret ingredient for successful teamwork is psychological safety—how team members treat each other—with two behaviors standing out: "equality in distribution of conversation turn-taking" (i.e., everyone has same amount of speaking time) and "high average social sensitivity" (i.e., empathy).[18]

In practice, team environments with psychological safety are ones in which members feel comfortable sharing ideas, taking intellectual risks, asking questions, and seeking feedback. They feel heard and appreciated; they know their voices are valued and that they will not be penalized for speaking up or "being wrong." The resulting team culture is one of engaged learning, openness, and curiosity. And, importantly, on psychologically safe teams, members share personal experiences, acknowledge fallibility, show vulnerability, and support one another.[19] In short, they make their shared humanity visible.

TEAMING IN THE ART MUSEUM

In 2009, soon after its residency program redesign, Brigham and Women's Hospital pioneered an innovative initiative using art museums as a space to enhance the practice of teamwork with their ITU teams. Initially co-developed by an art museum educator and a specialist in internal medicine,[20] the program leverages the expertise of both partners. The museum educator crafts gallery experiences in response to the team's needs and goals while the physician partner contributes relevant connections and observations regarding teaming and communication. The museum offers a beautiful space in which the team works collaboratively to explore works of art, make meaning together, and reflect on the nature of their interactions both in the museum and back at the hospital. Explicit goals include flattening hospital hierarchies, honing collaboration and communication skills, and developing an awareness of team dynamics.[21] The program, which has evolved over the past decade, is deeply informed by research on teams conducted by Edmondson.

The Brigham ITU museum program is designed and facilitated to support psychologically safe teaming experiences at the museum. Artworks are selected to address issues observed by the museum educator during rounds, or that might be important to hospital teams more generally. Carefully sequenced activities that invite collaborative meaning-making, personal and clinical stories, and reflections on personal values help jump-start a process that enables team members to better understand their respective roles, build interpersonal connections, and get to know one other as people. In each of the sessions, there is an intentional rhythm and flow that moves the group from a space of laughter and problem solving to one of open-hearted vulnerability and trust. Throughout the activities, the museum educator demonstrates the importance of reflective practice by inviting connections to their work at the hospital. Through the interplay between experience (doing) and reflection (thinking), team members can begin to acquire teaming skills and be inspired to reflect upon their own team's dynamics. An important part of the design is cultivating joy—providing opportunities to laugh, have fun, and relax. The goal is that everyone leaves the experience with a sense of renewal; a deeper understanding of themselves, one another, and their team dynamics; and the awareness of a set of skills that can be used in teaming situations going forward.

Figure 1. Gustave Moreau, *The Young Man and Death*, 1856–1865, oil on canvas, 85 × 48½ inches (123.2 × 215.9 centimeters). Harvard Art Museums/Fogg Museum. Gift of Grenville L. Winthrop, Class of 1886, Photo © President and Fellows of Harvard College, 1942.186

Figure 2. Felix Gonzalez-Torres, *"Untitled" (Portrait of Dad)*, 1991, white mint candies in clear wrappers, endless supply. Overall dimensions vary with installation. Ideal weight: 175 pounds. Photograph by Ruth Slavin/Installation view *Come as You Are: Art of the 1990s* at the University of Michigan Museum of Art, October 16, 2015, to January 13, 2016. © Estate of Felix Gonzalez-Torres/courtesy Felix Gonzalez-Torres Foundation

Figure 3. Dawoud Bey, in collaboration with Dan Collison and Elizabeth Meister, *Theresa, South Shore High School*, 2003. Chromogenic print 40 × 50 inches (101.6 × 127 centimeters) and audio recording. The David and Alfred Smart Museum of Art, The University of Chicago; Commission. © Dawoud Bey, Photograph © 2022 courtesy of The David and Alfred Smart Museum of Art, The University of Chicago and Sean Kelly, New York

Figure 4. Robert Colescott, *Emergency Room*, 1989. Synthetic polymer paint on canvas, 7' 6¹/₈"
× 9' 6¹/₈" (229 × 289.8 centimeters). Jerry I. Speyer and the Millstream Funds, Digital Image
© The Museum of Modern Art/Licensed by SCALA / Art Resource, New York, 70.1991 © 2022
The Robert H. Colescott Separate Property Trust / Artists Rights Society (ARS), New York

Figure 5.   Unidentified artist Indian, Uttar Pradesh, Mathura, *Standing Buddha Offering Protection*, Gupta period, late fifth century, red sandstone, 33^{11}/$_{16}$ × 16¾ × 6½ inches (85.5 × 42.5 × 16.5 centimeters). The Metropolitan Museum of Art, Purchase, Enid A. Haupt Gift, 1979

Figure 6. Rogier van der Weyden, *The Crucifixion, with the Virgin and Saint John the Evangelist Mourning*, c. 1460, oil on panel, left panel overall 71 x 36⁵/₁₆ inches (180.3 × 92.2 centimeters), right panel overall 71 × 36⁷/₁₆ inches (180.3 × 92.5 centimeters). Philadelphia Museum of Art, John G. Johnson Collection, 1917

Figure 7. Mequitta Ahuja, *Parade*, 2007, enamel on canvas, two panels, 96 × 160 inches (243.8 × 406.4 centimeters). Blanton Museum of Art, The University of Texas at Austin, Gift of Melanie Lawson and John F. Guess, Jr., in honor of Jeanne and Michael Klein, 2010 © Mequitta Ahuja 2007

Figure 8. Joan Mitchell, White Territory, 1970, oil on canvas, 111³/₈ × 88 inches (282.9 × 223.5 centimeters). University of Michigan Museum of Art, Purchase assisted by Friends of the Museum of Art and a grant from the National Endowment for the Arts. Photograph by Charlie Edwards © Estate of Joan Mitchell/courtesy Joan Mitchell Foundation

FRAMING EXPECTATIONS

Time is one of the biggest structural challenges for establishing strong teams in hospitals. Because of the rotational teaching model, "Just as you begin to develop cohesion . . . and get to know each other," states William Bynum, "you are off to a new group with a different set of personalities."[22] To address this challenge, the Brigham's museum-based team-building program is purposely scheduled at the beginning of a rotation in order to begin developing the informal relationships so important to teaming. Sessions begin with an evening meal at the museum. Team members arrive at different times. There is often a sense of rushing and then relief as individuals sit down, exhale, and begin to partake of the food. At the table, people usually sit next to someone they know or who shares a similar role. The conversation is generally lively, and the meal helps to provide a transition as the group moves from the hospital to the museum. The shared nourishment also offers a metaphor for the evening ahead, signaling that this is an experience in which participants will be cared for.

Following the meal, the group gathers in a circle for an overview of the session. Setting expectations and establishing a welcoming, inclusive, and nonjudgmental atmosphere are critical to laying the groundwork for psychological safety and an evening's success. The educator informs the team that this will not be a traditional art museum tour, but an experience designed to promote reflection on their team dynamics, communication patterns, and teamwork more generally. Knowing that people sometimes feel intimidated in art museums, she shares that their time together will be one of exploration and discovery in which there are multiple right answers and possibilities. She expresses a genuine interest in their thoughts and observations, and assures them that they will be using skills similar to ones used in the hospital. She hopes everyone will participate. At the same time, she invites them to notice how the team is working together in this new environment, and to notice their own participation on the team. Acknowledging hospital hierarchies, she suggests there are always opportunities for leadership, regardless of role—any of them might be the person who moves the conversation forward, who steps back so others can speak, who builds upon a colleague's observation, or who respectfully disagrees. She also recognizes that someone might be tired and feel "checked out." There is no judgment, but the invitation is to pay attention and to notice the impact of one's behavior on the team's dynamics.

BUILDING TRUST THROUGH PLAY

Building trust is essential for psychological safety. Stuart Brown states that "the basis of human trust is established through play."[23] Play promotes relaxation; is key to problem solving, creativity, and divergent thinking; and helps people enjoy one another. Each ITU session is launched with a playful warm-up exercise. The purpose is to offer a low bar for entry in a team experience that actively engages the whole group from the start and helps begin the process of learning just a bit more about each other. Warm-ups are also designed to encourage participation and laughter, which relaxes the group and prepares them for the rest of the evening.

In one particular session, having noted the role of nonverbal communication in the morning's hospital rounds, the museum educator decides to begin with "Pass the Gesture,"[24] an activity inspired by improvisational theater, and connects it to Zhan Wang's monumental stainless steel sculpture *Artificial Rock #85*.[25] It is one of two large-scale sculptures dominating a well-lit atrium in one of the more public spaces in the Museum of Fine Arts, Boston, though visitors walking by it often give it only a passing glance. The group begins exploring the abstract piece in silence. Inspired by classic Chinese scholars' rocks, the artwork is both textured and smooth. Nooks and crannies populate the surface, and the play of positive and negative space creates unusual shapes. A sense of movement is reinforced by reflective light that flickers across the metal surface. As team members walk around the piece, exploring it from different angles and perspectives, everyone is invited to think kinesthetically and to come up with a gesture that resonates with some aspect of the artwork. When everyone has thought of one, the team gathers in a circle. In silence, the first person passes their movement to the person to their left, who mirrors it back as precisely as possible. That second person then turns to the person to their left and offers their own, new gesture. The rhythm continues: the receiver reflects the given gesture back, then turns to their left to share their gesture, and so on. Throughout the activity, a variety of gestures are offered. Some are simple—such as the flicking of fingers to capture the reflective surface—while others might involve a full-body response to convey the overall structure or the complicated play of shapes. There is much laughter as team members mirror their colleagues' moves. When the circle is complete, the sequence is repeated one more time as fluidly as possible, creating a movement piece that embodies the team's collective creative response to the sculpture.

Afterward, the group is asked, "What did we do and what connections can you make to your work as a team on the ITU?" The group notices that the activity requires everyone to participate and to be fully present to one another. They also appreciate the variety of perspectives and gestures created by the group—noting that collectively the different responses capture some of the complexity of the piece. The interplay between offering and receiving is compared to hospital rounds and handoffs. A discussion ensues about the important, and often dominant, role of nonverbal communication in their work. And they consider the role of creativity when teams collaborate to understand and respond to a complex situation or problem. The museum educator remarks that the combined gestures have become a movement piece, and she wonders about the role of choreography in the hospital. How do they arrange themselves in space when rounding as a team? What role does a patient play? An attending shares that he always sits close to the patient's head so that when the team is sharing thoughts, the patient feels physically part of the team and the conversation. Playful activities such as "Pass the Gesture" help flatten team hierarchies, as everyone has the same task of receiving, reflecting, and communicating forward. Each person steps a bit outside of their comfort zone, as well as their designated hospital role.

Play can also be used as a way to create space for deeper, more reflective conversations which can help nourish trust. Nicholas Poussin's seventeenth-century painting *Discovery of Achilles on Skyros*[26] hangs in a grand salon-style museum gallery. The walls are covered in a patterned red cloth, and gold frames populate the space. This is a gallery filled with "important" Western paintings created to commemorate wealth, nobility, classical mythology, and religion. Inspired by *The Iliad*, Poussin's painting depicts an episode in the life of Achilles, the Greek Trojan War hero. The Oracle had foretold that Achilles would die in the war. In an attempt to escape this fate, his mother, Thetis, sends him to the island of Skyros where he masquerades as a daughter of King Lycomedes. Desperate for Achilles to return to battle, fellow soldiers Ulysses and Diomedes search for him everywhere. Poussin's painting captures the dramatic moment when Achilles is recognized. Disguised as merchants, Ulysses and Diomedes have come to Skyros with a trunk full of jewels and other treasures, in which they have hidden Achilles's sword. In the background, Lycomedes's daughters and Diomedes barter over baubles, while in the foreground Achilles unsheathes his weapon with an expression of glee and surprise. Ulysses, who witnesses the moment, has a joyful look of triumph, while a third daughter of Lycomedes recoils with an expression of dismayed horror as she realizes what has happened.

After arranging themselves in a semi-circle around the picture, the team begins by exploring the painting visually. Individuals offer observations and interpretations about body language, the array of emotions, and the relationships between the figures. Some are curious about the gender of the figure holding the sword (Achilles)—the figure is dressed as a woman, and yet the musculature of the arms read as masculine. When the group has examined the painting thoroughly, and curiosity is at its peak, the museum educator tells them the story. She then moves to the purposely playful part of the experience: creating a *tableaux vivant*,[27] "a living picture." One or two of the junior members of the team are made the "directors," and they assign each person the role of a character or an object in the painting. The group members then physically arrange their bodies to replicate the image as accurately as possible—nuances of gesture, body language, expression, and spatial relationships all need to be considered. The directors help refine poses to capture the moment in time that Poussin has represented. Once the directors are satisfied with the bodily reenactment, the team brings the painting to life as each character performs what they imagine happens next in the scene. Laughter, role reversals, and unexpected new ways of being together help the group members open up to one another.

Reflecting on the activity, the educator observes that the group participated in a long tradition of retelling a story across time. What makes the ancient Greek story of Achilles, retold by Poussin in the seventeenth century, resonant today? The group considers themes of fate, deception, being deceived by appearances, and moments when true selves are revealed. Pairing up, team members then discuss the role of stories, storytelling, and the painting's themes in their work together. An intern talks about imposter syndrome and the feeling they have that they are masquerading as a doctor. A senior attending remembers similar moments. A nurse reflects on the incredible shared responsibility the team has for holding patients' stories, especially at times when they are at their most vulnerable. The experience of play and reflection in the intimate setting of the art museum has provided an opportunity for the team to bond together around important aspects of their work, in a way not possible in the harried environment of the hospital.

SPEAKING UP AND COLLABORATION

A key teaming moment in every ITU museum session is an extended interpretive conversation. Fostering an environment where everyone feels safe enough to speak up is critical for effective teaming, and it requires an experienced facilitator. A warm stance of openness and authentic curiosity modeled throughout by the facilitator helps to create a respectful and welcoming space for exploration and discovery.

Museum educators have an array of facilitation tools at their disposal and choose strategically according to their goals. In the Poussin conversation, the educator used an inquiry-based approach supported by narrative information. For a teaming workshop, she opts for Visual Thinking Strategies (VTS). VTS is increasingly used in healthcare to hone observation and diagnostic skills.[28] VTS is useful for teaming because the structure welcomes all ideas equally and supports a nonjudgmental, respectful learning environment in which participants, regardless of hospital role, generally feel comfortable speaking up and sharing ideas—even provisional ones. The VTS inquiry-based process encourages a diversity of viewpoints and perspectives—a hallmark of effective teaming.

TEXTBOX 5.1

The Visual Thinking Strategies Method and Teaming

The Visual Thinking Strategies method[1] offers teams a structure for creating psychological safety and for engaging respectfully with one another.

A Visual Thinking Strategies conversation begins with silently looking at an artwork and is structured around three precisely worded open-ended questions:

1. *What's going on in this picture?* The open-ended question helps make the observational habits and mindsets of team members visible. One participant might notice the big picture, while another sees details. One person may be drawn to compositional elements and another to mood. It also signals that the team leader is not going to direct the process by telling the team where to begin.

---

2. *What do you see that makes you say that?* Asking participants to ground their interpretive ideas in evidence increases accountability and helps the group understand one another's thinking, while keeping the focus on the artwork (or other stimuli). It is a rigorous process that, with time, also allows assumptions, biases, and blind spots to surface in a nonjudgmental environment.

3. *What more can we find?* Giving a team the time and space to push beyond initial thoughts and ideas helps avoid premature conclusions. Some studies suggest that a common cause of misdiagnosis is a tendency to move too quickly toward a diagnosis.[2] Prolonged inquiry also creates space for quieter members of a group to participate. It allows for a range of ideas, some of them opposing, to surface in a collaborative learning environment. Psychologically safe environments are ones in which productive conflict can occur and be a source of greater understanding.

For a session on teaming, the museum educator chooses artworks that support multiple, even contradictory, interpretations and that reward sustained looking regardless of one's knowledge of art. As Dabney Hailey, founder of Hailey Group, LLC, states, it is the process itself that is the purpose.

NOTE

1. Dabney Hailey, Alexa Miller, and Philip Yenawine, "Understanding Visual Literacy: The Visual Thinking Strategies Approach." In *Essentials of Teaching and Integrating Visual and Media Literacy: Visualizing Learning* (2015). https://doi.org/10.1007/978-3-319-05837-5_3.

2. Jerome Groopman, *How Doctors Think* (Boston: Houghton Mifflin, 2007): 24.

In a VTS discussion, the facilitator is responsible for creating a team climate of respectful listening and engaged learning. Even though they may have expertise in art, they are curious and eager to learn from the observations and insights of the group. They aim to create a psychologically safe learning environment by (1) having an open stance and demonstrating active listening through body language and paraphrasing (and checking in for accuracy), (2) maintaining a respectful and appreciative stance in which no one idea is privileged, (3) demonstrating authentic curiosity and a desire to understand participant's thoughts and feelings, and (4) linking comments across the conversation by noting big ideas and points of convergence as well as alternative perspectives. A common trait on teams is a desire for affirmation (e.g., being told "Good job!") and a need to be right. When it becomes clear that the VTS facilitator is equally appreciative of all comments, the pressure to "get it" or to think about what one is going to say falls away, allowing for more attentive listening to one another and for focusing on the object at hand.

Figure 5.1 Oskar Kokoschka, *Two Nudes (Lovers)*, 1913, oil on canvas, 163.2 × 97.5 centimeters (64¼ × 38⅜ inches). Museum of Fine Arts, Boston, Bequest of Sarah Reed Platt, Photograph © 2022, Museum of Fine Arts, Boston, 1973.196

In a VTS discussion focused on Oskar Kokoschka's painting *Two Nudes (Lovers)*[29] (see figure 5.1), an ITU attending physician launches the group conversation by noting a possible contradiction within the artwork: two people seem to be moving in opposite directions yet are deeply physically entwined. The rest of the team dives in, enthusiastically exploring the possible relationship between the two figures, considering the context of the environment, and puzzling through the nuances of expression. To some, the pose is reminiscent of dancing. For others, this idea is contradicted by a somber mood reflected in the figures' facial expressions and the painting's color palette. Are the figures lovers? Is one figure protecting the other? Different interpretations related to gender emerge. Some wonder if the nakedness of the figures and the lush background allude to the Garden of Eden and the biblical story of Adam and Eve. The group discusses a tension between the strength and stability of the legs and a vulnerability in the expressions and unclothed bodies.

As they ponder the painting's emotional tenor, group members offer different readings. In the figure on the left some see anxiety, others despair. Looking at the figure on the right, a resident reads resignation in the downturned mouth and faraway gaze, while a nurse offers another interpretation. To her, the strong forward thrust of the left leg and the gaze suggest determination and a desire to move forward. Perhaps, an intern counters, one must accept something in order to move on. As the group investigates these ideas, participants note their own habits of thinking and observing. One resident remarks that she wants the image to be happy—that in her mind she keeps trying to see it that way, but the visual evidence tells another story. Another colleague considers the role of vantage point in shaping meaning. Throughout the discussion, the facilitator paraphrases what is said, asks the group to ground their interpretations in the visual evidence, and connects their ideas to one another across the arc of the conversation.

An interpretive conversation about a shared object of focus—here a complex work of art—can make individual thinking patterns, observational habits, and mindsets visible. When asked to reflect on the process ("What did we do? "What did you notice about how you worked together as a team?"), members comment on the value of hearing multiple perspectives, the importance of listening, and the benefits of not rushing to judgment or a conclusion. The group discusses how being present and listening to the perspectives of others helped them to see and think about the artwork in new ways. One participant compares the process to being in the hospital where there is a tendency to think in right/wrong binaries. Here, she says, she experienced how contrasting insights can deepen understanding and learned that welcoming multiple viewpoints can be a team strength, not a weakness. A diversity of lenses and entry points also helped team members recognize their own assumptions, blind spots, and possible biases. The process reinforces the importance of team interdependence and links back to morning rounds. When taking care of a patient, the team works together to figure out that patient's story. They make observations, ask questions, and consider multiple possibilities regarding a symptom such as shortness of breath. They discuss the importance of paying attention to things that might be overlooked—the architecture of feet, the sound of an expiration of breath (not just the inhalation), and nuances of skin color. As the attending remarks, "it takes more time but it's worth it."

Part of developing teaming skills is setting intentions for how you want to "show up." In this particular conversation, an attending physician (team leader) spoke first. Upon reflection, he acknowledged this and contrasted it to how he wants to participate at the hospital in the future, "to listen first and then respond." At the museum, he worried no one would speak and that silence would be contagious. His comment generated a discussion about the responsibilities of being a team member, different relationships with silence, patience, and the role of trust.

The Kokoschka painting was intentionally selected as an ambiguous image that might also generate conversation about complex relationships and feelings of vulnerability. Asking the group to think in metaphor and make connections to professional experiences creates space for participants to tap into emotional responses. For one intern, the piece evoked feeling fear about the unknown (for themselves and for their patients). Another person talked about the complex emotions of various stakeholders that surface when discussing discharge plans. For another the painting "captures how I feel everyday—dancing, trying not to misstep . . . but we do." Moments such as these can help bring group members closer to one another and offer insights into the personal concerns and experiences of individual team members.

CREATIVE EXPERIMENTATION AND COMMUNICATION

Within the design of a team-building workshop, creative activities can be a counterpoint to, or a springboard for, deeper personal discussions, depending where in the sequence of activities they are offered. Responding to artworks with sketching, sculpting, movement, poetry writing, or creative writing encourages alternative ways of exploring, discovering, and knowing. Sometimes there is a shared sense of discomfort ("I can't draw!"), which is another way of leveling the playing field.

Activities such as back-to-back drawing and group poems are particularly effective for honing teaming skills. Back-to-back drawing invites reflection on the importance and nuances of communication in teamwork. Finely tuned communication skills are not only necessary for patient care but are vital for working with colleagues. In this exercise, participants are asked to pair up with someone they don't know well or who has a different role on the ITU team. One person is the designated "describer" and one the "drawer." The describer leads the drawer (who keeps their eyes lowered) to an artwork of their choosing in a museum gallery. The "drawer" is seated with their back to the artwork, while the "describer" uses words to verbally convey what the artwork looks like. The "drawer" listens and draws what they hear described. The gallery comes alive with the sound of words—descriptions, similes, and metaphors. After seven minutes, laughter erupts as drawings are shared. Roles are reversed and the process is repeated with a new artwork. The activity concludes with reflection on the process and its relevance for working as a team on the ITU (see figure 5.2).

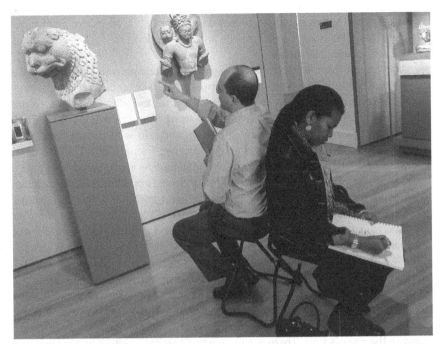

Figure 5.2 Back-to-back drawing, Museum of Fine Arts Boston, 2018. Photograph by Dr. Lisa M. Wong.

Back-to-back drawing encourages a group to think about the choices one makes when describing something—in this case an artwork—so that someone else can visualize it. The person describing has to consider where to begin, the sequence of information, which details to emphasize, and what words to use in order to describe with precision. The person drawing has to translate what they are hearing onto the page. They have to "listen in order to see"—something participants often connect to the act of seeing patients. The activity hones observation and communication skills while underscoring the interpretive nature and complexity of both.

Teaming requires building patience and trust, and back-to-back drawing in the museum provides an experience that allows the group to reflect on those ideas. For some, the act of being guided without seeing is uncomfortable, and this invites discussion about care and the dynamics of power. Teams consider what they have learned about communication from the activity, and its relevance for working with colleagues, patients, and patients' families. During reflections, parallels with morning rounds at the hospital are nearly always drawn: choosing what information to share when handing off patients and the importance of recognizing one's own habits of observation, describing, and listening. In one instance, a nurse suggested that the exercise highlights different disciplinary approaches and perspectives. She wondered if a nurse, because of their training and experience with patients, might

Strengthening Interprofessional Teams

be more inclined to begin with an overall description, while an intern might focus on a detail. Another nurse noted that she and her physician colleagues sometimes speak a very different language.

Teams often comment on the challenges of describing with specificity while using accessible language. A teaming communication "aha" occurs for most groups when someone acknowledges how important it is for the "describer" to consider their drawing partner's perspective—are they using language that is meaningful? It helps the group think about how they communicate with patients and with each other. Sometimes there are cultural or language barriers, or a lack of shared references. The importance of checking for understanding is reinforced. Groups acknowledge that listening is one of the hardest, and most important, skills to develop. There is laughter at a common inclination to jump ahead and draw predefined schema before the describer has finished talking.

The issue of questions often comes up: some ask if they have permission to ask questions during the back-to-back drawing activity, while others use them spontaneously. Others remark that they didn't think questions were allowed (the directions are purposely vague). This opens up a discussion about the role of questions on the team. Attendings may articulate their hope that everyone feels comfortable asking questions, but groups acknowledge there are sometimes barriers to doing so, including fear, not wanting to be perceived as "not knowing," and not wanting to waste the group's time. There is a recognition one has to intentionally create an environment in which questions are explicitly welcomed.

Group poems can be one of the most fun and playful moments in team-building workshops. They usually take place after an interpretive conversation and help prepare the group for deeper reflective discussions. After looking together at a work of art, participants, typically divided into groups of five or six, are given a strip of paper and invited to write a word, a phrase, or sentence that reflects an aspect of the artwork that resonates for them. (It might be an observation, a description, an emotional response, a snippet of dialogue, a metaphor, a question, a big idea, an association, etc.) What they each write will become a line of a poem. Each group, working collaboratively, arranges all their individual lines into a poetic sequence, which they then perform for their colleagues. When team members share their writing with one another, different ways of thinking are once again revealed; some team members take a metaphoric, abstract approach to the activity, while others are more literal and concrete in their responses. As one team member commented, "I loved creating something bigger and more beautiful together from multiple viewpoints." Creating "something bigger and more beautiful" offers a metaphor for their work as a team in the hospital and helps the group appreciate how each person contributes to the greater whole and to a shared sense of purpose.

In professional arenas, there is often pressure around performance and an accompanying feeling of being judged. In the context of the museum, performance becomes a place of creative play, experimentation, and risk-taking. When groups present their poems, team members show sides of themselves that may never emerge in their professional domain. A talent for beatboxing, interpretive dance, singing, or just plain silliness may surface. Hierarchies can slip away when a chief resident or an attending is willing to let go and perform without reserve, or when a medical student or intern with a love of language or creative writing helps guide the team. In this context, all are liberated from right/wrong thinking and the fear of making a mistake, a common sentiment back at medical school or the hospital.

Artifacts from the museum experience provide a touchstone for more engaged—and sometimes even joyful—ways of working together. Poems go back with them to the hospital. Some hang on the walls of the team workroom, and others have been collected into a shared binder by the ITU head nurse. One team that had a particularly exuberant experience together reports that, years later, they still laugh together when they encounter one another in hospital settings.

KNOWING ONE ANOTHER

A key element for psychological safety is a team's willingness to share personal stories—to allow themselves to be known by others on their team.

After play and laughter, collaborative problem solving, and reflection, the educator usually introduces a free-choice experience purposely tailored to encourage personal and professional reflections. Once again, the group is invited to think in metaphor by using an artwork as a catalyst for insight and connection. The invitation to think through metaphor allows a participant to modulate their response according to their sense of emotional safety as they move back and forth between their own personal reflections and the object.[30] In this activity, called "joys and struggles," participants explore the galleries and select a work of art that resonates with the prompt, "Find a work that speaks to a joy or a struggle you experience in your work life." As they share their chosen objects with teammates, stories about gratitude, uncertainty, grief, caring, work-life balance, loneliness, love, transitions, and self-doubt fill the galleries.

Often one person will share a truth that cracks the group open, as in the case of a resident who chose the painting *Wounded Amazon* by Franz von Stuck.[31] In the painting, the figure of an Amazon with shield in hand—surrounded by centaurs killed in battle and clutching her bleeding breast—dominates the canvas. For the resident, the work visualized her sense of work sometimes being a battle with no clear victors, and the wounds—so close to the heart—she carries as a result. In another example, an attending physician, inspired by a small, transparent glass sculpture holding a delicately detailed flower with roots, told a story about not fitting in with the dominant macho culture of his community. His childhood experiences compelled him to define his own identity, strengths, and core values. He related to the sculpture's combination of delicacy and strength, qualities which he also admires in many of the team's patients. When someone in the group shares their own vulnerabilities, especially a senior member of the team, it models courage, humility, and a shared sense of humanity. When a leader demonstrates a willingness to be vulnerable, to acknowledge fallibilities, junior members of the team may reconsider the pressure and/or the fear of being perfect or invincible

The "joys and struggles" activity works best when done in suites of galleries with a variety of artworks in terms of style, medium, culture, and period. In one session, an intern selected a work representing a Hindu deity. For her the piece reflected both a joy and a struggle. She spoke of her struggle of being far from her close-knit family in India, particularly her elderly grandparents about whom she worried. Religious practices were an important part of her family life growing up, but in her pursuit of medicine, she distanced herself from that part of her upbringing. Recently, though, she found herself returning to her earlier faith, finding that it connected her to her grandmothers and provided sustenance in the challenging work of her chosen profession. Not only did the team hear about important aspects of her life, they also learned about her cultural traditions, which may have been unfamiliar to some in the group.

Part of what makes art such a rich resource for teambuilding workshops is its capacity to stimulate multiple meanings and connections. In one session, Julie Blackmon's photograph *Baby Toss*[32] resonated for an attending physician, an intern, and a medical student on a team. The medical student related to the expression of fear on the baby's face and the feeling of being thrown "into a vortex." But the image also captured her belief that someone on the team would be there to catch her. The attending spoke about the joy of being a teacher and mentor whose role is to help medical students, interns, and residents move beyond their comfort zones in order to grow. Worried that he sometimes pushes interns to grow too quickly, he spoke of the vulnerability and humility of being entrusted with the learning and growth of others. The intern related to the older child standing to the side with a hat pulled over their eyes. Unlike the baby, this child's feet are on the ground. The intern identified with this figure because, despite being in a state that is relatively more stable, they still feel like they are operating blindly with so much yet to learn (there was much laughter in the room, especially from other interns, when she shared this idea).

REFLECTION

The previously described team-building workshops conclude with a final reflection during which team members consider their own participation, share observations about the dynamics of their team in the museum, and set an intention for working together back at the hospital. The range of responses includes the importance of listening, embracing the diversity of perspectives, breaking down hierarchy, and gratitude for their colleagues. An intern bravely acknowledges, "I tend to only listen to people whom I think are important. Tonight, I learned everyone has something to say." Another states, "Everyone brings a different perspective to interpretation and the same holds true for patient care as well, which shows the importance of having many diverse views." Someone else shares, "We [doctors and nurses] all have an important perspective that needs to be heard [in order] to do what's right for our patients."

Over and over, team members express that they appreciate the opportunity to get to know one another as people. In the words of one participant, "[we] hear about people's thoughts on issues unrelated to medicine and learn from those perspectives." Group members set intentions to be more curious about one another, seek out moments of shared joy and laughter, and have fun.[33] Most movingly, they talk about cultivating gratitude and caring for each other as well as for their patients. An intern says he will return to the hospital with a mental image of *Baby Toss* and a sense of trust; rather than feeling shame or castigating himself when he makes a mistake, he will reassure himself that the team is there to support him. An attending reflects on "the importance of seeing colleagues in a personal way. (It gives) me insight into how they work and interact with others. I learned I need to connect more and give feedback/support." And a chief resident promises, "I will look for individuals struggling."

LEADERSHIP MATTERS

Repeatedly, members of ITU teams report back that *how* they work together after a museum team-building session is different. A participant writes that she is continually surprised by "the level of intimacy that is reached [after a session], despite structure, time pressures, and a team that has both older and younger members." Nurses and physicians feel more connected, there is an increased level of comfort among team members, regardless of role, and, according to Linda Delaporta, head ITU nurse, "interactions are more collaborative." She firmly believes that the design of the workshop "teaches [the team] how to work together. . . . They develop team-building skills, without even being aware of it. . . . It changes the dynamic of the team back on the unit itself . . . it truly does. They'll be laughing about something or make mention of the poem they pulled together."[34] She highlights the value of being able to get to know one another outside the constraints and stresses of the hospital.

In promoting new ways of being together and creating psychologically safe environments, leaders have a crucial role to play. As Amy Edmondson remarks, psychological safety cannot be mandated; rather, team leaders must lead by example. "Psychological safety," she writes, "is a shared sense developed through shared experience."[35] In the art museum, team participants share an experience of working together in a psychologically safe learning environment that is carefully designed and facilitated by the museum educator. Because of the interprofessional makeup of ITU teams, many individuals—particularly nurses, attendings, and senior residents—have the opportunity to participate in the museum team-building workshops more than once. Some attending physicians have been part of the program since its inception in 2009. They not only advocate for the value of the program within the ITU; they support the museum educators by taking actions that contribute to an environment of trust and participation. In interpretive conversations they acknowledge their own blind spots, show appreciation for the insight of others, model personal risk-taking by sharing their own stories and vulnerabilities, and reinforce important relevant connections to their work in the hospital.

With a long-established history, the museum program has increasingly become an integrated part of the ITU culture. The program both reinforces and amplifies the ITU's commitment to teaching and teamwork. As this chapter is being written, ITU nurses at the Brigham have been moved to COVID-19 wards. Delaporta says they cannot wait to return to the ITU and to the museum sessions. "It's different," she says. "We miss the interpersonal connections. On the ITU, we are part of the team. And good collaboration is vital to patient outcomes."[36]

The hospital is hectic and demanding. By contrast, the art museum offers a space to pause and reflect. Surrounded by works of art that are testaments to the complexity, resilience, and richness of human experience, team members can establish a culture of collaboration, trust, reflection, shared responsibility, and care. With a carefully conceived lesson plan and the guidance of a skilled facilitator, they can begin to practice the art of teaming.

TEXTBOX 5.2.

Interview with Dr. Joel Katz

Corinne Zimmermann conducted this interview with Dr. Joel Katz, Vice Chair for Education and Director, Center for Visual Arts in Healthcare, Brigham and Women's Hospital, on May 3, 2022. Katz is a leader in the field of museum-based education for health professionals. In 2003, Katz and colleagues partnered with art museum educators to create Training the Eye: Improving the Art of Physical Diagnosis, a popular course offered at Harvard Medical School. Since then, he has been the guiding force behind several museum-based programs at Brigham and Women's Hospital including the newly founded Center for Visual Arts in Healthcare at Brigham and Women's Hospital. The interview is presented here in an abridged and edited form for this publication.

How did the Integrated Teaching Unit museum workshops come into being?
The faculty, residents, and nurses suffered through miscommunication and misdirection typical of a busy academic medical center, and we realized that we could do much better at teamwork and team building for ourselves and our patients [in the mid-2000s]. We considered various proposals, but I felt the most effective way was going to be at the art museum.

Why the art museum?
The hospital can be a highly stressful and challenging environment. Everyone has very rigid roles, too often without shared expectations.

In academic medicine, people are locked into roles for which they are extremely well trained. But they can't really actualize their skills because of communication and teamwork breakdowns. We have incredibly hard-working and talented people who just don't connect with each other. We don't hear much about the quality of individual providers being poor. We hear a ton that the communication is poor. And so that's the challenge.

The museum setting opens people to experiences that get them out of their rigid thought processes and deeply ingrained habits. We can test new approaches without feeling threatened. It opens minds to new ways of thinking. It helps participants identify vulnerabilities and biases in themselves (and others), which may not have been apparent. The museum brings people to the same level. You don't need to be an artist to participate. You don't need to be an expert in the history of art or the history of medicine. You simply need to show up and look and share. In the museum, you can lose your inhibitions and learn to converse and connect in new ways that are directly applicable to the work environment.

Taking the providers outside of the hospital and planting them somewhere else is beneficial in itself. People get to know colleagues in ways they otherwise wouldn't take the risks of doing. The art museum workshops provide a window into what people's lives are like outside the hospital, to what they value and appreciate, and what they bring to the table.

I once joined a museum workshop with a team that included a physical therapist I had worked with for ten years. I knew his first name, but that was it. For ten years, I'd been consulting with him about my patients and occasionally fielding questions about his patients. Then we went to the museum, and I suddenly discovered that he builds furniture on the side and that he has two kids at home who have very similar interests to my kids. He's passionate about politics—not my politics, but politics. Now we've become close friends. We have coffee, and we get together inside and outside the hospital. I feel like he understands my perspective, and I value his. Most importantly, when around patients, we talk directly to each other. We now have a much more productive and closer communication style.

I particularly love it when a group looks at and discusses abstract art together. It helps open a window on how differently the world can be seen by different people.

Hospital rounds after the museum visit feel very different. Before a visit, a nurse may sit quietly and not say much during team rounds. But after the team's time together looking at art, that nurse might start the conversation or challenge what people are doing. The experience allows each of us to slip out of our very hierarchical roles, to really improve communication, and feel positive about our contributions and what we do.

The ultimate benefit is that the patient notices consistent communication and positive interactions among the team.

Any advice for others interested in doing this work?

One of my passions is working closely with museum educators. My advice is to find a museum educator you can partner with, lay out the problems your team is having, and engage them in exploring solutions. I feel like I am only effective because of what museum educators have taught me. They are almost like the radiologists of medicine; they can see things we can't see. I have learned so much from them. And that's the secret to any successes our programs have had.

NOTES

1. Ted A. James, "Teamwork as Core Value in Healthcare," https://postgraduateeducation.hms.harvard.edu/trends-medicine/teamwork-core-value-health-care; https://www.hrhresourcecenter.org/HRH_Info_Teamwork.html.
2. Jennifer Weller, Matt Boyd, and David Cumin, "Teams, Tribes and Patient Safety: Overcoming Barriers to Effective Teamwork in Healthcare," *Postgraduate Medical Journal* 2014, no. 90: 149.
3. Rebecca Mitchell, Vicki Parker, Michelle Giles, and Brandan Boyle, "The ABC of Health Care Team Dynamics: Understanding Complex Affective, Behavioral, and Cognitive Dynamics in Interprofessional Teams," *Health Care Management Review* 39, no. 1 (2014), cited in Rebecca Greenberg, "Teamwork: The Heart of Healthcare," *AAMC Reporter* (May–June 2016): 7.
4. Arthur Feldman and Kenneth Ludmerer, "Solving One of Graduate Medical Education's Problems: A Loss of Thoroughness," *Journal of Graduate Medical Education* 9, no. 3 (2017): 287.
5. Feldman and Ludmerer, "A Loss of Thoroughness," 287.
6. Liselotte N. Dyrbye, Colin P. West, Daniel Satele, Sonja Boone, et al., "Burnout Among U.S. Medical Students, Residents and Early Career Physicians Relative to the General U.S. Population," *Academic Medicine* 89, no. 3 (March 2014): 443–51.
7. Feldman and Ludmerer, "A Loss of Thoroughness," 288.
8. https://www.brighamandwomens.org/medicine/general-internal-medicine-and-primary-care/hospitalist/about-us.
9. Joel T. Katz and Shahram Khoshbin, "Can Visual Arts Training Improve Physician Performance?" *Transactions of the American Clinical and Climatological Association* 125 (2014): 336.
10. Katz and Khoshbin, "Can Visual Arts Training," 336.
11. Amy C. Edmondson, *Teaming: How Organizations Learn, Innovate, and Compete in the Knowledge Economy* (San Francisco: John Wiley & Sons, Inc., 2012), 13.
12. Edmondson, *Teaming*, 26.
13. Edmondson, *Teaming*, 128.
14. Edmondson. *Teaming*, 51-57.

15. Amy Edmondson, "Psychological Safety and Learning Behavior in Work Teams," *Administrative Science Quarterly* 44, no. 2 (June 1999): 354.
16. Edmondson, *Teaming*, 118.
17. Charles Duhigg, "What Google Learned in Its Quest to Build the Perfect Team," *New York Times*, February 28, 2016, https://www.nytimes.com/2016/02/28/magazine/what-google-learned-from-its-quest-to-build-the-perfect-team.html (accessed June 16, 2022).
18. Duhigg, "What Google Learned."
19. Duhigg, "What Google Learned."
20. Under the leadership of Joel Katz, the ITU museum program was started by Ray Williams, a museum educator, and Mary Thorndike, an internal medicine specialist. Corinne Zimmermann, museum educator, began leading the program in 2012. Over the years, numerous museum educators and medical educators have helped guide the program.
21. Katz and Khoshbin, "Can Visual Arts Training," 336.
22. Rebecca Greenberg, "Teamwork: The Heart of Healthcare," *AAMC Reporter* (May-June 2016): 7.
23. Stuart Brown, "Play is More Than Just Fun," TED Talk, 2008, https://www.ted.com/talks/stuart_brown_play_is_more_than_just_fun/transcript?language=en.
24. This activity, created by the author (Zimmermann), is described in Katz and Khoshbin, "Can Visual Arts Training," 336.
25. https://collections.mfa.org/objects/490951/artificial-rock-85?ctx=ad0cab90-695f-4422-95ff-b6b687d2a1aa&idx=0.
26. https://collections.mfa.org/objects/32968/discovery-of-achilles-on-skyros?ctx=fa0edd61-641a-49bc-b862-1e6b3b260b58&idx=0.
27. Shannon Murphy, "Tableaux Vivant: History and Practice," *Art Museum Teaching* (December 6, 2012).
28. Gauri Agarwal, Meaghan McNulty, Katerina Santiago, Hope Torrents, and Alberto J. Caban-Martinez, "Impact of Visual Thinking Strategies (VTS) on the Analysis of Clinical Images: A Pre-Post Study of VTS in First-Year Medical Students," *Journal of Medical Humanities* 41, no. 4 (2020): 561-72.
29. Oskar Kokoschka, Austrian, 1886–1980, *Two Nudes (Lovers)*, 1913, oil on canvas, 163.2 x 97.5 centimeters (64 1/4 x 38 3/8 inches), Museum of Fine Arts, Boston, Bequest of Sarah Reed Platt, 1973.196.
30. Elizabeth Gaufberg and Ray Williams, "Reflection in a Museum Setting: The Personal Responses Tour," *Journal of Graduate Medical Education* 3, no. 4 (2011): 549; Parker Palmer, *A Hidden Wholeness: The Journey Toward an Undivided Life* (San Francisco: Jossey Bass, 2004): 92.
31. https://harvardartmuseums.org/collections/object/143495?position=4.
32. https://www.jacksonfineart.com/artists/502-julie-blackmon/works/44095.
33. In a lovely (and humorous) extension of the conversation about Julie Blackmon's photograph, team members recreated the photograph on a quad in front of the hospital and sent the photograph of their "tableau" to Corinne Zimmermann, who led their session.
34. Personal communication with Linda Delaporta, March 15, 2021.
35. Edmondson, *Teaming*, 136.
36. Personal communication with Linda Delaporta, March 15, 2021.

6

Confronting Bias

In "Diversity is Not Enough: Advancing a Framework for Antiracism in Medical Education," Sonja Solomon et al. write, "Racism is deeply entrenched in American healthcare."[1] It is well established that racism, bias, and discrimination have profoundly negative consequences for patients from historically marginalized populations, including lack of access to quality care and treatment, and higher rates of disease and premature death. Racism and discrimination also have negative consequences for trainees and professionals who are underrepresented in medicine, leading to higher rates of social isolation, moral injury, burnout, depression, and attrition—all of which impacts patient care. Studies show that BIPOC patients have better outcomes when treated by health professionals with similar ethnic or racial backgrounds. However, as Solomon and others argue, increasing diversity is not enough, as the effects of structural and institutional racism are too pervasive and deep. Instead, she argues for a paradigm shift in which antiracism is "the foundation upon which we build an equitable learning environment." "Problems rooted in racism," she writes, "demand solutions grounded in anti-racism."[2]

This chapter focuses on confronting bias. In it, we highlight the work of Dr. Kamna Balhara, Assistant Residency Program Director in Emergency Medicine at Johns Hopkins University Hospital, who, along with her colleague Nathan Irvin, is making systemic changes to the residency program there by formally integrating an antiracism framework into the residency curriculum.[3] Balhara has a longstanding passion for the arts and humanities, and museum-based pedagogies are integrated throughout her work in this area. Discrimination in healthcare—and in museums—takes many forms, including sexism, ageism, ableism, homophobia, transphobia, classicism, and more. The lessons Balhara offers provide inspiration for how museum-based pedagogies, when sensitively and mindfully employed, can play a role in helping to dismantle structural and institutional racism within healthcare and beyond.

This chapter begins with an interview with Dr. Balhara in which she illuminates the problem of health inequities and racism in the health professions and discusses the groundbreaking programs incorporating museum-based practices that she and Irvin have pioneered to prepare interns and residents to address health inequities, racism, bias, and discrimination. Following the interview, we focus on Share Tools, an online platform created by Balhara and Irvin in 2021 that provides resources and tools informed by museum-based practices and narrative medicine to support antiracist pedagogies.[4] To provide "a picture of practice," we then detail a museum workshop sequence co-developed by Balhara and Zimmermann.

A CONVERSATION BETWEEN CORINNE ZIMMERMANN AND DR. KAMNA BALHARA

Corinne:
Tell us a little bit about yourself, and the art museum–based work that you are doing.

Kamna:
I am an emergency physician who practices in Baltimore at Johns Hopkins. I'm also one of the assistant residency program directors. In that role, I've been very lucky to find support within our department to integrate arts-and-humanities-based work into teaching our residents.

When I was an undergrad, I was a French major. Before medical school, I got a master's degree in French cultural studies and lived in Paris for a year. That year really challenged me; it made me question my assumptions. I chose to write about painter Édouard Manet and poet Charles Baudelaire, and how they represented women. As I was writing and exploring their works, I started to wonder, "Why did I choose the work of these men to understand the experiences of women?" It made me realize that I had assumed that the authoritative voice on women's experiences would be male. I had failed to question traditional power differentials. The best thing about that realization and that experience was it really pushed me to be curious and critical. It was a year dedicated to looking at art, and it was magical.

When I went to medical school, I thought that chapter of my life was closed—left behind for the forward momentum of medical training. It took me longer than I would have liked to realize that art-based approaches to education for physicians and future physicians could be truly integral to my work. As a woman and as an immigrant, navigating a life in academic medicine, I have needed avenues for introspection, for critique, for exploring the experiences of sometimes being an outsider—art allows this processing and expression. Art and literature always offered me avenues to give voice to and explore my own inner conflicts and experiences. That's what I'm trying to bring to my work with residents and fellows.

At Hopkins, we are working on three major initiatives. The first is Health Humanities at Hopkins Emergency Medicine, what we call H3EM, which offers humanities-based curricular programming to emergency medicine residents and involves an interprofessional team of healthcare workers. I co-direct this initiative with my colleague Dr. Nathan Irvin, and our goal is to apply the humanities toward helping residents understand and address the human experiences of health and illness. We also seek to build cultural humility in patient-centered care to better serve Hopkins patients and the surrounding Baltimore communities. We also have a speaker series featuring healthcare workers, artists, and activists. It's really important for us to translate this art-inspired introspection and discussion into action, so we have a small grants program that awards residents working at the nexus of social medicine and the humanities, as well as the Creativity in Medicine Award for those who want to submit creative works in poetry, photography, mixed media, etc.

The second major initiative is a year-long, longitudinal distinction track in the health humanities, offered to any resident or fellow in any specialty at Hopkins. I lead this in conjunction with my mentor and colleague, Dr. Rachel Salas. I believe the humanities will have relevance to the trainees' careers, their clinical practice, and their future lives as educators or clinicians. Through this track, we are committed to generating cross-specialty dialogues across the hospital on the culture of healthcare and health equity.

Thirdly, Dr. Irvin and I recently launched Share Tools, an online platform which applies museum-based and narrative approaches to support education around antiracism for health professionals and trainees.

Corinne:
You're doing amazing work. It's multi-pronged, which is inspiring, especially within one institution. What are the needs and problems that you are trying to address?

Kamna:
The three complementary initiatives build upon each other. At first, I didn't know the scope of what our residents needed, and I didn't know the scope of the issues we could address through the arts and humanities until I engaged experientially in the work. But I believed if we engaged our residents with the arts and humanities through our curriculum, we would create space for them to reflect, process their experiences, and question the world around them. This is often at odds with the way in which medical education is conducted. There's a right answer. There's a very specific hierarchy. Training is tough and traditional attitudes are "suck it up and get through it." I really wanted to create space to make the intangible tangible. I always worry about the disconnect between us and the patients we care for. I see the humanities as a bridge to making those relationships more human and personal.

Early on, we did some pilot sessions with our emergency medicine residents. In subsequent years we selected themes for H3EM's curriculum based on responses and identified areas of interest from our residents. From there, we had to convince others at our institution of the value of this work and demonstrate its currency for academic medicine. The longitudinal health humanities distinction track, offered across the institution, now additionally ensures that there are opportunities for true integration of the arts and humanities into medical education through formal avenues for training, and not just for emergency medicine residents.

Corinne:
It sounds like engaging residents to identify needs was critical to developing the program in a responsive way.

Kamna:

Yes, I think that's been the key to how we've been able to get buy-in from our learners. We keep the curriculum very flexible and iterative. We build and adapt. As situations change, or if there are major events in medicine or the world, we don't have any problem adapting or inviting people who can speak to the current moment. I think keeping it current to the realities of our residents is really important for engagement.

Corinne:

Staying close to your residents' experiences, how do you think bias and racism has affected them?

Kamna:

I think it works on multiple levels. Calling out structural racism is so important because it is both embedded in the system—impacting our experiences in medicine as a whole—and is also granular, impacting our interpersonal encounters. There's a lot of great literature on how structural racism and bias are embedded in each step of the process of medical training. Medical students who identify as BIPOC remain grossly underrepresented in medical school, especially when you think about the proportion of the US population who identify as Black, Hispanic, and/or Native American. And we know even less about the representation of people that identify as members of the LGBTQIA+ community because of pervasive stigmas and mistreatment in healthcare fields. Structurally, racism has a huge impact in terms of access and opportunities, mentorship, and being able to get to where you want to go. Experiences are very different, depending on what race or ethnicity you might identify with. That's the macro aspect of it.

As to the micro, I think experiencing bias or racism is common for our residents. It's common for our nurses. It's common for our faculty. And when you encounter that on a day-to-day basis, it's destabilizing and demoralizing. Residency is really rough. It's a time when your whole identity is going through multiple transitions. You're busier than you've ever been. You may not have time for hobbies or the people you care about—the things that make you *you*. And so to be "othered" when at work is extraordinarily isolating. I have witnessed multiple instances myself—a resident being told to "go back to where they came from," or to "speak English" when they're communicating perfectly clearly. Additionally, some residents feel like they have to hide their cultural identity—their true selves—so others don't make assumptions about their professionalism based on outdated or racist preconceptions. I think it affects their journey through medicine on a structural level, but it also affects their day-to-day experiences—how they identify and their sense of belonging in medicine.

How do we equip them to respond and to navigate this, so that they do not have to feel they are constantly shouldering that burden? And for those who witness it, are they going to suffer moral injury in staying silent or complicit? How do you empower them to respond? It's really important to intervene at this stage of training, because all these disparities in representation, promotion, and retention persist after residency. This is a really crucial time to get people actively thinking about these questions, because they're going to be the future leaders and decision-makers in the field.

Corinne:
Could you talk specifically about how your programs address these issues?

Kamna:
I think it happens at two levels. It's about personal engagement, and it's about structural change. Each of the sessions for our residents are designed in this exact way. We incorporate activities that are grounded in art museum–based education to inspire personal engagement, discussion, and reflection. Then we conclude by tying the experience to their clinical practice, with recommendations or data drawn from evidence-based medicine, to equip them to translate that reflection into action—it could be action in their personal lives or collective action to make structural change. I'll give you an example. Especially with COVID, we've seen our patients who are unstably housed navigating a lot of issues. And there's also a lot of compassion fatigue toward these patients. We thought it would be important to have a session on that. There's a beautiful series of photographs from a *Seattle Times* project "Portraits of Homelessness"[5] with captions written by the subjects of the photographs. It's a series of images of folks who are suffering from unstable housing combined with their stories. We use those photographs to get people to look closely. We ask them, "What is one thing about this person that you're curious about? What do you want to know, and why?" Then we transition to a conversation about being unstably housed within the context of the pandemic and use evidence-based literature to talk about that. We get the residents personally engaged and then loop back to the clinical environment so that they think about the issues we discussed in the session in a more active and empathic manner. As a result, a group of our residents is now working on a collection of tools to be made available to emergency department physicians to help them understand the resources available in the community for patients with unstable housing. Out of this one conversation on unstable housing came a very tangible change. That encapsulates what we are trying to do.

There's a great framework by Sonja Solomon and colleagues that we apply to our work. They propose that antiracist or health equity work in medical education should have four steps: seeing, naming, understanding, and acting. To see, we have to observe and look closely. And with art, we're doing just that. Then we're asked to name what we see. And this is the uncomfortable part. That's where Parker Palmer's concept of the third thing is so valuable.[6] Third things are works of art, poems, and objects that allow us to explore a topic indirectly through metaphor. The artwork provides space for us to make very direct and uncomfortable statements, to name the injustices that we either endure or see around us. And then the third step, understanding, is about making meaning together with a methodology like VTS [Visual Thinking Strategies] where you reflect and build meaning collaboratively. Because VTS asks us to support our ideas with evidence, you have to consider why you believe something. It invites us to interrogate ourselves and our preconceptions. And what I really love about VTS is the leveling of hierarchies, which allows the collaboration that is necessary to the final step: acting. Medical education is so hierarchical, with power differentials between the teacher and the learner. But when you bring a group of healthcare professionals and trainees and teachers from different specialties or disciplines together to talk about a work of art, you're not asking or expecting any of them to have any prior knowledge. As a result, hierarchies are flattened. I think having these conversations around art as equals, as partners, allows for remodeling relationships that would traditionally prevent us from pushing for change or that would prevent us or make us afraid of challenging the status quo. I think that collaborative spirit in these endeavors is really special.

Corinne:
That was going to be my next question: Why art? Are there other stories you could share that help us see the value of art and museum-based practices for antiracism work?

Kamna:
Yes. I am going to talk about a session with Robert Colescott's extraordinarily provocative and uncomfortable painting *Emergency Room*[7] (see figure 4). It was eye-opening for everybody involved. We began the session by looking at the artwork together using VTS. It was done over Zoom due to the pandemic, but you could really feel palpable tension and discomfort. And I will tell you, there was stunned silence. Then one person spoke, then another person spoke, and it just snowballed. And you saw people struggling out loud with how to say things that made them uncomfortable. But I think that brought us all closer. Afterward, in response to a resident's suggestion, we created an online anonymous forum for residents and other staff to share experiences with discrimination that they may have had. It was eye-opening, first for people to start to feel "Okay, I'm not alone in going through this," and second, for others to realize "I can't believe my colleagues *do* go through this." Multiple residents were inspired to write about their own experiences with prejudice, and these were then shared broadly with the department. That led to some dialogue-building with our nursing staff as well. From that single thirty-minute conversation about Colescott's painting, we opened a larger dialogue across the department. Some of our residents are trying to publish their work as well. I think that dialogue is going to propagate well beyond our department.

Corinne:
It sounds like people took that experience and pushed it forward in so many ways. Did you have any conversation or reflection about their experience of discomfort?

Kamna:

Yes, much of the benefit comes from the debrief itself, when people say, "That made me uncomfortable" or "I didn't like that, but I still felt like there was something I wanted to share."

Corinne:

Did people recognize that the discomfort was necessary?

Kamna:

Yes. One of the main themes that came out of collecting formal feedback and doing a focus group with our residents was *this has to keep happening*. People appreciated the experience of being pushed out of their comfort zone in a supportive and respectful space. Another major theme was they felt it was transformational, both at an individual level and for the culture of the department.

Corinne:

A question many of us doing this work have is about creating sustainable change. Do you feel that your emergency department is moving toward that?

Kamna:

Yes, I think structurally we notice this in a few ways. I think one of the most valuable ways to measure cultural change is the image we put forth to the next generation. When medical students come to interview for a position in our program, our residents often talk to them about H3EM as "our humanities program." They really own it and see it as a strength, and they use it as a selling point for our residency program. And interviewees ask about it. I think that's a tangible way in which it has become part of our identity and it's something we're proud to offer.

Current residents are also generating new ideas for carrying it forward. As part of a fourth-year mini-fellowship, one resident has elected to create an arts and humanities track, and hold an arts-and-humanities-based conference for emergency medicine residency programs.

Corinne:

I'm curious if you have observed a positive impact on patient care.

Kamna:

That is the hardest aspect to capture. When we did our focus group and collected written feedback, many of our residents said they now spend more time with patients, that they're more curious about their patients, and they ask questions they would not have thought to ask before. The most important feedback would be from the patients themselves. We have a grant from the American Association of Medical Colleges grant to design simulated scenarios with standardized patients to give us feedback on skills we think are relevant to the humanities.

Corinne:
What are some of those skills that you're hoping to measure?

Kamna:
One of them is cultural humility. The second is interprofessional practice—the ability to genuinely work as an equal partner on your team and to see your patient as a member of that team. And the third aspect is being able to navigate bias. In the simulated scenarios, we've peppered the patient's chart, as well as the verbal handoff, with biased language or elements that can create misconceptions and assumptions. Then we record these encounters and evaluate how the participating residents navigate those sources of bias. We're positing that those exposed to the humanities may have a leg up in navigating these issues.

Corinne:
How did you prepare yourself to do this work?

Kamna:
I think the most important thing for me is framing it as a learning experience for myself. I've done some art history work, but I'm not a museum educator. I think one important thing for me was realizing the limits of my knowledge and understanding. Now I approach this work with a growth mindset and really invest in partnerships with folks who are museum educators, or scholars in the humanities, in addition to other members of the healthcare team and patients themselves. The Harvard Macy Institute Art Museum-based Health Professions Education Fellowship was extraordinarily valuable in that regard. The other important thing was learning to own my own blind spots because the conversations that we have with our residents or learners often open my eyes. I can't tell you the number of times we've had a conversation and I think, "I did not see it that way until you brought it up." But I think that really speaks to the value of museum education methodologies for leveling hierarchies while engaging with compelling works of art. The teacher can learn something all the time.

Corinne:
Those moments are gold.

Kamna:
Yes, it really brings me joy when someone points out something that is new to me.

Corinne:
Right, as opposed to getting defensive, or whatever else someone might do. Circling back, I can imagine that people involved in healthcare would be really interested to know how you have gotten buy-in from your administration?

Kamna:

We really wanted to be responsive to the needs of our learners. To make that argument, we had to prove that the learners wanted our emergency medicine residency arts and humanities program, and found it valuable. In 2018, we did six pilot sessions, for which we just told residents, "Hey, hang out after the conference. Bring your lunch. This is totally elective, but here are some things we're going to talk about." And we minimized the amount of additional prep time. If we had them read something, we ensured it was really brief. We wanted to make sure each session was self-contained, that you could just drop in, and that it was very convenient. We did sessions with a variety of media and themes.

We documented the numbers of learners who participated each time and captured formal feedback immediately after these sessions. We asked what participants wanted to see more of. We took that data to our program leadership and said, "Here's some preliminary data demonstrating that there's a desire and potential positive impact, and this is something that is lacking." In my case, my department chair and program director were extraordinarily supportive. And it was a lot easier for them to say, "Okay, let's make time in the curriculum," because there was some preliminary work.

Corinne:

Where did the funding come from?

Kamna:

We are, again, very, very fortunate. Our chair was willing to give us a budget to start to build these three initiatives. Luckily, much of the art in Baltimore is accessible free of charge. We use our budget for speakers' honoraria and a grant program to enable our residents to reflect and move this work forward, as well as for our creativity and medicine awards. Grant funding is out there, but it is limited. But I do think compared to five years ago, there are many more opportunities now. In addition to the American Association of Medical Colleges grant for the simulations, the Macy Foundation supported our Share Tools work.

Corinne:

What advice do you have for other health-professions educators or art museum educators interested in doing this kind of work?

Kamna:

We need to prepare to answer questions about how we measure impact. But are we doing ourselves a disservice by trying to measure impact using the traditional metrics of academic medicine?

Corinne:

It's a struggle within the field. There are other tools, but right now, they're not as valued by many leaders in the health professions who value quantitative methods only. We need to find or create the right tools to measure this work.

Kamna:

Yes. Also, we try to keep the art relevant to our community because so much of our work is about helping providers feel closer to the communities they serve. I think it's important to have works of art that either originate from these communities or can be viewed locally, such as murals or sources of public art. I try to make sure there's a diversity of subjects, themes, media, and artists.

I cannot stress enough the value of partnerships. It is impossible to do this work without interdisciplinary partnerships. We brought in folks who are violence intervention specialists who have also been victims of gun violence. We bring in patients. We bring in other members of the healthcare team to participate in the conversations. For anyone who's in the health professions seeking to do this, finding partners in your community—museum educators, community artists, or activists— is super important.

Corinne:

What about art museum educators? What advice do you have for us?

Kamna:

Be aware that we have limited time and need to show clinical relevance. If students can apply the lessons to their clinical practice, it helps getting buy-in. Working in partnership is really important. The museum educator brings expertise about the art, about designing amazing experiences, while someone in the health professions can ensure that this great experience is something that connects to and can be applied to patient encounters or to research. The input and expertise of museum educators is so important, and the choice of partner is important, too. We want someone who will help us think creatively about our goals and who will be responsive to our needs. They have to care.

AN INTRODUCTION TO SHARE TOOLS

Share Tools (Supporting Humanities-based Anti-Racism Education for Health Professionals), funded by the Josiah Macy Foundation, is a valuable resource for health-professions educators and museum educators developing programs to confront and mitigate bias. The comprehensive website includes core concepts related to antiracism, a glossary of key terms, links to research and pertinent articles, and teaching modules employing museum-based and narrative medicine practices. Many of Share Tools' activities and underlying ideas will be familiar to readers of this book. Examples include how one might use a personal response tour, group poems, or interpretive conversations to support dialogues about health disparities, racism, discrimination, and biases.

Because these necessary conversations can be difficult, they must be embarked upon with humility, intention, and care. The Share Tools website offers suggestions for how to prepare oneself to facilitate such discussions. The first step is to conduct a self-assessment, as recognizing our own assumptions, biases, and privileges is essential. Educators who come from positions of privilege, especially, must invest in learning as much as possible about how structural racism and systemic inequities shape all of our experiences and inform the learning spaces and environments in which we participate. Loretta Ross, a human rights activist, who advocates for a practice of "calling in," recommends that self-assessment include self-forgiveness. If we recognize that this work is relational, that it requires a learning mindset, that mistakes and missteps are opportunities for learning, we will likely be more open and nonjudgmental toward others.[8]

A stance of openness, curiosity, and respect are important for creating learning spaces that encourage individuals to share their perspectives and experiences, if they choose to do so. Boundaries are necessary; as facilitators we aim to hold people accountable with empathy rather than shame. Part of establishing boundaries is framing the museum experience and setting some agreements. We generally acknowledge that the conversation may cause discomfort or hurt. The discomfort is often intentional; the hurt is not. The most important thing is for each individual to take care of themselves: to pause, to take a break, to leave if necessary. Agreements can include making a commitment:

- to be present for one's own experiences and the experiences of others
- to actively listen with respect, compassion, and curiosity (listening to understand does not mean agreement)
- to embrace discomfort and mistakes as opportunities for learning
- to assume best intentions (but acknowledge impact)
- to take care of oneself and others

For this work to be transformative and sustainable, the experiences need to be ongoing. Ideally, antiracist pedagogies should be woven across all learning. Part of preparing is knowing who is in the room and anticipating directions a conversation might take. Because antiracism work is fundamentally relational, it helps if your groups already work together regularly and, through this, have already established a culture of trust.

The workshop sequence we describe next has been used with a group of health-professions educators who have participated in an ongoing community of practice for several months. We have also used it with interns and residents who participate together in a medical humanities program. The sample workshop is ninety minutes long. This can be a constraint but the dedication of time to the topic signifies its importance.

PICTURE OF PRACTICE

The workshop leader(s) begin by letting the group know that the session will be an exploration of racial inequities in healthcare, as well as an invitation for the group to think about their own experiences, assumptions, and biases. We acknowledge that the conversation could be difficult and state that if it is activating for anyone, they should feel free to step away or do whatever they need to do to take care of themselves. We share a set of agreements and confirm everyone is comfortable with them.

Warm-up (three minutes)

To bring everyone to a place of embodied presentness, we invite the group to take ten breaths together, raising their hands over their heads on each inhale and bringing them down on each exhale.

Close Looking and Reading (twenty minutes)

We often begin our sessions with an experience of close looking. In a modification of an activity developed by Balhara and Irvin, we pair a carefully selected image and a poem.[9] The pairing of a visual image with text that is read aloud allows for multiple entry points for different kinds of learners. After someone gives voice to the poem, we invite the group to look at the photograph and read the poem on their own with these guiding questions in mind:

- When you view the image and read the poem, what feelings or thoughts arise? What associations/connections exist between the image and the poem?
- Please take a few minutes to write down your thoughts.

The group returns to share their ideas.

Reflection

In one example, we juxtaposed Gordon Parks's photograph *American Gothic*[10] with Lucille Clifton's poem "Study the Masters."[11] *American Gothic* depicts Ella Watson, a cleaning woman whom Parks met at the Farm Security Administration in Washington, DC, while he was documenting the lives of African Americans as part of a Farm Security Administration fellowship. She stands erect in front of a large American flag holding a mop and a broom—the tools of her trade. The title references, and challenges us to reimagine, Grant Wood's painting of the same name, which is considered by some to be an iconic image of America.[12] Clifton's short poem paints a word portrait highlighting and celebrating the labors of her Aunt Timmie. The group's discussion explored themes of privilege, invisibility/visibility, gender, "America," and dignity. Following the discussion, we ask the group how the image and the poem might resonate or be relevant to the practice of healthcare today.

INTERPRETIVE CONVERSATION AND SYSTEMS THINKING ROUTINE: ROBERT COLESCOTT'S *EMERGENCY ROOM*

The next activity focuses on Robert Colescott's painting *Emergency Room*. As discussed by Balhara in our interview, we know the painting can be challenging for viewers. Knowing that, we scaffold the experience; we move from thinking about our own personal identities to considering the roles of systems in our lives.

We each hold many identities. We may define ourselves by our ethnicity, our gender, our age, our race, our political beliefs, our professions, our passions, and more. Each person is invited to think about core aspects of their identities and write down ones they are willing to share. In groups of two or three, individuals take turns sharing their list. Their partner(s) then selects one they are curious about and says, "Tell me more." Suggestions for open-ended questions can be shared to help guide the conversation.

Next, we invite the group to consider how as individuals we are embedded in systems and to examine how those systems shape our identities. To structure the conversation, we use a modified Thinking Routine from Project Zero, "Art to Systems and Back,"[13] with Robert Colescott's large painting *Emergency Room*. We begin the conversation by sharing some information: Robert Colescott was an African American artist who painted this image in 1989. The painting is large—seven feet by nine feet—and Colescott meant for it to provoke the viewer, to make us uncomfortable, and to wrestle with things we may not want to confront. Colescott used exaggeration in his work because he said, " Overkill is probably the way it really is, if you have the guts to really look at it."[14]

Art to Systems and Back

Step 1: What do you notice about the work? Gather as many observations as possible.

Step 2: What civically related systems—systems that affect people's lives as members of a community—does this work invite you to think about?

Step 3: Select one system you'd be interested in thinking about further. What are the different parts of this system—the different elements that are involved in it?

Step 4: If you wanted to change this system, what parts might you focus on?

Step 5: Reflection: What did you learn about the artwork, the system you investigated, or yourself?

After a discussion about the many racial and cultural stereotypes Colescott's work depicts, groups identify a range of systems including medical (healthcare), legal, religious, environmental, economic, and housing. Often the system our participants choose to focus on is healthcare, leading to discussions about ways the healthcare system humanizes or dehumanizes patients and staff, and the sharing of suggestions for proactive steps that can be taken to combat "othering."

Reflecting on the experience, participants mention how engaging with the artwork enabled them to think deeply about cultural stereotypes, racism in healthcare, the perpetuation of violence through systems, and their own discomfort and biases. In the words of one participant, "Breaking down BIG problems into component parts stimulates my sense of agency, activates problem-solving and optimism."[15]

LOVING-KINDNESS MEDITATION ADAPTED FROM RHONDA MAGEE

The work of racial justice is hard. It can feel overwhelming. In her book *The Inner Work of Racial Justice*, law professor Rhonda Magee posits that a practice of embodied mindfulness and self-compassion can offer healing and strength. She writes, "As we set out to look deeply into racism with mindfulness, we need to maintain a commitment to meet whatever arises—including our own and others' emotions—with an uncommon level of kindness and love, and with a genuine wish for healing. We need to develop and embody radical compassion and the will to be a space within which racial truth can be spoken and heard."[16] We conclude our sessions with an adaptation of one of her loving-kindness meditations.

Once participants have found a comfortable seated position, the facilitator invites everyone to gently rest their eyes and to "come home into the body." As people relax into and focus on the restorative sensations of breathing, they are invited to find a place of quiet appreciation—and to "feel into what is well, good, and at peace within you at this moment . . . (to) sense into the strength that exists in you now."[17]

As the group dwells in the healing powers of the breath, the facilitator gently guides them to now reflect on moments in their journey when they might have experienced or witnessed injustices or suffering, to notice the sensations in the body and to "allow yourself to feel and sense into the part of you that can meet your own suffering with kindness. . . . Say to yourself gently, 'In this moment I acknowledge . . . suffering in my mind, body and community. . . . (S)uffering is part of the human experience. . . . I deserve some support and kindness in this moment.'"[18]

She continues:

> Now sense into your compassion for yourself in this moment, your desire to be free of any feelings of *dis*-ease. [If you so choose] allow one hand to come to rest over your heart, and one hand to come to rest over your lower belly. As you do, breathe in and out and sense into the support that your own compassionate touch brings.[19]

She concludes by inviting participants to recite to themselves phrases from a traditional loving-kindness meditation:

> May you be filled with loving-kindness,
> May you be well in body and in mind,
> May you stay safe,

Confronting Bias

May we each be safe from inner and outer dangers,
Truly joyful, easeful, and free.[20]

NOTES

1. Sonja R. Solomon, Alev J. Atalay, and Nora Y. Osman, "Diversity Is Not Enough: Advancing a Framework for Antiracism in Medical Education," *Academic Medicine* 96, no. 11 (November 2021): 1513.
2. Solomon, Atalay, and Osman, "Diversity is Not Enough," 1514.
3. Kamna S. Balhara, Michael R. Ehmann, and Nathan Irvin, "Antiracism in Health Professions Education Through the Lens of the Health Humanities," *Anesthesiology Clinics* 40, no. 2 (June 2022): 287–99.
4. https://www.sharetools.org/.
5. https://projects.seattletimes.com/2017/portraits-of-homelessness/.
6. Parker Palmer, quoted in Elizabeth Gaufberg and Maren Batalden, "The Third Thing in Medical Education," *The Clinical Teacher* (May 17, 2007): 79.
7. K. S. Balhara and N. Irvin, "'The Guts to Really Look at It'-Medicine and Race in Robert Colescott's *Emergency Room*," *JAMA* 325, no. 2 (2021): 113–15.
8. Loretta Ross, TED Talk, https://www.ted.com/talks/loretta_j_ross_don_t_call_people_out_call_them_in?language=en.
9. https://www.sharetools.org/courses/systemic-racism-and-impact-on-the-health-of-a-community.
10. https://collections.artsmia.org/art/100557/american-gothic-gordon-parks.
11. Lucille Clifton, "Study the Masters," *Callaloo* 22, no. 1 (1999): 54.
12. https://www.artic.edu/artworks/6565/american-gothic.
13. Shari Tishman, Carrie James, Flossie Chua, David Perkins, Emily Piper-Vallillo, and Alexa Beil, "Art as Civic Commons," Project Zero, Harvard University, http://www.pz.harvard.edu/sites/default/files/ArtC%20Handbook%2007-26-21.pdf.
14. J. Hamlin, "Painter Gets the Last Laugh: A First in Venice, a Show in Berkeley," *San Francisco Chronicle*, May 12, 1999, cited in Balhara and Irvin, "The Guts."
15. Anonymous participant in professional development workshop, April 8, 2022.
16. Rhonda V. Magee, *The Inner Work of Racial Justice* (New York: TarcherPerigree, 2019): 28.
17. Magee, *The Inner Work*, 279.
18. Magee, *The Inner Work*, 78.
19. Magee, *The Inner Work*, 159.
20. https://www.mindful.org/loving-kindness-to-support-racial-justice-work/.

7

Caring for the Spirit

Ray Williams

> Yea, though I walk through the valley of the shadow of death, I will fear no evil: for thou art with me; thy rod and thy staff, they comfort me.

—Psalm 23:4 (KJV)

THE LANDSCAPE

Today, the United States is one of the most religiously diverse nations on earth. According to a study published by the Pew Research Center in 2015, 53 percent of Americans consider religion "very important" in their lives, and another 24 percent say it is "somewhat important." A total of 55 percent of those surveyed pray at least once daily, and 72 percent believe in heaven. Christians account for 70.6 percent of the US population when all branches of this complex religion are considered together—Catholics account for a subset of 20.8 percent. Nearly 23 percent of the sample were unaffiliated with any religious tradition, describing themselves as atheist, agnostic, or "nothing in particular." Other major world religion affiliations in the United Stated include Judaism (1.2 percent), Islam (0.9 percent), Buddhism (0.7 percent), and Hinduism (0.7 percent). Muslim and Hindu populations are the fastest growing in the United States.[1]

The patients who come to American emergency rooms, cancer treatment centers, and nursing homes are from all over the world, and of course the ratios of hospital patients who identify with any of these faith traditions will vary widely by region. Clinicians who are committed to providing culturally responsive care may find this diversity daunting. To further complicate matters, beliefs and practices may vary widely within any major religious tradition—even within a family. For example, older members of immigrant families may adhere more closely to the traditions of their country of origin than do those who have grown up in the United States. This tremendous range of religious expression across generations and traditions argues strongly for the need of a spiritual assessment protocol as part of patient care, a position argued by Dr. Christine M. Puchalski, founding director of the George Washington Institute for Spirituality and Health in Washington, DC. Puchalski's Spiritual History Tool is introduced in this chapter. This assessment will help clinicians avoid stereotypical assumptions about beliefs and practices based on race and ethnicity. It may also alert them to patients with a history of conflict or damage caused by participation in a religious community. Hostility or indifference to spiritual expression may be revealed when inquiring about a patient's spiritual history.

The tremendous variety of spiritual beliefs and experiences makes the aspiration of "cultural competence" unattainable; healthcare providers are now advised to adopt a stance of "cultural humility," to be aware of many different religious beliefs and practices, and to signal their openness to responding to individual needs. The art museum with culturally diverse collections is a unique site for gaining an introduction to many of the world's religious traditions.

Unlike other chapters in this book, this chapter is signed because of its personal nature. Nevertheless, it has benefited from conversations about personal losses, religious beliefs and skepticism, and museum-based teaching that my co-authors have generously shared. Readers will note that this chapter resonates with our writing elsewhere on cultural bias, story, professional reflection, and well-being. I begin with a personal story. After a brief overview of a series of museum visits designed for a palliative care team comprised of nurses, social workers, chaplains, and physicians, we will consider how art museums with ritual objects and religious imagery from many different traditions might provide insights and information about beliefs and practices that support culturally responsive work in healthcare settings. The beauty of some of these objects and their resonance with human experience may, at times, lead clinicians to find meaning that affirms their own values and offers insight into the challenges they face in the work of healing and, inevitably, losing patients in their care.

A PERSONAL HISTORY

My grandmother Clyde Padgett Johnson was born in 1898 and died in 1996. More than twenty-five years after her death, I still wrestle with the tensions between our family's values and our interactions with the healthcare system. I wonder why there was no real conversation about what to expect, what to hope for. Such stories, with all their unanswered questions and shocking images and misunderstandings, stay with us—apparently sometimes forever. We remember small acts of kindness; we perseverate on careless words, on hands without gentleness.

The family had gathered around Clyde's bed in the nursing home: my aunts from Pennsylvania and California, my uncle and parents from in-state, my siblings and cousins. We got caught up on family news, told stories about Clyde locking herself out of the house, sang some favorite songs from the Methodist hymnal. Eight years earlier, my grandmother had fallen and broken a hip and had a stroke—I'm not sure in what order, as such details are easily forgotten. She had not been able to walk for years; now, she did not speak. In our memory she was strong and funny—always up for a sewing or gardening project—but here, she was shockingly small . . . fragile. I think the physical care for my grandmother was fine. Her pain was under control. We were waiting, offering our loving presence to this person who had meant so much in our lives.

On the third day of our vigil, a chipper blonde nurse came bustling in. She checked Clyde's vital signs and announced, "I think she's looking better today! She may pull through yet!" There was a shocked silence in the room. How could a nurse so completely misunderstand our presence, our love, and our faith? How could anyone put stock in "vital signs" when looking at the wasted body of a ninety-eight-year-old? This miscalculation signaled a profound ignorance that made me question everything about her medical judgment. In my story, that thoughtless nurse plays the part of the villain.

I am grateful for the differences in a more recent story of loss. When my father died last year, an emergency room physician stayed after her shift to wait for my mother and sister to arrive at the hospital. She had arranged for a private space for them to be with Dad, ignoring COVID-19 protocols that had kept him isolated in the nursing home. The doctor explained that this time, Dad was dying. She provided an outline of what to expect, gave them the option of leaving or staying as long as they liked, and arranged for the nurse to provide regular updates, cold drinks, and snacks. In the story that helps my family come to terms with Dad's death, those thoughtful caregivers are our heroes.

TEACHING IN THE MUSEUM

Perhaps because their years of training cultivate a primary identity as scientists, many healthcare professionals are wary of any reference to religion in their work setting. This discomfort was evident during a memorable conversation I had in the museum with a group of nurses, residents, and senior physicians specializing in women's health. We had been thoughtfully considering a colonial-era Peruvian painting that featured a miracle-granting statue of the Virgin Mary. At the end of our wide-ranging conversation, which included noting elements of Christian iconography and considering historical information about the impact of the Catholic Church on Indigenous peoples in South America, a member of the group said, "This makes me think of a patient I took care of for several weeks. When she was ready to leave the hospital, she gave me a prayer card! And I just didn't know what to say." She did not know how to interpret this gift and felt that, by accepting the prayer card, she would be seen as affiliating with a religious tradition that was not meaningful to her. I suggested that the patient had felt cared for and wanted to express a reciprocal desire to show care and concern in her own vocabulary, which was rooted in Catholicism. What do we say in such situations? "Thank you."

Palliative care teams, in my experience, are much more comfortable communicating about issues of religion and spirituality. After all, they work closely with chaplains, professionals who are specially trained to conduct a spiritual assessment, support patients and families of diverse beliefs and cultures, and bring in religious leaders from the community who can provide specialized rituals or who share a common language with the patient. Chaplains are also available to provide spiritual support for healthcare providers who suffer from burnout, grief, post-traumatic stress, and other occupational hazards. Chaplains are often the heart and soul of the team.

My first experiences working with chaplains took place in 2006 in Providence, Rhode Island, in the galleries of the Rhode Island School of Design's Museum of Art. I had contacted a local hospice organization and offered to design a retreat or workshop at the museum to honor the important work they were doing. A group of six chaplains and social workers responded to my invitation. In a preliminary planning conversation, I learned that every three months about sixty patients died under the care of those hospice professionals. The deaths piled up so relentlessly that they had trouble even remembering certain individuals, and they found this to be a source of moral distress. We agreed that I would design a series of quarterly workshops, each of which would include looking for beauty, sharing an interpretive conversation, learning about various cultures and their understanding of death, and a brief, nondenominational ritual that centered a reading of all the names of people the group had served that quarter. It was deeply moving to see the galleries activated on behalf of these caring souls and to think of the comfort their work brought to so many patients and families. In one memorable session, toward the end of the year, one of the participants shared a portable shrine she had made after being introduced to the Buddhist bodhisattva of compassion, Guanyin, "the one who regards the cries of the world." She had put an image of Guanyin at the center of a folded cardboard triptych that she had decorated with colorful paint and words of reassurance. She quietly shared that she had also incorporated Guanyin into her personal practice.

In 2021, Dell Medical School at The University of Texas at Austin started a new fellowship in palliative care. Leaders of this program wanted to build a quarterly series of visits to the Blanton Museum of Art as a way of building cohesion among the interprofessional team of fifteen nurses, social workers, physicians, and chaplains. They wanted opportunities for professional reflection and self-care to be a throughline in every session.

We thought about the contours of the fellowship year and agreed that the first session, to be held in late summer, would be dedicated to "Convening the Community." In it, we used personal response prompts to help members of the team begin to know one another beyond their shared work. We heard about values and grandmothers and spiritual questions and memories. We spoke and we listened carefully, without questioning.

The second session focused on "Courage" and recognized that any story of courage must include an element of fear. One group looked at a narrative painting based on the Old Testament story of Esther's courageous advocacy for the Jewish people, celebrated each year in Jewish communities through the festival of Purim. The other group looked at a painting based on the ancient musician Orpheus, who went to Hades, the underworld, to rescue his newly wed, newly dead wife, Eurydice. Both of these stories of courage in the face of death have inspired artists, filmmakers, and musicians for centuries. To add a playful note and encourage social connections, each of the groups performed a Readers' Theater script based on the stories, complete with kitschy costume accessories.

"Memory and Absence" was the theme for the third session, inspired by the preoccupations of Colombian artist Oscar Muñoz, whose work in photography and video invites conversations about growing up, how places change over time, lost loved ones, and our tendency to lose the details of our memories over time.

The final session of the year, on the theme of "Caring for the Spirit," was designed to encourage play, mindful practices, and expressions of gratitude. One especially meaningful activity asked participants to pair up and sit facing one another, look carefully at one another's face, and make a continuous-line drawing of their partner without looking down at their paper or lifting their pencil. After laughingly sharing the "portraits," the paired participants were invited to share specific things they appreciated about their partner.

The sessions developed for the palliative care team in Austin were not tightly focused on religious expression. This reflects the limitations and opportunities of the collections available at the Blanton Museum (primarily European, Latin American, and modern/contemporary art), as well as the emphasis on building community and supporting self-care requested by the fellowship's co-directors in our planning. However, representing the religiously pluralistic society in which we live today is vitally important in efforts to develop more culturally responsive healthcare. Museum educators working with collections that have similar gaps may need to resort to high-quality reproductions to introduce beliefs and practices from Judaism, Islam, Hinduism, Buddhism, and other traditions. Of course, when working with more global collections, educators should incorporate works of art from these traditions in a robust, balanced, and respectful way. Teaching with ritual objects and religious imagery requires careful preparation, with an eye to both cultural specificity and human themes that resonate with a diverse audience. Group leaders must also be intentional in their use of inclusive and conditional language, giving every participant room to feel welcomed as their authentic self.

GRIEF AND THE BUDDHA'S TEACHING

It is 2016, and I am in the company of a dozen museum and medical professionals at the Metropolitan Museum of Art. We are in New York City for a conference exploring the emerging trend of collaboration between art museums and medicine. We have come from all over the country to learn from one another and to imagine new ways that our institutions and systems might become more helpful, more humane. The individuals in my group have signed up for a session on how the art museum might support caregivers whose work involves proximity to suffering and death. The museum people have the occasional, limited experience of death typical of our contemporary, medicalized culture; the physicians have seen . . . so much. We have all known grief and loss.

I ask the group to look together at a fifth-century red sandstone sculpture of the Buddha (figure 5). He is standing, relaxed, and serene. His subtly carved garment presses against a perfect body. His cropped hair has sprung into snail-like curls, and I am reminded of a story in which the snails of the forest crawled onto Siddhartha's shaved head to protect him from the blazing sun so that his meditation could continue undisturbed. Elongated earlobes suggest the heavily jeweled earrings, now removed, that he would have worn as a young prince; although some would say that the emphasis on the Buddha's ears indicates his superlative ability to listen. The sculptor manifested a reverence for the sensuous human figure typical of South Asian art and drew on a list of metaphors traditionally used to describe the Buddha's transcendent beauty. This masterwork shows the Buddha with eyes shaped like lotus petals, a torso like a lion, and long, well-formed arms that reach the knees—physical traits mentioned in canonical descriptions of the Awakened One.[2] We cannot help but be moved by this realization of human beauty and the many stories that surround the life of the Buddha.

"I have learned a story from Buddhist tradition that I would like to share with you," I say. "It's a teaching story that has something to tell us about grief and loss."

Long ago, when the Buddha lived, a daughter was born to a poor household, to the Gotami family. The child was frail and could not thrive. She was called Kisa, "the frail one." She was often overlooked, neglected. Most of the rice went to Kisa's brother.

As soon as it was decent, Kisa was married off and sent to live with her in-laws. The young bride must have had a moment of hope for what her new life might bring, but she was treated like a servant by her new mother-in-law. Kisa kept her eyes down and her hands busy. It was only when the new life growing in her womb became apparent that the family began to look at Kisa with a glint of respect.

The baby came, and Kisa was transfixed, transformed—even happy. This little boy needed her, only her. They looked into each other's sparkling eyes and laughed! When the baby cried, Kisa had whatever was needed.

But the child fell sick with a fever—and died. Kisa could not take this in. She clutched the boy's body to her own and let no one come near. Beside herself, her long hair exposed and unkempt, her clothing torn and dirty, she crossed the threshold of her husband's house and went into the streets. Most people took one look at her and moved away. Finally, one kind man approached and said, "Sister, if you will come with me, there is a great Teacher not so far from here. He may be able to help you." Mutely, Kisa followed the man to a place in the forest where people had gathered. She knew the Teacher at once and pushed her way through the crowd, shouting wildly and thrusting her burden forward: "Teacher! My baby is sick. Do you have the medicine we need?"

The Buddha looked at Kisa. He saw her, through and through. He knew this story. "Perhaps I can help you, Child. Go back into the village. Bring me a mustard seed for the medicine. But remember: This mustard seed must come from a household that has not known death."

Having a plan, a possibility, helped bring Kisa back to herself. She was determined to get the medicine her baby needed. But throughout that long day, knocking at household after household, Kisa heard the stories of loss. "My husband . . . our mother, just last winter . . . my little brother . . ." Settling among the roots of a banyan tree and seeing the lamps of the village being lit, Kisa was able to look at the child's body and see it for what it was. Her tears bathed that body, and she prepared to let it go.

Having fulfilled her duties, Kisa returned to the forest. And the Buddha saw her, clearly, with compassion. The Frail One joined the community that followed the Buddha, and she offered loving-kindness and comfort to many in need. Until the end.[3]

We pause for a moment to let the meaning of the story find its way to us . . . to dry our eyes and regain our composure. Perhaps we were imagining the possibility, the inevitability of our own losses. Who would we be in those moments of grief? Perhaps the medical professionals among us were also remembering patients and families, moved by the beauty of the sculpture and the emotion of the story to feel those losses in a new way.

I invite others to speak of memories, feelings, faith, or questions: "We are all part of such stories sooner or later, aren't we? This community of loss is vast. We wonder how we will face grief and loss, when the time comes." I remind the clinicians in the group that even when they cannot offer a cure, their experience of death and their insights can be helpful to patients and families whose experience is much more limited:

A death in the family is a major event that must be processed over time by those left behind. Many of us search for meaning by repeatedly telling the story of suffering, medical interventions, courage, prayers, rituals, and last words. As you reflect on your interactions with families and patients nearing the end of life, ask yourself, "How will my character be described in the story this family tells about the death of their loved one in the hospital?" They will be telling their story long after the healthcare professionals have forgotten that individual death and attended to many more people facing death and loss.

The ancient story of Kisa Gotami's loss asks us to imagine the worst—the loss of a beloved child. It honors the intensity of human love and grief, and it provides a model for our contemplation. In the story, the wise teacher (or healer) does not counsel or resist, but offers an active, compassionate presence in the face of irreparable loss. Kisa feels seen and understood. She is given a small task that she can manage, a process that will eventually help her feel less alone in her pain. She is able to rejoin the community in a new way.

TENDING TO THE SPIRIT

Research shows that patients who can draw on spiritual resources cope more effectively with their illnesses, are more likely to follow medical orders and practice healthy behaviors, and are generally more hopeful. As they face suffering and

serious illness, patients may need prayer, rituals, time for confession and atone-
ment, or the opportunity to mend relationships. When religion and spirituality are
understood to be a natural part of care, staff members of diverse faith traditions
may feel more secure in offering useful information from their own experiences,
thus becoming important resources for a team committed to offering spiritually
informed care. Members of a healthcare team may feel a stronger connection
with patients, colleagues, and their own traditions in a climate in which religion is
acknowledged.

Physicians are trained to focus on saving lives, but reasonable people understand that not every ailment can be cured and that death is, indeed, inevitable. Still,
we want some company, a compassionate presence, on this hard path. We do not
want to feel abandoned by our doctors as we face our last weeks and days of life.
We want to be seen and understood. Our spirits need to be cared for, even when
our bodies cannot be made whole. There is much that a kind and experienced guide
can do to help us navigate, but the current healthcare system, with its emphasis on
efficiency and the limited, action-oriented, scientific paradigm of medicine today,
often lets us down in our hour of need.

We know that in times of trouble—suffering, fear, grief—many people confront existential questions: "Why me?" "Am I going to die?" "What will happen if I
die?" People of faith may ask, "How could God allow this to happen?" In their book
Making Health Care Whole: Integrating Spirituality into Patient Care, Christina Puchalski and Betty Ferrell argue that caring for the spirit is just as much a professional
responsibility as caring for the body and mind:

> Particularly when people are faced with a life-threatening illness, questions
> about meaning and purpose in the midst of suffering arise. It is not uncommon
> for people to question God, fairness, and life choices. People often undertake
> a life review, where issues related to their life, relationships, and self-worth
> might arise. Spiritual issues include hopelessness, despair, guilt, shame, anger,
> and abandonment by God or others. These issues can provoke deep suffering,
> which can result from people feeling alienated from themselves, others, God,
> or from their ultimate source of meaning.[4]

The authors provide the FICA Tool for taking a patient's spiritual history to be included in their chart, a process that provides important information to the care team
and signals to the patient that conversations about religious or spiritual questions
are possible in the medical setting.[5] The information-gathering questions include:

- Faith and Beliefs—Do you consider yourself spiritual or religious? Do you have
  spiritual beliefs that help you cope with stress or pain?
- Importance and Influence—What importance does your faith or belief have
  in your life? Do your beliefs influence your decisions about your healthcare?
- Community—Are you part of a spiritual or religious community? Is this of
  support to you and how?

- Address in Care or Action—How would you like me, your healthcare provider, to address these issues in your healthcare? What action steps do you need to take in your spiritual journey?

Puchalski and Ferrell remind their readers that "historically, spirituality was an integral part of the mission and practice of healthcare institutions and providers. The medical model of practice in healing prior to the 1900s was service-oriented compassionate care. Medical care was primarily supportive and palliative, with limited options for curing disease. Healers utilized a holistic approach of physical, psychological, social, and spiritual care."[6] With all of the benefits science has brought us, we may have lost sight of these other important dimensions of care.

Just one hundred years ago, many people still died at home; the family may have cared for their sick and elderly for years, supported by occasional visits with their family doctor. Multi-generational households were far more common, and family caregivers were present for all the inevitable markers of decline and eventual death. After a death, neighbors of all ages visited the home, or funeral home, to see the body one last time. The nostalgic image I invoke here may be grounded in middle-class Protestant Christianity in the United States, but in all times and places people have had to integrate the experience of suffering and death into their lives. What wisdom have we earned through the millennia of facing sickness, old age, and death—sights that motivated Prince Siddhartha to renounce material pleasure in search of enlightenment, aspects of human experience we see all around us today?

ART, RESONANCE, AND WISDOM

Every world religion offers stories, wisdom, a worldview, and rituals that help the grieving live on for a while. These religious narratives are often represented in images, and these rituals often make use of objects. Many museums house works of art that are no longer used in a religious setting, thereby becoming rare sites where one may learn about diverse religious expressions. Where else do we have the opportunity to learn about the world's religions? Public school curricula offer cursory information, if any, as many in the general public embrace the inaccurate belief that teaching about religions violates the First Amendment's principle of separation of church and state. Among health professionals, only a small percentage will have taken a religion course at the university level, because they must prioritize the science courses required for advanced study.

In closing, let's consider a painting of the Crucifixion by Rogier van der Weyden from around 1460 (figure 6). Although made to support Christian beliefs, how might it speak to any of us today? It is one of the most profound representations of grief I have ever seen. The austerity of the setting—blood-red banners against grey walls that isolate the silent, tormented figures—and the timeless quality of the scene make for an intensely affecting image. It breaks our heart, even as it speaks to our own experience. We recognize this grief that knocks Mary off her feet. We see the signs of torture and suffering on the body of Jesus. We feel John's sorrow, even as he dutifully steps forward to support the stricken mother.

Whether or not this experience of grief is familiar, the artist makes the situation crystal clear. I asked my six-year-old daughter to look at a reproduction of the painting with me on the website of the Philadelphia Museum of Art. Right away, Clyde says, "She's falling because she's so sad. She's praying, but her eyes are open; she's got two tears. He's sad, too. He's holding her. He has three tears. I can't look at the blood. My eyes start watering, and I feel sad. I just can't talk about it." This work of art presents a story of intense suffering, the grief that comes with the loss of a loved one, and promises the reward of being with God in heaven. Our eyes start watering, and we feel sad, just like Mary—another mother who had to hold the lifeless body of her own son, forlorn and waiting to understand the meaning of . . . all this.

Religious beliefs and practices have led to some of the most profoundly moving, beautiful creative expressions in human history. (Religions have also been the source of conflict and damage as well, it must be admitted, but that is not our focus here.) Liturgical music, the architecture of sacred spaces and their adornment, sacred texts, and ritual objects are all made with devotion and an eye toward perfection. We have seen that images of the Buddha embody a cultural ideal of human perfection. The calligrapher who transmits the sacred words of Allah through a Qur'an, together with the artist who creates the intricate ornamentation of "carpet pages," seeks a perfection in form suited to the miraculous origin and ultimate truth of Allah's revealed message. The visual vocabulary developed to represent the many Hindu gods shows us that these beings are extraordinary—with extra arms, shape-shifting powers, and the elaborate garments, jewelry, and offerings of food and flowers that devotees present. Those of us who take time to look and wonder will find something that resonates with our own experience and questions, something to help broaden our sensibilities and nourish our humanity, perhaps even something of the transcendent.

In addition to becoming more aware of the spiritual needs of patients and their families, healthcare providers may themselves find elements of the various traditions helpful in maintaining their own well-being. The art museum is a unique setting for getting acquainted with the spiritual beliefs and practices that have helped people in many times and places pursue a good life. It is not necessary to "convert" to or wholly embrace any particular tradition; we may find something of personal value in any of the religions we encounter through ritual objects in the museum. If we are looking at art from Buddhist traditions, we may find teachings about the letting go of desire or mindful eating to be useful in our daily practice. If we are considering silver candlesticks or whimsical spice boxes made for use in Jewish celebrations of Shabbat, we may decide to protect time for rest, reflection, and a special meal with our own family and friends. Islam may remind us to center our connection to the divine, to pray on a regular basis, to submit to things beyond our control. Christianity offers a powerful story of suffering, death, and transcendence; the suffering of Jesus has meaning, and the image of resurrection offers hope. Hinduism, with its understanding of the divine as endlessly changing and available to us in many forms, as well as its belief in reincarnation—another chance!—may offer a sense of possibility that serves any of us well.

The world's religions are often referred to as "wisdom traditions." When we reach the limit of what data and information can do for us, wisdom becomes a meaningful element in caring for one another and ourselves. We can be grateful that this wisdom is available to us all, as we seek to understand the big questions of human experience, the mysteries, and the meaning of our lives. When we accept the invitation, when we enter with an openhearted stance, the art museum becomes a place that is alive with familiar concerns, inspiration, and perhaps, even comfort.

NOTES

1. Pew Research Center's Religion & Public Life Project, "America's Changing Religious Landscape," 2015, https://www.pewresearch.org/religion/2015/05/12/americas-changing-religious-landscape/.
2. Geshe Jampa Gyatsho, "The Thirty-Two Marks and Eighty Exemplifications of the Sambhogakaya," *Buddhist Himalaya: A Journal of Nagarjuna Institute of Exact Methods* III, no. I & II (Kathmandu: 1990–1991).
3. My telling of this traditional Buddhist story was adapted from Sarah Conover, *Kindness: A Treasury of Buddhist Wisdom for Children and Parents* (Spokane: Eastern Washington University Press, 2001), 7-10.
4. Christina M. Puchalski and Betty Ferrell, *Making Health Care Whole: Integrating Spirituality into Patient Care* (West Conshohocken: Templeton Press, 2010), 5.
5. Puchalski and Ferrell, *Making Health Care Whole*, 198.
6. Puchalski and Ferrell, *Making Health Care Whole*, 11.

8

Nurturing Well-being

Art museums have long offered visitors solace and sanctuary. Social scientist John Falk writes that enhancing well-being is the most fundamental value of museums.[1] In the past five years, the authors of this book have received an increasing number of requests from across the health professions for museum experiences to enhance student and staff well-being and to foster connection and relationships. Coming to the art museum for a responsively designed workshop dedicated to wellness and compassion can be a moment to pause and to exhale, to recenter and connect. This chapter provides examples of lesson plans and activities explicitly designed to help participants cultivate connection, relationships, and community; connect to meaning and purpose; activate core values and strengths; and build habits of gratitude and joy. (Mindfulness and self-compassion, two longstanding practices for nurturing well-being, are explored in chapter 9, "Practicing Mindfulness.") It weaves together many themes found throughout this book. Regardless of the topic, a running thread across all of our work is a commitment to offering care and nourishing the soul.

A PROFESSION IN CRISIS

In her illuminating and at times laugh-out-loud-funny book *We Are All Perfectly Fine: A Memoir of Love, Medicine, and Healing*, internist Dr. Jillian Horton writes "medicine is so fucking hard."[2] Recounting her personal experience of burnout, she describes working in a toxic culture in which she and her colleagues—characterized by Horton as highly conscientious and often perfectionistic—learn to become "excellent at compartmentalizing."[3] Everyone seems fine until they are not. In describing her own journey through burnout, Horton draws an analogy to cutting onions: "Cutting those onions is like me and medicine. In the first few years, everything burned. Then one day the pain just stopped. That was a warning sign, and I missed it."[4] In experiencing distress, Horton is not alone. In 2019, the World Health Organization identified burnout as an occupational syndrome characterized by physical and emotional exhaustion, feelings of depletion, a sense of isolation and detachment, and negative feelings or cynicism about one's job—all of which can lead to a loss of purpose and meaning.[5] Art museums surround visitors with beauty, creativity, and imagination—a complex range of human experiences. By helping healthcare professionals slow down and engage attentively with artworks, with themselves, and with each other, art museum workshops can provide a moment to pause—to step away from an often intense professional environment—and to recharge some of the emotional energy depleted by the demands of their profession.

TEXTBOX 8.1.

Burnout and Moral Injury in Healthcare

In 2019, Harvard University released a report calling physician burnout a public health crisis.[1] It is an issue that affects all clinical disciplines, levels of training, and professional life stages. The consequences of burnout include practitioners leaving the field, increased medical errors, and diminished patient satisfaction. Burnout costs the healthcare system billions of dollars every year.[2] Factors that contribute to burnout include "too much work; a lack of autonomy, recognition, sense of community and trust; and misalignment between personal values and organizational values."[3] In their widely read opinion piece "Physician's Aren't Burning Out. They're Suffering from Moral Injury," Simon Talbot and Wendy Dean argue that rampant burnout is, in fact, produced by a dysfunctional healthcare system.[4] Moral injury, which Liz Gaufberg describes as "a violation of deeply held moral beliefs, often in relation to trusted institutions and individuals," is a widely experienced systemic issue in which organizational and financial structures of modern healthcare make it challenging for providers to practice patient-centered care in accordance with deeply held values.[5] Talbot and Dean write, "The increasingly complex web of providers' highly conflicted allegiances—to patients, to self, and to employers—and its attendant moral injury may be driving the healthcare ecosystem to a tipping point and causing the collapse of resilience."[6]

In order for larger medical organizations and systems to flourish, individual providers must flourish, but the presence of moral injury, chronic stress, and overload in healthcare create poor conditions for provider well-being. As the field has evolved over the last decade—from "an era of distress" (characterized by ignoring the problem of provider distress) to greater awareness of the personal and organizational costs of burnout and moral injury—programs focused on cultivating resilience and well-being practices such as mindfulness have become more available.[7] Today, there is an increasingly loud call "to stop blaming the individual"[8] in response to the perception that the onus of change is being placed on the individual provider versus a dysfunctional system. The underlying message is that

---

practitioners should learn to better tolerate ever-increasing workplace stress and demands.

System change can be slow. Dr. Tait Shanafelt argues that both organizational strategies and personal strategies are needed. But activating individual interventions without meaningful organizational change to address larger systemic issues can reinforce healthcare professionals' feelings of frustration and even anger.[9] A healthy organizational culture would provide increased flexibility, autonomy, and resources, and recognize the human needs of healthcare professionals. It would support the personal efforts of healthcare workers. And it would recognize that caregivers—like all humans—will make mistakes and experience doubts and uncertainties. A culture shift that values vulnerability, compassion, and self-compassion would encourage a growth mindset in which shaming and blaming and compartmentalization are replaced by support, learning, and transformational growth. Cheryl Woods Giscombé, Associate Dean of the University of North Carolina Chapel Hill School of Nursing, reminds us that "structures are made of people, not robots."[10] The healthcare system of today is the environment that is shaping the next generation of providers. A commitment to organizational *and* individual wellness should be part of a "core organizational strategy."[11]

NOTES

1. Partnership with the Massachusetts Medical Society, Massachusetts Health and Hospital Association, Harvard T.H. Chan School of Public Health, and Harvard Global Health Institute, "A Crisis in Healthcare: A Call to Action on Physician Burnout," 2018, https://cdn1.sph.harvard.edu/wp-content/uploads/sites/21/2019/01/PhysicianBurnoutReport2018FINAL.pdf.
2. Pien Huang, "What's Doctor Burnout Costing America?" *NPR*, May 31, 2019, https://www.npr.org/sections/health-shots/2019/05/31/728334635/whats-doctor-burnout-costing-america (accessed June 15, 2022)
3. Catherine Florio Pipas, *A Doctor's Dozen: Twelve Strategies for Personal Health and a Culture of Wellness* (Hanover: Dartmouth College Press, 2018), 4.
4. Simon G. Talbot and Wendy Dean, "Physicians Aren't 'Burning Out.' They're Suffering from Moral Injury," *STAT News*, July 26, 2018, https://www.statnews.com/2018/07/26/physicians-not-burning-out-they-are-suffering-moral-injury.
5. Dr. Elizabeth Gaufberg, personal communication, May 11, 2022.
6. Talbot and Dean, "Physicians Aren't 'Burning Out.'
7. Tait D. Shanafelt, "Physician Well-being 2.0: Where Are We and Where Are We Going?" *Mayo Clinic Proceedings* 96, no. 10 (October 1, 2021): 2682–93.

8. Tait Shanafelt, "Physician Burnout: Stop Blaming the Individual," *New England Journal of Medicine Catalyst Innovations in Care Delivery*, June 16, 2016, https://catalyst.nejm.org/doi/full/10.1056/CAT.16.0806.
9. Nikitha Menon, Mickey Trockel, Maryam Hamidi, and Tait Shanafelt, "Developing a Portfolio to Support Physicians' Efforts to Promote Well-being: One Piece of the Puzzle," *Mayo Clinical Proceedings* 11 (November 2019): 2176.
10. Personal communication on May 20, 2022.
11. Shanafelt, "Physician Well-being 2.0," 2686.

CONNECTION AND COMMUNITY

Art museums, as we have proposed throughout this book, can be productive learning environments for reflection and meaning-making for medical school students. In these years, students begin the ongoing process of professional identity formation, defined as "the moral and professional development of students, the integration of their individual maturation with growth in clinical competency, and their ability to stay true to values which are both personal and core values of the profession."[6] As we have detailed, the practice of medicine today comes with great challenges. Brown University physician and educator Hedy Wald and her research colleagues ask, "How can we best support the complex iterative process for a humanistic, resilient health care professional? How can we effectively scaffold the necessary critical reflective learning and practice skills for our learners to support the shaping of a professional identity?"[7] One pedagogic strategy is to help students develop their reflective capacities through creating supportive opportunities for reflection during which students can share experiences and process feelings, emotions, and concerns with one another and their mentors. Wald et al. argue that building and strengthening those capacities during medical training can help students develop mindsets and practices that can be protective in times of stress throughout their professional journey.[8]

In 2017, as part of an arts and humanities initiative at a Boston area medical school, first-year students visited a local art museum for a restorative evening of community building, reflection, and renewal. The session included a repertoire of creative art-making and gallery experiences intended to help the group slow down, exhale, and have fun. By the end of the evening, students envisioned the museum as a place that could help them maintain their humanity during the intense process of medical school. At the beginning of their second year, after beginning rotations at teaching hospitals across the city, the students returned to the museum with a request for a session focused on transitions. They hoped the museum visit might also provide an opportunity to stay connected with one another as they were no longer in classrooms together and were dispersed across the city. Entering clinical rotations can be a stressful and demanding time. Students join the busy world of hospitals, where they are confronted with the limits of their current knowledge and with real-life situations. In working with patients and families, they encounter a wide range of physical and emotional suffering and, often for the first time, death. The transition can be hard, and their peer group may not be as available as when everyone was on campus together.

The workshop, planned by a museum educator, with valuable input from the group's student leader and faculty adviser, begins in the museum's studio space. A basket of index cards and markers sits on a table outside the studio's door. Before they enter, students are invited to write on an index card a word capturing an emotion or thought they would like to release, and to then attach the card to a suspended clothesline. As students read words written by their classmates, including "stress," "fatigue," and "doubt," murmurs of recognition and "oh yeahs" can be heard. In the studio, tables are laden with simple yet colorful art-making supplies, as well as food and drink—offerings of different forms of nourishment. As they eat, the museum educator reads aloud Wilsawa Szymborska's poem "In Praise of Dreams"—a series of couplets in which the poet imagines wondrous capabilities.[9] Students are then invited to make a three-dimensional object responding to the prompt "In my dreams . . ." This metaphor-based activity encourages students to think about what's important to them. It also allows them to step off the page of their daily lives and imagine possibilities for their own personal and professional lives. Sharing their three-dimensional creations and the stories behind them sparks camaraderie and enhances a sense of connection. Laughter helps everyone relax.

As the group moves into the galleries, they continue exploring the power of metaphor and using artworks as catalysts for sharing and processing thoughts, emotions, and experiences. Everyone receives a handmade tag with the prompt "Find a work of art that speaks to a hope or an uncertainty for the coming year." Talking about challenges and vulnerabilities can be hard, perhaps even counterintuitive. Learning to name emotions and feelings, and reflect on their meaning, can help with cultivating a responsive versus a reactive stance to difficult situations. Filled with complex, layered, meaningful objects, art museums are repositories for generative "third things," a term coined by Parker Palmer. Third things are multivalent reflective stimuli such as artworks, poetry, literature, music, etc., that invite us to explore topics through metaphor. Palmer writes that "in Western culture, we often seek truth through confrontation. But our headstrong ways of charging at truth scare the shy soul away. If soul truth is to be spoken and heard, it must be approached 'on the slant.' . . . Mediated by a third thing, truth can emerge from, and return to, our awareness at whatever pace and depth we are able to handle."[10]

The group concludes the evening with a powerful musical experience, led by the student leader. Prior to the workshop, students were asked to capture sounds from their hospitals on their phones. Standing shoulder to shoulder in a circle, they begin playing their recordings one at a time. Slowly, a murmur of voices builds into a cacophony of electronic beeps, footsteps, and more voices. Using only gestures, the student leader slowly brings the volume of sounds down, until the group is standing in silence. She steps into the middle of the circle and invites her classmates to echo

Nurturing Well-being

each line as she sings a rendition of a Navajo prayer, "Now I will walk in beauty / Beauty is before me / Beauty is behind me / Above and below me."[11] After repeating the song a few times, she subdivides the students into three groups and conducts them to sing the song as a round. Mirroring the playing of the sounds of the hospital, the harmonizing voices fill the space, and then they, too, are slowly brought down. At the end, the group stands for several minutes in silence. Some have tears in their eyes. The silence is broken by hugs, laughter, and someone declaring, "I didn't know how much I needed this."

Building reflective capacities and communities of support is crucial throughout one's professional life. The years of internship and residency can be particularly challenging. Current literature documents an ever-growing culture of loneliness and isolation within the practice of healthcare.[12] Cultivating connection and community is one of the most powerful possibilities offered by art museums. Social scientist Arthur Brooks writes that art is essential because of its capacity to "provoke in us the full range of experience and emotion."[13] In designing workshops to promote care and nurture well-being, some of our overarching goals are to create experiences that invite individuals, if they so choose, to share and reflect upon experiences, emotional responses, and deeply held feelings in a supported space. Core museum-based practices used with healthcare groups, such as a personal response tour or sharing reflective stories in response to narrative prompts inspired by artworks, can bring people together in surprising ways. Team members feel more bonded to one another, and students recognize the value of emotional support systems. Several months after engaging in one of our programs, a resident participant reflected how the design of the workshop created an unexpected sense of intimacy within the group. Exchanging personal stories inspired by an artwork with another resident led to a desire to know one another better. "He is now one of my best friends," the resident concluded.

(RE)CONNECTING WITH MEANING AND PURPOSE

Having a sense of meaning and purpose helps us connect to something that is bigger than ourselves. Too often, meaning and purpose can get lost in the hectic pace and the increased organizational demands of contemporary healthcare. There is little time for reflecting upon and learning from one's experiences. Yet it is through reflection that learning and personal growth happen; it is through reflection that a habit of mindful self-awareness and meaning-making can be cultivated. Stepping back and processing an experience can enrich its significance for us.

To begin a workshop focused on renewal and restoration of meaning, a group of interns and residents, accompanied by an attending physician, gathers in the art-making studio of a museum. In preparation for an activity called "Stepping Stones," each person is given a large piece of paper, a collection of stones, some markers, and strands of ribbon.[14] Everyone is then invited to create a map of the

Nurturing Well-being

stepping stones, the moments of their personal and professional journey, that have brought them to this point in time. In creating their map, the educator encourages participants to reflect upon significant experiences and decisions, and to consider both positive moments and ones that might have been more difficult. The maps can take any form that feels authentic to the maker—not all journeys are linear. After fifteen minutes, everyone shares their map in groups of three. The activity spurs insights and surprises. Taking a "balcony view" of one's journey, reflecting on and discussing the choices one has made, and connecting the past with the present can renew or clarify one's purpose, as well as prompt awareness about future possibilities and directions.

For the next activity, an interpretive conversation, the museum educator selects a work of art chosen to inspire the group to both consider and actively write their own story. On the right panel of Mequitta Ahuja's enormous diptych painting *Parade*,[15] a larger-than-life-size figure of a woman strides to the right with a look of determination and purpose (figure 7). She walks barefoot on what looks like a pebbled surface and is surrounded by lush vegetation rendered primarily in blacks and grays. A hint of blue sky anchors the background and highlights her face in profile. Behind the figure, a voluminous explosion of hair, extending across both canvases, comes alive with active mark-making and bursts of color and light.

The artwork's left panel is filled with vertically layered striations of colors dripping down the canvas. They are framed on the left by a curve of golden yellow paint. The range and diversity of mark-making fills the painting with a sense of energy and vibrancy. As the group gathers in front of this compelling artwork, the museum educator asks them to take it in for a few minutes and explore it from different angles and vantage points. Participants are then invited to share what they find themselves drawn to; for some, it is the feelings evoked by the image (awesome, powerful, inspiring), for others it is the dynamic marks and colors, and for many it is the figure. Together, they begin to construct a narrative about who this woman might be. They are curious about where she might be coming from and where she might be going. The group agrees that this is a woman who is actively moving toward something— perhaps her future? Her body language and gaze convey strength, as does the activated swirl of hair that seems to propel her forward. The more they look, the more significant her hair becomes—pinpoints of sparkling white paint evoke associations of stars and the cosmos. One person shares that the figure represented is a person of color, and that within the Black community, hair has meaning. Building on this comment, the educator provides some background on the artist. Mequitta Ahuja, who is of South Asian and African American descent, imagines hair as a "space of infinite creative possibilities . . . a space of abstraction or imagination." Ahuja states, "The idea of exaggerating my hair comes out of the cultural space that hair has in the lives of Black people and the way it has embodied our changing ideas of standards of beauty as well as political consciousness."[16]

There is a lot of puzzling within the group over what looks like a mini explosion where the two canvases meet—could it signify creativity? A rebirth of some sort? A coming into being? There is also a lot of speculation about the relationship between the two panels—one is abstract and the other more representational. The group notices color affinities between the vertical drips of paint and the figure's brightly colored clothing. The group speculates whether the abstract, blurry colors on the left go through the prismatic explosion in order to cohere into three-dimensionality on the right. Or perhaps the left side represents elements of the woman's past? The somber colors—shot through with brighter hues—and the textured ground upon which the figure walks lead some to wonder if perhaps the figure is burdened by parts of her history. They imagine that the right panel embodies a sense of hope, that the colors on the left are being transformed and reframed into sources of energy and beauty.

After a satisfying exploration of the painting, the educator provides the group with some information about the artist's process. Mequitta Ahuja uses her own body as source material which she says is "largely related to my unusual ethnic heritage and wanting, needing, to have imagery in the world that reflected my identity."[17] Ahuja calls her practice "automythography," which she defines as "a strategy I use to counter limiting frameworks." "It is," she writes, "the expansive and inclusive process of self-construction and self-representation, a creative form in which I gain and enact my agency."[18]

Drawing inspiration from Ahuja, participants are invited to reflect on the concept of automythography and to enact their own agency by writing their own stories (not their resumes, they are cautioned), which they then share with one another in pairs. The prompt invites the group to both remember and imagine: What is my story so far? Where do I want to go? What matters? The stories that emerge speak to personal and professional values, and the choices one might make in order to find expression for deeply held commitments. The years of internship and residency can be hard. Giving oneself permission to imagine and to voice "what comes next" can help free someone who feels stuck. Sharing dreams and aspirations, actively listening and being listened to, and holding one another's stories can help to create a community of care and support. Furthermore, research has identified the cognitive activity of "imagining," envisioning one's ideal life, can contribute to a greater sense of well-being.[19]

Throughout museums, one can find works of art that speak to life choices, and there are many possible artworks that can help participants reconnect with meaning and purpose across all stages of one's career. For example, a painting such as Noah Davis's *Painting for My Dad* can be accompanied with the prompt, "Write about standing at a threshold."[20] Reflecting on moments of transition, and the choices we have made, can remind us of different moments in our journey, and strategies we might have called upon to move forward. Commissioned portraits can also be productive for this kind of experience. How has a person chosen to be represented? What values are expressed? How do they want to be remembered? We often pair a discussion of a portrait or self-portrait with a reading of Mary Oliver's

Nurturing Well-being

poem "Summer Day," which reminds readers that crafting a life (or a profession) requires thought and intention.[21] The pairing offers a stimulus for reflecting upon what brought each individual in the group to the practice of healthcare. Responses are often surprisingly diverse and can range from a desire to alleviate suffering, to conducting research in a quest to cure diseases, or to satisfy familial and cultural expectations.

In sharing personal narratives, we may also invite stories of difficult circumstances or decisions. A sculpture of the Hindu god Ganesha (see figure 4.1) or a painting of St. George and the Dragon can call up times of overcoming obstacles or finding courage in the face of impossible seeming tasks. When someone in the group, especially a leader or a mentor, shares their own experiences of struggle and doubt, it can be a gift to the others. In her book *Wintering*, essayist Katherine May reminds us that:

> We have seasons when we flourish and seasons when the leaves fall from us, revealing our bare bones. Given time, they grow again.[22]
> Here is another truth about wintering: you'll find wisdom in your winter, and once it's over, it's your responsibility to pass it on. And in return, it's our responsibility to listen to those who have wintered before us.[23]

"Finding one's wisdom" speaks to a process of naming, reflecting, and learning. When one is struggling, hearing about the "seasons" of another's professional journey can help normalize a situation. Recognizing that others have faced similar obstacles and learning to treat oneself with kindness are the foundations of self-compassion which research shows contributes to a sense of well-being.

ACTIVATING CHARACTER STRENGTH(S) AND VALUES

Each one of us possesses virtues and character strengths that can provide guidance as we navigate the complexities of life. Research on well-being suggests that knowing and enacting these virtues and strengths helps us lead personally meaningful lives, and increases happiness and flourishing. The Jubilee Center's resource "Framework for Character Education in Schools" defines character as "a set of personal traits or dispositions that produce specific moral emotions, inform motivation and guide conduct."[24] In the framework, these personal strengths are associated with virtues. Examples include intellectual virtues such as curiosity and judgment, moral virtues such as compassion and integrity, civic virtues like honesty, and performance virtues like teamwork.[25] In their research in the domain of positive psychology, Martin Seligman and colleagues identified a constellation of twenty-four strengths and virtues that we all have—in lesser and greater degrees. They propose that within that constellation we each have "signature" strengths— strengths that feel essential to who we are—and that when enacted can contribute to flourishing.[26] Strengths are not rigidly fixed, and one can intentionally develop traits they would like to cultivate.

The following museum-based activity invites an interprofessional group (students, interns, nurses, and physician mentors) to identify their signature strengths and consider how these might serve them in the practice of medicine. The activity reminds participants that they carry within them strengths and values that can aid them in the face of challenges or difficult decision-making. It also offers a reminder that finding opportunities to express core strengths and values can contribute to one's sense of living a meaningful life that is good. The museum educator begins by inviting participants to take the VIA Survey of Character Strengths, available for free online or alternatively by providing a handout with the twenty-four strengths and their definitions.[27] Everyone identifies a top strength as well as one they would like to further develop. She then introduces the group to a creative pruning activity. After selecting one of the qualities they have identified, everyone freewrites for three minutes about why the trait is important to them and how it might support them in their professional lives. Once they are done, they are asked to count the number of words on their page and delete half of them. They repeat the step by pruning the shortened text in half one more time. The final prompt is to circle five to eight of the remaining words that have the most relevance. By pruning the extraneous words, everyone discerns something essential about what their chosen strength means to them. For the next step, they are given a piece of heavyweight cardstock and asked to write their strength at the top. The circled words—sometimes a list, sometimes a phrase—are then transcribed below that. Examples include: appreciation of beauty and excellence: "inspires possibility, want to do, be better"; love of learning: "Inner reward system, appreciation of discovery"; creativity: "letting go, freedom, air, colorful journey." In a lovely twist, one group member used both sides of the blank card to capture her experience of humor as having different dimensions: "powerful playful and creative" and "disarms and deflects, it's playful deception," reminding us all that every strength potentially has more than one manifestation.[28]

In a final step that builds complexity, everyone is invited to explore a gallery and select an artwork that resonates with their strength and to consider the connections. The museum educator then collects everyone's squares of cardstock in a basket and invites each person to choose one at random. Participants explore the gallery again to select a work of art that speaks in some way to a colleague's prompt. They each share their selections with the group. In one example, a nurse selected a colleague's card with the strength "love." The prompt read, "tending with care, appreciating the beauty within," and he chose a fifteenth-century stained glass panel depicting Christ washing the feet of the disciples. The artwork inspired him to consider how a practice of care informed by love could help one maintain humility and connect to the deep humanity we all share, regardless of circumstances. His colleague, who had written the prompt, had selected an intricately carved wooden panel depicting intertwining floral motifs and figures, which provoked a meditation about the skill and care—the love of one's craft—the artist brought to the task of transforming a humble piece of wood into art. It inspired her to think about how she expresses her love for the "craft of doctoring." In one session, the activity led to a discussion about the tension caused by choosing a work of art to resonate with someone else's words. Was it a form of appropriation? However, when asked how it felt to be on the receiving end of the activity, everyone concluded it felt like a gift. We discussed how the activity could be a metaphor for the many possible ways a strength could be expressed. Seeing one's strength through the eyes of another, mediated by metaphor, can amplify someone's understanding about the meaning, and the possible expressions, of that strength. When participants leave the museum, the personal card (and perhaps a photo or postcard of the selected artwork[s]) can function as a touchstone to remind them of their inner capacities and/or intentions.

CULTIVATING JOY AND GRATITUDE

> We shake with joy,
> we shake with grief
> What a time they have, these two
> housed as they are in the same body.[29]
>
> —Mary Oliver

In her poem "We Shake with Joy," Mary Oliver reminds us human beings have an amazing capacity to hold joy and sorrow simultaneously. Cultivating a practice of joy matters in healthcare, as "joy is not just humane; it's instrumental. . . . The gifts of hope, confidence, and safety that healthcare should offer patients and families can only come from a workforce that feels hopeful, confident, and safe. Joy in work is an essential resource for the enterprise of healing."[30] In designing gallery experiences, we seek to offer moments that will introduce or spark joy. In the following example, an interprofessional group of healthcare workers participating in an immersive museum-based workshop focused on flourishing begin with a warm-up designed to frame the session.

It's early evening at a local museum. Golden light filters through large windows into an atrium space where visitors enjoy one another's company in the museum's cafe, read on benches, and explore two large sculptures. On one side, tucked away from the space's main flow, there is a surprising sight. Several people—some wearing medical scrubs—are walking around with sticky notes attached to their bodies. In this creative warm-up, developed by Stanford's d.School,[31] a handful of sticky notes is given to each person in the group. Everyone responds to the prompt "How are you feeling . . . really?" by writing down one feeling per note for as many feelings as they are experiencing. The goal is to acknowledge that we can hold multiple emotions simultaneously, and that feelings can be nuanced. Participants also respond to a second prompt: "What gives you joy?" Again, the goal is to write as many responses as possible, one idea per note. As a next step, the group is asked to post their handwritten notes to their bodies. This unexpected instruction leads to some creativity, as notes are posted on faces, arms, legs, and torsos. They are then instructed to begin walking around the space. At the sound of a bell, everyone stops and turns to the person closest to them. Conversations begin as partners query one another about what is written on the various sticky notes, and the space comes alive with voices, curiosity, laughter, and sometimes hugs. "Tell me about home" asks someone in response to reading "homesick." Other snippets of conversation include, "Tell me about your dog," "Tell me about your grandmother," "Tell me about a memorable patient," and "Tell me about fishing." The bell rings again, participants circulate, and the process is repeated, allowing everyone to interact with someone new. This warm-up invites the group to tune into their emotional states, find connections, and learn a bit more about each other. In one moment of unexpected bonding, the first thing everyone wrote in response to "How are you feeling . . ." was tired. The group burst into laughter and took a photograph. "This is one of the best moments of internship," joked a participant. The activity welcomes expressions of joys, sorrows, and personal truths. Playfulness, chance, and care are intentionally designed into the process to create a space of vulnerability, openness, and curiosity. The exercise allows these professionals to interact as people and lays the foundation for deepening connections that will lead to sharing more profound emotions later in a session.

When we design museum workshops, we seek to create experiences that help stimulate a sense of "collective effervesce," a term first used by sociologist Émile Durkheim and defined by Adam Grant as "the sense of energy and harmony people feel when they come together in a group around a shared purpose." "Peak happiness," Grant writes, "lies mostly in collective activity."[32] Individual and collective joy can be manifested through a range of activities. Interpretive conversations which invite us to slow down, be present, and attend to an artwork closely as we work to collaboratively build meaning can often lead to a state of flow in which the demands of one's life can slip away for a moment. There is satisfaction in working through a complex visual puzzle together. Other activities that we have described throughout this book, including group poems, creating tableaux, and improvisational storytelling, embrace play as a catalyst for joy.

There is a strong connection between finding joy and living one's life with meaning and purpose. When we engage works of art to share and receive stories about what matters to each of us, or about challenges we might face, we invite the possibility of being more open and vulnerable with our colleagues. Giving ourselves permission to be vulnerable may lead to creating deeper bonds and relationships. In a meditation on joy, columnist David Brooks proposes that "vulnerability is the only means we have to build relationships, and relationships are the only means we have to experience joy."[33] When healthcare organizations and medical schools support the integration of museum-based workshops with an eye to fostering relationships, joy, and community into their programs, they are making a systemic change that demonstrates care.

Nurturing Well-being

Joy is a habit that can be cultivated, and habits take practice. In *The Book of Delights*, poet Ross Gay catalogues a year of finding small pleasures every day.[34] With time, Gay began to see joy readily. Leaning into joy, though, doesn't come easily. For some people it might feel self-indulgent, particularly in the face of great suffering. Perhaps some of us are hardwired to remember the negative. Angela Williams Gorrell writes, "Joy, like other emotions longs to be shared. . . . Not only do we need permission to be honest about emotions like sadness, anger, and fear, we need permission to be joy-filled. And we need this permission from other people and ourselves. . . . We need other people to help us recall, recognize, and reflect on the good."[35] As museum educators, we intentionally give our groups permission to find and remember joy. Inviting individuals to seek and reflect upon a work of art that sparks joy for them or that resonates with a joy in their professional life can help reframe potentially difficult situations. Naming a joy and sharing it helps remind us of ways to nourish and replenish our spirits. Sometimes the act of sharing itself can call up associated feelings of well-being.

Joy can also be found in the practice of gratitude. Gratitude encourages savoring, which literature on flourishing defines as "the capacity to attend to, appreciate, and enhance the positive experiences in one's life."[36] Like joy, gratitude can become a practice—one that has been shown to promote flourishing. Simple exercises, such as naming three things that one is grateful for, can increase a propensity for gratitude, as well as promote a general sense of psychological well-being.

We often conclude museum sessions with exercises that cultivate gratitude. A favorite—"And I Noticed"[37]—begins with reflection in a quiet gallery or a space filled with beauty. The educator invites the group to stand in a circle and to tune into their senses. She then guides them through a process of taking a few deep cleansing breaths together to center themselves. The invitation is to then reflect upon the present moment or the experience of the workshop, and to complete the phrase "And I noticed . . ." One by one, each person shares their observations aloud: "And I noticed generosity and laughter," "And I noticed a sense of peace within," "And I noticed how much I enjoy my colleagues," "And I noticed we are funny, and caring and thoughtful," "And I noticed the beauty of different perspectives." The activity which invites attentiveness and reflection often leads to expressions of appreciation.

Expressions of appreciation in the workplace are important. They can help contribute to a psychologically safe and inclusive environment where colleagues feel acknowledged and respected. In another concluding gratitude exercise, pairs team up to make two-minute blind contour drawings of one another. In this drawing activity, participants are asked not to look at the page or lift their drawing pencil while capturing their partner's likeness. The process ensures a drawing will not be realistic, while slowing us down to really pay attention to one another. The process also helps bypass any tendency to judge or critique oneself. Looking attentively at someone, or being on the receiving side of someone else's gaze, might initially cause a bit of discomfort (and nervous laughter). But drawing simultaneously, with attention and care, can help us see one another with new eyes. Attention, writes mindfulness teacher Tara Brach, "is the most basic form of love. By paying attention we let ourselves be touched by life, and our hearts naturally become more open and engaged."[38] As partners exchange drawings with one another, they are asked to share some words of appreciation for their colleague. Once again, joy—in the form of laughter, smiles, and expressions of thanks—fills the room.

Tyler VanderWeele, Director of the Human Flourishing Program at Harvard University, provides research-based evidence that the practices of savoring, gratitude, and joy can promote flourishing.[39] The act of savoring implies slowing down and reflecting with attentiveness, practices that are core to the interpretive conversations as described throughout this chapter and book. Interpretive conversations can also nurture cognitive flexibility, self-awareness, and the ability to explore multiple perspectives and reframe situations capacities that also contribute to "wellness of mind."[40] Gathering with colleagues away from the classroom, hospital, and clinic can help spark new ways of being with each other. The museum environment, rich with objects that speak to the broad range of human experience, provides a context that—with the guidance and care of skilled facilitators—enables opportunities for more openness and vulnerability than is typically possible in hospital and clinic environments. Our commitment to building community and supportive relationships, in the words of a healthcare colleague, helps "foster a sense of interdependence instead of rugged individualism."[41] At the end of one of our sessions, a resident commented that she valued museum-based workshops because she felt cared for: "We spend our days taking care of others. When we come to the museum, I feel like you are taking care of us." We come to this work with enormous gratitude and with a deep desire to create experiences for our healthcare colleagues which contribute to their sense of well-being and to their capacity to flourish. We hope they leave our sessions feeling they matter, that they are valued, respected, appreciated, and loved.[42]

TEXTBOX 8.2.

Art and Well-being: An Interview with Cheryl Woods Giscombé

Corinne Zimmermann and Ruth Slavin conducted an interview with Dr. Cheryl Woods Giscombé on May 20, 2022. Giscombé, trained in nursing and psychology, is the Associate Dean of the PhD Division & Program at the School of Nursing at the University of North Carolina (UNC) at Chapel Hill and the Levine Family Distinguished Scholar of Quality of Life, Health Promotion, and Wellness. She is a health equity researcher who studies interventions to reduce stress and stress-related disparities with a focus on underrepresented populations. She is a Josiah Macy Fellow and was part of the inaugural cohort of the Harvard Macy Institute's Art Museum-based Health Professions Education Fellowship. The interview is presented here in an abridged and edited form for this publication.

Nurturing Well-being

Cheryl, can you tell us a bit about how you became involved with museum-based practices for healthcare?

When I took the Program for Educators in Health Professions offered by the Harvard Macy Institute, I participated in an art museum elective. I love the peaceful environment of art museums, but I had never been a huge "art museum person." And I literally fell in love. Because of those experiences, the Museum of Fine Arts Boston feels like a spiritual home. I was then invited to be part of the inaugural Harvard Macy Institute's Art Museum-based Health Professions Fellowship. Now when I give presentations, or teach a class on stress management, resilience, and burnout prevention, I incorporate art. Often I begin with a photograph of a landscape that I know people will find restorative. I invite the group to look in silence, then ask them what comes to mind. Overwhelmingly, they'll say things like "calm," "peaceful," or "tranquil." Then I invite them to reflect on how often they experience states of calm, peace, or tranquility at work (or in their lives). Usually they say "never" or "only sometimes." We can then brainstorm ways to access those feelings and change their work environment. One way I introduce these practices into the workflow is to begin a meeting—for example, a curriculum meeting—with an art-museum-based activity such as Visual Thinking Strategies (VTS) or some kind of reflective practice like the image meditation I just described. It changes the energy in the room. It helps us be more present and listen more respectfully.

Why do you think museum-based practices are so helpful for addressing stress, health disparities, and burnout—all of the things that you focus on in your work?

One of my favorite concepts in social psychology is heuristics, which are cognitive shortcuts. That's what resonated with me when I was first introduced to VTS. VTS is such an effective way to help people become better, more comprehensive observers. It helps people begin to see their own biases. They learn about themselves, and they learn about others. And then they can extrapolate that learning to the patient experience.

Is there a story you could share that would help us see the value of art-museum-based practices when working with either nursing students or other healthcare professionals?

I was the co-leader on a grant with UNC-Chapel Hill's School of Social Work, where we educated psychiatric nurse practitioners and master's in social work students together. It's a behavioral health integration project that prepares them to work with more diverse populations. We brought them to UNC-Chapel Hill's Ackland Art Museum twice. I partnered with museum educator Elizabeth Manekin, and in one example, we selected a picture of an older gentleman and, perhaps, his wife who's giving him medication. They're in an old rural house. All kinds of ideas about ageism came up, as well as ideas about poverty, about class. We wanted to create an experience that allowed students to notice what comes up for them and their classmates. We're training them to work with diverse populations, so the process helps them understand what they're bringing to a situation.

One of the artworks I have loved exploring with students during COVID is the *Mona Lisa*. Everybody's like, "Oh, yeah, the *Mona Lisa*, I've seen that." They think they know it. And every single time I've used it the group sees something new. It helps students see right away how frequently we use cognitive shortcuts, make assumptions, and pass over things we think we already know. I love how looking at art can train us to slow down and see with new perspectives.

In medicine, physicians and nurses, we need to act quickly which sometimes leads to misinterpretations. You might think someone has an earache, but it's something else. Cognitive shortcuts help us be more efficient as we move through the world, but we need to develop a reflective self-awareness to know when we need to pause and check.

If you were to take that thread and weave it back to mindfulness, flourishing. . . . What are the intersections for you?

Art can be a tool for mindfulness. When we ask students to look at art and think together, they become focused on the present moment. Everything slows down. When they actively listen to their peers' thoughts and observations, they're showing compassion, using empathy. Often, they realize "Wow, I didn't see that." We try to extrapolate that experience to day-to-day activities where you think you know someone, but you don't. Or you think you know what they're about to say and dismiss it without really listening. You might miss something valuable. Using open-ended inquiry to look at art can help us practice being nonjudgmental, and remind us to be more present in the moment. Students see more deeply, and hopefully, they're seeing one another, and their patients more deeply.

Could you talk a little bit about how museum-based practices might support flourishing and mindfulness?

We're so tense, rushed, and tight that we miss out on beauty, and breath, and all that comes with them. The art museum is a place that can open us up, connecting with our vulnerability, the artist's vulnerability, the humanity of what's before us in a work of art. The universal qualities of art effectively get to the core of who people are and help us to remember our common humanity.

As a leader, what is your vision for the role that museum-based practices might play in the education of nursing students going forward?

Everything! Caregivers can get lost in other people. And they can get lost in the acuteness, the chronicity of illness in the hospital setting. When students enter the world of hospitals, they need to be reminded both of the fullness of life and to stay connected with who they are. We all need constant reminders to stay in touch with our own humanity, the humanity of the work we do, and the human being in front of us. I think art can help us do that.

NOTES

1. John Falk, *The Value of Museums: Enhancing Societal Well-being* (Lanham, MD: Rowman & Littlefield, 2021).
2. Jillian Horton, *We Are All Perfectly Fine* (Toronto: HarperCollins, 2021), 5.
3. Horton, *We Are All Perfectly Fine*, 5.
4. Horton, *We Are All Perfectly Fine*, 6.
5. World Health Organization, Burn-out an 'Occupational Phenomenon': International Classification of Diseases," https://www.who.int/news/item/28-05-2019 -burn-out-an-occupational-phenomenon-international-classification-of-diseases (accessed June 15, 2022); Rhitu Chatterjee and Andee Tagle, "Burnout Isn't Just Exhaustion. Here's How To Deal With It," https://www.npr.org/2021/03/08 /974787023/burnout-isnt-just-exhaustion-heres-how-to-deal-with-it.
6. Michael W. Rabow, Rachel N. Remen, Dean X. Parmelee, Thomas S. Inui, "Professional formation: Extending medicine's lineage of service into the next century," Academic Medicine 85, no. 2 (2010): 310. https://www.academia.edu/24028393 /Professional_Formation_Extending_Medicine%CA%BCs_Lineage_of_Service _Into_the_Next_Century, cited in Hedy S. Wald, David Anthony, Tom A. Hutchinson, et al., "Professional Identity Formation in Medical Education for Humanistic Resilient Physicians: Pedagogic Strategies for Bridging Theory to Practice," *Academic Medicine* 90, no. 6 (June 2015): 755.
7. Wald et al., "Professional Identity Formation," 753.
8. Wald et al., "Professional Identity Formation," 753.
9. Wislawa Szymborska, *View with A Grain of Sand* (Orlando: Harcourt Brace & Company, 1993): 87.
10. Parker Palmer, *A Hidden Wholeness: The Journey Toward an Undivided Life* (San Francisco, CA: Jossey Bass, 2004), 90–94.
11. Gregg Smith, "Now I Walk in Beauty," https://heatherhoustonmusic.com/song /now-i-walk-in-beauty-a-navajo-prayer/.
12. Arthur C. Brooks, *From Strength to Strength: Finding Success, happiness, and Deep Purpose in the Second Half of Life* (New York: Portfolio/Penguin, 2022), 120.
13. Arthur C. Brooks, "Art Should be a Habit, Not a Luxury," *The Atlantic*, January 27, 2022, https://www.theatlantic.com/family/archive/2022/01/art-consciousness -happiness-exercise/621374/.

14. Activity introduced to authors by Elizabeth Gaufberg.
15. Mequitta Ahuja, "Parade," 2007 Enamel on canvas, two panels, 96 x 160 inches. Blanton Museum of Art, The University of Texas at Austin, Gift of Melanie Lawson and John F. Guess, Jr., in honor of Jeanne and Michael Klein, © 2010 Mequitta Ahuja 2007.
16. Minneapolis Institute of Art, *Tress IV*, https://collections.artsmia.org/art/108869/tress-iv-mequitta-ahuja.
17. Elephant, "5 Questions with Mequitta Ahuja," https://elephant.art/5-questions-with-mequitta-ahuja/.
18. Lamar Dodd School of Art, "Mequitta Ahuja: Automythography," https://art.uga.edu/galleries/mequitta-ahuja-automythography.
19. Tyler J. VanderWeele, "Activities for Flourishing: An Evidence-based Guide," *Journal of Positive Psychology & Well-being* 4, no. 1 (2020): 82.
20. Noah Davis, *Painting for My Dad*, 2011, Collection of the Rubell Museum, Miami.
21. Mary Oliver, "The Summer Day," https://www.loc.gov/programs/poetry-and-literature/poet-laureate/poet-laureate-projects/poetry-180/all-poems/item/poetry-180-133/the-summer-day/ (accessed June 22, 2022).
22. Katherine May, *Wintering: The Power of Rest and Retreat in Difficult Times* (London: Riverhead Books, 2020), 68.
23. Katherine May, *Wintering*, 122.
24. Jubilee Center for Character and Virtues, "A Framework for Character Education in Schools," 2017: 2, https://www.jubileecentre.ac.uk/userfiles/jubileecentre/pdf/character-education/Framework%20for%20Character%20Education.pdf (accessed June 22, 2022).
25. Jubilee Center for Character and Virtues, "A Framework," 5.
26. The VIA Institute on Character, "Character Strengths," https://www.viacharacter.org/character-strengths-via (accessed June 22, 2022).
27. The VIA Survey of Character Strengths is available at https://www.viacharacter.org/account/register.
28. Permission to quote granted by Ray Williams, Dr. Nicole Farmer, Dr. Anson Koshby, and Dr. Samantha Gallivan.
29. Mary Oliver, "We Shake with Joy," Reprinted by the persmission of the Charlotte Sheedy Literary Agency as agent for the author. Copyright Mary Oliver 2009 with permission of Bill Reichblum.
30. Donald M. Berwick, "Forward," in Jessica Perlo, Barbara Balik, Stephen Swensen, Andrea Kabcenell, Julie Landsman, and Derek Feeley, *IHI Framework for Improving Joy in Work* (Cambridge, MA: Institute for Healthcare Improvement, 2017): 4.
31. Sarah Stein Greenberg, *Creative Acts for Curious People* (California: Ten Speed Press, 2021), 116–17.
32. Adam Grant, "There's A Specific Kind of Joy We've Been Missing," *New York Times*, July 10, 2021, https://www.nytimes.com/2021/07/10/opinion/sunday/covid-group-emotions-happiness.html.
33. David Brooks, "The Difference Between Joy and Happiness," *New York Times*, May 7, 2019, https://www.nytimes.com/2019/05/07/opinion/happiness-joy-emotion.html.
34. Ross Gay, *The Book of Delights* (Chapel Hill: Algonquin Books, 2019).

35. Angela Williams Gorrell, *The Gravity of Joy* (Grand Rapids: William B. Eerdmans Publishing Company, 2021), 173, cited in Tish Harrison Warren, "How to Cultivate Joy Even When It Feels in Short Supply," April 24, 2022, https://www.nytimes.com/2022/04/24/opinion/easter-season-joy.html.

36. Tyler J. VanderWeele,"Activities for Flourishing: An Evidence-Based Guide," *Journal of Positive Psychology and Well-being* 4 (2020): 81.

37. Inspired by Jessie Scholsser Smith.

38. Tara Brach, "Attention—The Most Basic Form of Love," July 17, 2014. https://www.tarabrach.com/attention-the-most-basic-form-of-love/.

39. VanderWeele, "Activities for Flourishing," 4.

40. Nikitha Menon, Mickey Trockel, Maryam Hamidi, and Tait Shanafelt, "Developing a Portfolio to Support Physicians' Efforts to Promote Well-being: One Piece of the Puzzle," *Mayo Clinical Proceedings* 11 (November 2019): 2173.

41. Meg Chisolm, personal communication, May 23, 2022.

42. Dr. David Olawuyi Fakunle states that we all want to experience what he calls the "existential determinants of health"—to be acknowledged, appreciated, respected, understood and loved. "Prioritizing Flourishing: Our Greatest Public Health Opportunity" Conference, April 29, 2022, Johns Hopkins Bloomberg School of Public Health.

9

Practicing Mindfulness

In the introduction to his 2017 book *Attending: Medicine, Mindfulness, and Humanity*, physician Ronald Epstein considers his professional and personal journey to mindfulness.[1] During medical school, he was profoundly struck by connections between seemingly disparate events such as a senior physician noticing and calmly addressing a serious and urgent development during a surgery, and another mentor's compassionate and painstaking interview of a patient with a head injury. "I saw how awareness, flexibility, and attention are crucial for all clinicians, regardless of specialty or profession."[2] Years later, as a working physician in academic medicine, Epstein describes feeling confident he had acquired the knowledge and skills to be a good physician. Yet, as he observes himself in action, he notices that "sometimes I practiced with clarity and compassion, and other times impatience, distraction, unexamined emotions, and defensiveness got in the way. Lacking a guidebook, I had to look inside myself." He continues, "I came to three conclusions—good doctors need to be self-aware to practice at their best; self-awareness needs to be in the moment, not just Monday-morning quarterbacking; and no one had a road map."[3]

Long after these initial insights, Epstein was invited by his dean at the University of Rochester to create a mindfulness program for physicians. He collaborated with Michael Krasner and other colleagues to pilot the program for seventy clinicians at risk of burnout. Epstein describes how the development team's model of excellence addressed knowledge and skills necessary for excellent care, but also the "qualities of caring, and the clinicians' resilience and well-being—showing how these three domains were linked and how practicing mindfulness—could affect all three."[4] Following up on Epstein's groundbreaking 1999 article "Mindful Practice" in the flagship *Journal of the American Medical Association*, in 2009 Krasner, Epstein, and colleagues published another *JAMA* article—this time reporting on the first set of positive program outcomes.[5]

Since then, Epstein and his like-minded colleagues have been leaders in providing evidence-based, practical "road maps" to understand, teach, and advocate for the importance of mindfulness in medical care. In doing so, they build on the foundational work of scientist and meditation practitioner Jon Kabat-Zinn. In 1979, Zinn founded the mindfulness-based stress reduction program, known as MBSR, at the University of Massachusetts. This program initially focused on providing insights and mindfulness training for people living with chronic illness, pain, or other conditions, with the goal of improving their day-to-day lives. Proof of MBSR's efficacy has given rise to programs around the world and also stimulated new research agendas in neuroscience and psychology that cumulatively support mindfulness as an evidence-based practice.[6] Zinn's initial goal was to establish a rationale and a set of practices for mindfulness detached from any religious tradition in order to develop and test a model which would be acceptable in the West, and particularly, within Western medicine.[7] Today Zinn speaks openly and with passion about MBSR and other mindfulness practices' debt to over twenty-five hundred years of thought and practice within Asian traditions, particularly Buddhism.[8]

The art museum offers an interesting and unique setting for mindfulness. While taking full advantage of the museum environment, this chapter focuses on using works of art as unique resources to introduce and gain experience with different mindfulness ideas and practices. Activities and sequences include practices for grounding in the body, exploring attention and awareness, and compassion. Each activity or sequence addresses one or more aspects of the widely used definition of mindfulness offered by Zinn—"paying attention on purpose, in the present moment, non-judgmentally"[9]—while examining the particular opportunities offered by working with art in the art museum.

GROUNDING IN THE BODY

Quieting the mind, finding a calm center within, or creating a moment of stillness can be difficult for anyone who works in healthcare. The experience of a day in which things happen in rapid succession may lead to a sped-up feeling, as if one is trying to compete with time itself. Bodily sensations and needs, as well as emotions that arise, may be pushed aside in order to meet the many demands of a day. The following sequence of museum-based activities explores grounding in the body as an essential foundation for mindfulness, as well as introducing a focused-attention breath practice. In preparation for this experience focused on the senses and the body, the museum educator has carefully chosen works of art, gallery spaces, and materials to appeal to the senses. For each activity, she has handwritten a few keywords or made a small drawing on a piece of mat board as a visual organizer for each person. Participants can also use this board as a private space to record thoughts, and participants take it with them as a small memento.

Welcoming a group of fourth-year medical students and two physician-educators, the museum educator invites them into an open, spacious gallery and asks them to stroll around the space slowly, taking time to notice the works of art. Most of the artworks are very large contemporary pieces; many suggest landscapes, while others are more fully abstract. They are generously spaced in relation to one another, interspersed around the room's windows and seating. She asks the participants to look for a work of art that they think could provide "a place to rest."

After everyone has identified a potential work of art, the educator welcomes the group to a circle of gallery seating, and asks "Where are your feet?" People laugh at this rather odd question—borrowed from Ronald Epstein—and look down at their feet.[10]

Looks like everyone has found their feet! So please have a seat and get comfortable. The purpose of this question is to ground you in the here and the now. We are going to start by doing a short meditation together—about five minutes. You may get distracted; that happens to most everyone. As you notice your mind straying, gently return to paying attention to your body and your breath.

When you are ready, please close your eyes, or, if you prefer, you can soften and lower your gaze. Take a few easy breaths, in and out—easy breaths.

Without looking, use the index finger of one hand to slowly trace around each finger of the other hand—as if you were drawing the outline of your hand, as you may have done as a child.[11] Notice the slow gentle touch of one of your fingers tracing the outline of your other hand. When you have finished, switch hands and repeat. You may notice the texture and temperature of your hands, or feel a warm, tingling sensation as you find and trace the edges of your hands.

Let your awareness linger in your hands as you continue to breathe in and out, without effort, letting your awareness move with your breath, as it enters and leaves your body.

(Throughout, the museum educator uses a warm, calm tone of voice and sets a slow, rhythmic pace, with time elapsing between prompts.)

Keep breathing comfortably and naturally and imagine that you can follow your breath to all parts of your body.

Simply follow the breath. No effort; just relax and allow the breath to come and go.

As you breathe, notice how your feet are supported by the ground.

Notice where your body is supported by the seat.

Continue to breathe, letting the breath flow in . . . and out . . . without effort.

You may be aware of discomfort or tension in your body.

Allow the awareness of these sensations.

Allow these sensations to rise and fall as your breath continues to rise and fall.

Use your breath to accept things as they are today in your body.

Now, as you continue to breathe, I invite you to find a place in your body that feels good today. Take a moment to stop and notice this place where you can appreciate and rest in your body.

I invite you to pay particular attention to a place where your body feels sturdy and ready to support you.

Use the steady rhythm of your breathing to center and rest peacefully in your body.

Keeping in mind a place to center and rest; I invite you to simply breathe and rest in your body for a silent minute.

(The museum educator allows a timed minute to elapse.)

When you are ready, open your eyes. Look around and in silence, walk to the work of art you chose before that could be "a place to rest" for you today. Settle in to spend time looking at the artwork in silence. Let your eyes wander while you breathe and look.

As you breathe and look, perhaps you can find a connection between the sturdy, peaceful place I hope you found inside you—and a place to rest in the artwork.

After five minutes, the group reunites to see and hear about the works people chose—people are invited to share about their choice, their experiences, and what they noticed during this multi-part activity. When everyone has had a chance to share and reflect, the educator leads the group to an adjacent gallery.

For the second activity, the museum educator has chosen three works of art that evoke strong sensory responses by visitors due to their texture, size, or allusions to the human body. Strategies of looking, reflection, and inquiry will be used—first individually, and then through sharing in small groups—to explore the connections to the body and to medicine. Unlike the focused attention practice described earlier, that involved returning to the breath over and over again, this plan invites different elements of perception, feeling, and thinking to intertwine while keeping a focus on self-awareness and sensory perception.

The museum educator gives the directions for participants to visit the three different works of art and choose one that attracts them. Once they have chosen, they are instructed to move around the work and look closely, reflecting for ten minutes on a set of four questions handwritten on their mat board:

1. Look for traces of making. Imagine the movements your own hands would make in creating this work and textures you might feel.
2. How does this work relate to the human body in scale, materials, and ideas?
3. What associations or impressions arise in response to looking?
4. What connections to medicine can you make based on your own experience living in a body, and also caring for others?

Further instructions encourage them to take notes or make drawings about their ideas: *"These can be private or (eventually) shared as you wish."* After ten minutes pass, they will gather with those who chose the same work of art to share their responses in a small group.

The participants examine the three works of art:

Standing Figure by Alberto Giacometti is an approximately two-foot-high bronze sculpture of an attenuated female figure, posed with one foot slightly forward. The work's surface shows traces of the artist's hand in the pinches and bumps he made in the original wax model, as well as the impression of "molten wax" from before it was cast in metal.[12]

Untitled, 2005 by Mark Bradford is a large-scale multimedia work, approximately eleven feet tall by sixteen feet wide, in which the process of layering scraps of found paper—such as maps and bright-colored sticky notes—is combined with adding and subtracting paint and other materials. The artist's

Practicing Mindfulness

time and labor making this dynamic and immersive work can be discovered in the layers.[13]

Untitled, 1965 by Robert Morris is a mixed-media work that is approximately six feet square. Its aluminum-painted canvas panels include inlays of zinc, lead, and Sculp-metal, a metallic clay that hardens to metal. At the center of the work, two nearly life-size arms and hands reach toward each other but do not quite touch. Smaller squares below them have the impression of a pair of gloves (in black), an additional impression of two tiny hands (in gray), and a yellowish-brown photographic plate with an image of a fired bullet from one of the artist's previous works.[14]

When sharing in small groups, participants offer observations about changes in their perception of the works as they physically moved around them or considered the different prompts. Some recurring themes are vulnerability and mortality, joy and exuberance, human limitations, ambiguity and complexity. In response to the fourth prompt, one of the senior physicians comments that during medical school and residency you are constantly challenging your own body and mental stamina. You may even feel you are not doing a good job of caring for yourself, while learning about the human body and caring for patients. The trainees respond with their own thoughts, clearly appreciating this tacit invitation by the senior physician. With five minutes left, the educator prompts the other groups, if they have not already done so, to consider the connections to medicine.

Bringing the groups together, the museum educator invites people to share reflections about their perceptions or responses to the activity. Participants often note that they appreciate the opportunity to write and reflect knowing that their thoughts may be kept private if they choose, but they also enjoy the discussion and sharing. Wrapping up, the educator invites questions about the art and the artists, calibrating the length and depth of her answers to the group's interests and the time left.

To bring this exploration of grounding in the body to a close, the museum educator has planned one more short activity. The group enjoys the physical break of moving from one end of the museum to the other and being invited to relax and enjoy the break. Arriving at their destination, they arrive in a large airy space and gather in front of a painting by Kehinde Wiley.[15] The educator invites them to stand together and close their eyes for a minute of breathing while returning to the theme of "resting in the body." She invites them to put their body in the pose of the young man in the painting, noticing especially the position and feeling of his face and hands. The group gazes upward at the luminous portrait of a young Black man. He, too, gazes upward, standing in a relaxed but alert pose, his face and hands particularly illuminated. He extends his hands in front of him with his palms up and slightly outward, his fingers gently curling. A vivid background of painted vines and flowers completely fills the space behind and around him, and a few twine around the man's lower body.

Practicing Mindfulness

The museum educator invites everyone to have a seat, and, without too much thinking, write in response to two prompts:

"My heart knows . . ."
"My body knows . . ."

Responses, when shared, include the following:

My body knows the peace that is radiating from him.
My heart knows joy in looking at this image.
My body knows the deep sorrow that is also present with this intense beauty.
My heart knows about the courage it takes, trusting another person.
My body knows the gentleness in this man's pose, I feel like he is invoking kindness.
My heart knows how to recognize goodness.
My body knows how it feels to stand in a posture of attention and trust, asking and receiving.
My heart knows I am seeing this person in a dream, like someone or something I have lost.

People are clearly engaged and moved by this artwork, so the educator keeps her closing simple. She shares that Kehinde Wiley collaborated with his model, Keshawn Warren, to create this portrait, and that Mr. Warren chose this pose based on a famous painting of a Christian saint, St. Francis.[16] She reads a statement by the artist: "My desire is that the viewer sees the background coming forward in the lower portion of the canvas, fighting for space, demanding presence. Almost as if the painting itself becomes an embodiment of a type of struggle for visibility, and this might be considered the main subject of the painting."[17]

The educator thanks everyone for coming to the museum, for their openness and sharing, and expresses the hope that some of what they did together today may be useful for them as they take care of themselves and care for others.

This museum teaching plan incorporates ideas and practices from mindfulness meditation writers and teachers to introduce basic breathing and body awareness techniques.[18] The first activity utilizes a "focused awareness" approach using the breath as an "anchor" for roving attention. Introducing the ideas of rest as available both in the body and in a personally resonant artwork invites participants to slow down and pay attention to their bodies and their senses. The second activity—looking at an artwork and responding to four prompts—is based in kinesthetic response, and its instructions to notice thoughts, associations, and feelings is a beginning practice of "open awareness," though quite highly structured. Choice is employed as a technique across both of these sessions to enhance participants' conscious attention to themselves—what they are drawn to—and to the works of art. Finally, breath and resting in the body are revisited briefly, followed by a concluding practice evoking paired awareness of body and heart to bring closure to their experience. Complementing the arrival practice, which invited internal focus, the second practice offered time for private thinking and writing, while the third practice, "my body knows, my heart knows," reconnects the group, as everyone looks, responds, and shares in the moment about the same work of art, yet from uniquely personal vantage points.

ATTENTION AND AWARENESS

At its most fundamental, mindfulness is paying attention. Yet, as Jon Kabat-Zinn notes, mindful attention goes beyond thinking: "Your thoughts will only be a part of your experience. Awareness means seeing the whole, the entire content and context of each moment."[19] In considering the next museum sequence of activities, it may be helpful to differentiate between two widely recognized general types of mindfulness practice—focused attention meditation and open monitoring meditation, also known as focused awareness and open awareness. Many participants may already have some experience with a focused attention practice—in which participants repeatedly return to a specific focus—such as mindful breathing and the body scan. Open monitoring meditation invites a broader focus "allowing and acknowledging any experiences that might arise during mediation."[20] Neuroscientist Daniel Siegel speaks about freeing the mind,[21] while Kabat-Zinn writes about the idea of "open spaciousness of awareness."[22]

Investigations into the nature of consciousness have a long and rich history in both Eastern and Western traditions, but anyone reading this can conduct their own short thought experiment on focused and open awareness in everyday life. First, imagine searching for an item in an unfamiliar grocery store. You must tune out the many distractions around you—the overloaded cart blocking your path, the laughing baby, the giant "sale" signs, the piped-in music—in order to focus on finding the item. You try to maintain goal-oriented "top down" attention.[23] Change the scene and imagine being at a concert: your awareness of being surrounded by people, the music reaching your body and the feelings it generates, your shoulder touching the person next to you, subtle changes in the lighting. At the concert, you may even have felt a diffuse but palpable connection to every other person having this experience with you.[24] The varied elements of the experience do not vie for your attention, but rather seem to be available to you as an experience of the whole, without requiring a sense of effort. This common experience may give us a sense of open awareness.

At the museum, the educator waits to greet the arriving participants with a handful of maps. After they have shed their coats, she welcomes them and describes their warm-up activity, a short museum-based version of one created by physician and writer Ronald Epstein.[25] Using gallery maps that she hands out, they will pick a destination of their choosing in the museum—anywhere—and head off to it.

She asks if everyone has a phone or a watch; people smile—they are doctors, so most have both! She gives the instructions: "Take five minutes to get to your chosen destination, using the map. This is your starting point. Your activity is called 'Ten

Minutes of Red.' Start a ten-minute timer and look for everything red. This is your sole purpose and focus for those ten minutes. Jot a brief word of two, if you wish, about what you find. After ten minutes, please take about five minutes to make your way back here."

Twenty minutes later, people return, chatting easily to each other. Some are smiling; others look rushed or irritated. The educator invites them to talk in pairs or threes about the experience, and then to share with the whole group. Most people enjoyed moving around the museum freely, but for some the focus was irritating as they noticed things they wanted to look at, but they had to keep scanning for red. Some entered the "game" mindset and competed with themselves to find all the red they could, even race-walking through the galleries. One person, laughing, says they used to paint and therefore got involved in the question, "When is red *red*, and not orange or purple?"

The museum educator acknowledges the potential tension between getting to *wander* but not getting to *wonder*—and having to keep a narrow attention focus. She invites them to consider the way their brain feels in the grocery store and concert experience examples described earlier, and the way that other thoughts—"What red is *red*?"—interrupt even our most focused top-down thinking.[26] The next activity will invite them to slow down through a short, preparatory meditation and then practice an "open awareness" exercise with a work of art. The group walks together to a nearby gallery and takes their seats with their backs facing a large abstract canvas that the educator has selected for the open awareness activity.

As we get started, I want to share a description of mindfulness: "being aware in the present moment, without judgment." So, we will be noticing what it is like to have a moment-to-moment awareness, fluid and flexible, in which one does not get stuck judging oneself or one's thoughts or feelings. Whatever arises in your mind is okay. Let's get started. When you feel ready, simply close your eyes, or soften and lower your gaze.

I invite you to use your breath to gently settle into your body.

Easy breaths, no special effort.

Relax from your day into your breath and your body.

Let the gentle waves of your breath reach all the way through your body from the top of your head, down to your feet.

Allow the breath to soften your body wherever it goes, wherever you are aware of the breath.

As you breathe, you may notice sensations, such as the room's temperature and how you may feel the temperature differently in different parts of your body.

You may notice other images coming to mind.

Or you may be aware of emotions in the present moment that are "left over" from your day.

You may be preoccupied with a specific thought or a jumble of thoughts.

Whatever you sense, see, feel or think, just let it be what it is . . . whatever it is.[27]

It may help to name these sensations, images, feelings, or thoughts.

You don't need to resist them, nor do you need to attach to them. Just let them come and go.

Imagining having a mind which notices without getting stuck, here is an image to consider.

A small spring runs over mossy ground and into a piece of bamboo, shaped into an open pipe. Water flows down the open bamboo pipe which tips slightly downward into a simple wooden bucket. When the bucket is full, it tips over and the water flows out into a small stream. All day the water flows in, the bucket tips, and empties and the cycle starts over with no visible effort.

Take a moment to imagine the ease with which this bucket fills and empties.

Now take an additional moment to breathe, continuing to breathe, continuing to let your sensations or thoughts come and go. (Timed silent minute.)

When you are ready, open your eyes and turn your stool around to face the painting behind you. We are going to spend time looking at this painting by artist Joan Mitchell.

Spend time letting your gaze rove freely across this large painting. As you look, notice what parts of the painting interest or attract you the most. Allow yourself to see what part might draw you in and spend time there. For the next four to five minutes, look at one area for as long as you want. Move your eyes around the painting to wherever you want to go and stay there as long as you like. While you are looking, pay attention to your sensations, feelings, thoughts, and perhaps images as they come, staying with them as long as you like, then like the water in the fountain, simply let them move on.

The participants take five minutes to explore Joan Mitchell's *White Territory*, a very large abstract painting (over nine feet tall and over seven feet wide) that has both "quiet" and energetic areas of color and mark-making (figure 8).[28] Though the color white is predominant in both the background washes and dynamic areas of thick smears and brushstrokes, other colors found in the work include deep pine greens, luminous golds, and turquoise blues, with additional marks in gray and black. In this sequence, the breath meditation inviting open awareness is intended to prime people for relaxing and looking, and to enjoy "filling and emptying" their mind. They choose their pace by moving when they get restless; their only task is to look while paying attention to the painting and to their interior experience.

Back together in front of the painting, the educator asks everyone to prepare to describe to others where on the canvas they lingered and what they experienced. She offers the metaphor of telling about "a walk that you took, and now want to tell someone else about—describe what you saw, sensed, felt, and thought." Participants narrate this in varied ways. One, a musician, describes his perception that the painting has four distinct quadrants—or movements—and that he became taken with imagining what kind of music would be in each part. As he did this, he felt a sense of the whole *and* the parts, just like in music; he found that experience really enjoyable. This sense of four distinct areas shaped the experience of others too; many noticed, in particular, the long, slightly conical, deep green, vertical shapes filling the work's upper left quadrant, comparing them to sentinels or judges, relatively stable and still. Others were attracted to an area of turquoise blue surrounded by gold and white marks, seeing it as a ball of energy, or experiencing the feeling of a sunny day. Another person recounted spending all their time in one part of the painting where there were "drips and dribbles," and spent a lot of time thinking about the artist making these marks—experiencing a sense of time recorded in them. The last person to share said this painting "was" her most recent evening of emergency department service, and she correlated the feeling, colors, and brushwork to four distinct experiences. Her stories of both the painting and her doctoring were filled with observations of connections and dissonance.

The diverse and rich individual responses to this chosen artwork testify to its complexity and the participants' attention to it. They were intrigued by the invitation to suspend judgment, practice a fluid and moment-to-moment attention, and share their impressions with others. The educator closes with a discussion of the visit's activities, revisiting focused awareness and open awareness meditation approaches, and answering questions about the artist or the work. She shares that Joan Mitchell has described her paintings as sensory impressions conveying a felt sense of landscapes that also represent what one writer termed the artist's own "internal weather."[29]

How does this relate to clinical medicine? Ronald Epstein writes about the different kinds of thought processes that may be helpful to clinicians. These include being self-aware and developing the ability to monitor one's inner states or thoughts while still focusing on the patient. The physician's ability to maintain a receptive, nonjudgmental stance toward both themselves and the patient is also valuable in perceiving accurately. In reading Epstein's descriptions, one imagines an open, agile awareness which is calm and adaptable.[30] Time, and the lack of it, strongly shape the moment-to-moment experience of doctors and others working in healthcare. However, time in and of itself is not sufficient to convey the care and attention that build trust between doctor and patient.[31] Epstein writes, "When physicians are present, patients feel that spaciousness."[32] This museum experience provides an opportunity for participants to explore focused attention and open awareness, and to build skills in noticing the differences.

COMPASSION

There is widespread consensus that compassionate care is fundamental to excellence in clinical care. Yet, as more fully described in Chapter 8: Nurturing Well-being and Chapter 3: Cultivating Empathy, working conditions, burnout, and other issues present obstacles to mindful, compassionate care. This is true for physicians at all levels of training and practice, but particularly for trainees, who frequently voice personal stories related to these issues in museum workshops. A fourth-year medical student speaks movingly about struggling to maintain her equilibrium in the face of daily challenges so that she can achieve her goal of being a competent, kind, and compassionate doctor. Another speaks of witnessing deep suffering, questioning whether he has matured enough as a caregiver to face such suffering; he wonders how to acquire the skills to be present as a compassionate witness for his patients.

Several students with the same mentor comment that they have been advised not to "go over the empathy cliff" without really understanding the alternative. Ronald Epstein beautifully describes this dilemma in the following passage:

> During training, supervisors and colleagues warned me of the danger of becoming too involved with patients. Patients die, and they are ravaged by unspeakable tragedy, depredation, and abuse. Getting too close to the edge of this vortex feels dangerous. You fear that you'll lose perspective and degenerate into a mass of emotional jelly. Clearly though, boundary situations demand a greater sense of presence—not less. Only with a radically tenacious sense of presence can a clinician maintain the sense of intimacy necessary to truly be there with a suffering patient. In medicine, trainees hear little about how to do this.[33]

Epstein subsequently describes the ability to be present as arising in the physician's capacity for mindful self-awareness, emotional regulation, and "mentalization"—the ability to dispassionately consider their own thoughts. He observes that with these in place, physicians can connect with their patients and enjoy the richness of practicing medicine without fear. He notes that these capacities do not protect the physician from strong and sometimes difficult emotions, but rather prepare them to remain connected with themselves and others during these times. He writes of his own evolving sense of presence—"At first, presence was an individual experience for me; only later did I realize that it was shared"—and his realization that "a shared connection can unite the physician and patient."[34]

This museum teaching plan was created to explore the physician's role in witnessing suffering and loss, as well as to consider the practical value of the third main type of mindfulness practice: compassion practice.[35] The first section is presented here as an annotated outline. The featured artwork, *The Death of Leander* by Guilio Carpioni, has been chosen because of its subject matter: the tender and beautiful depiction of a scene showing witnesses to a young man's death.[36] In this small, vivid oil painting, a dramatic scene takes place among churning ocean waves. Four sea nymphs and a merman surround a young man, whose skin has a pale bluish-green hue that contrasts with the sea creatures' warm, rosy flesh. Together, the nymphs support his body in a piece of white cloth. The facial expressions and body language of the attending figures suggest a range of emotions. In the upper righthand corner, rising behind and above the group, is a stern, bearded man holding a trident and the reins on two surging horses, whose bodies merge with the whitecaps of the waves.

1. Welcome and Framing

    The educator welcomes the group of third-year medical students; she knows they have come straight from their internal medicine rotation at the Veterans Affairs Hospital and invites them to share what they were doing right before they left. Their responses mix serious topics with humor as they take the invitation to arrive, connect, and relax.

The educator leads a shorter version of the breathing meditation, starting with grounding in feet, seat, and breath, inviting participants to catch up with themselves, relax, and enjoy the time at the museum.

2. Looking
   A. First Impressions

   She gives each person a piece of matboard, saying, *we will take a few minutes to just look—this is about first impressions. Please feel free to make notes for yourself if you wish.*

   Typically, the arrival conversation, breath exercise, and undirected time to look and gather first impressions help people to settle in and spark curiosity about this dramatic painting.

   B. Guided Looking

   Now, let's see what we can learn together by taking on different aspects of this work, and having a closer look. There is a lot to see and puzzle over here. The educator uses a basket of handwritten cards from which each person chooses a prompt to guide them in looking again with a specific purpose in mind. These include:

   What draws your eye? Does your eye keep coming back to a particular place? What movement do you notice?

   Take a good look at the textures and colors and notice where they repeat. What do they contribute to the painting?

   Take a good look at the many figures. You may want to consider gender, body language, and facial expressions as you consider what's happening. Who is looking at whom and what might those looks convey?

   What is your impression of the overall scene? What might be happening?

After giving everyone time to look, the educator invites comments. Although the group has been looking for over ten minutes at this point, once people begin talking again, they become deeply absorbed in the rich descriptions, as each becomes more aware of how particular elements shape the scene. Pace, tone, and expectations of participation and willingness to think more deeply have been established. Their comments have served to engage each more deeply with some of the entry points to empathy (eye contact, facial expression, body language—see chapter 3: Cultivating Empathy).

3. Checkpoint: Pause and Assess

   The educator's choices have modeled close and patient looking and have suggested some lenses to use—this is often helpful for those who might need some vocabulary and structure for looking. Participants have shared their observations and impressions. The museum educator transitions by asking, *before we leave describing, what else is there to notice that hasn't been mentioned?*

She pauses for responses, and then asks, *what is your biggest question at this point?*

Usually, participants have already moved toward interpretation and are curious about the story behind this dramatic scene. The museum educator answers any factual questions—such as the date the work was made, the artist's name, etc.—saving the story and the painting title for last.

4. Sharing the Story

This is a painting depicting a Greek story of gods and mortals and incorporating elements from later European literature and plays based on this same story.

Hero and Leander lived across the Hellespont—a narrow body of water that connects the Aegean Sea to the Sea of Marmora—from each other. They met when Leander attended a summer festival for the goddess Aphrodite held on the island where Hero lived. It was love at first sight. Hero, however, was a priestess of Aphrodite's temple, and her life was dedicated to serving the temple and the goddess. Nevertheless, she and Leander became lovers.

Each night throughout the summer, Leander swam across the Hellespont, following the flicker of a torch that Hero placed in her tower to guide his way. One night, a strong storm turned the sea turbulent and blew out Hero's torch. Without the light to guide him, Leander lost his way and drowned. He was found by sea beings as we see here and placed on the shore on Hero's island.

Some versions of the story say that the god Poseidon, who ruled the seas and their winds, caused the storm. In other tellings, he commands the sea nymphs and a merman who find the drowned man, leaving us with questions about agency, fate, and loss.

5. Reflection

This is a list of some ideas to prompt introspection and connections to medicine: the museum educator will select among them depending on the themes and ideas that the participants have offered so far. Most specifically, if the discussion has already opened out toward clinical connections and personal experiences, she will support this direction and move on to the closing discussion or written reflection in part VI, "Witnessing and Medicine."

Does knowing the story change the way you see this work of art? (This story deals with loss, death, care, fate, and a malevolent god. The museum educator links responses to participants' earlier ideas and observations.)

What does the artist show us about the human experience of loss and death?

What connections to clinical experiences (care, death, loss, the physician's role) does this work bring up for you? What past experiences and stories might relate here?

6. Witnessing

You have touched on the fact that in this painting, only one of Poseidon's horses and the merman stare out at the viewer. We talked about "witnesses" to the action within the painting and also witnesses that look directly out to us, the viewers. Those in this painting are pretty much all witnesses, but they are paying attention to different things, as you have already described.

If you had to pick one figure that you identify with, which one would it be? Describe the connection for you. (Medical students virtually never identify with Poseidon, who surveys the scene, but do sometimes—in response to this identification question—refer to him as "the attending.")

This aspect of the conversation usually provides some reflective and even humorous moments as participants gently evaluate their own roles (subservient, watchful, cautious, distressed, in charge, compassionate). It also provides a relaxed moment before the final reflection if they haven't yet gone into depth about clinical connections and their role.

7. Closing: Witnessing in Medicine

Based on the tone, direction, and individuals' disclosures or lack thereof in discussion, the educator invites participants to reflect out loud (or, privately, in writing) on their thoughts about accompanying people during times of pain or suffering, or as they or their families face loss and death.

To begin the next activity, the group walks together to the South Asian gallery and settles in front of a tenth-century sculpture, *Vishnu as Varaha the Cosmic Boar*.[37] The main figure, Vishnu, with the form of a man and the head of a boar, is many times larger than the multitude of figures, garlands, and architectural details that surround him. Though one of his four arms is missing and there is other damage on this sculpture, the beautiful, rounded form of Vishnu—one leg forward and body slightly twisted—attracts and holds everyone's attention. Originally made for a temple exterior ledge, the dozens of surrounding figures and decorative details—carved in high relief—emerge from the oblong piece of sandstone.

The museum educator once again starts by giving everyone time to look and then asks people in the circle to each take a turn describing what they are noticing or wondering about. People mention the size of the central figure versus the surrounding ones and note a partially damaged figure of a woman sitting atop Vishnu's upraised snout. They identify several lotuses: one arches over Vishnu's head, another supports his raised foot and is, in turn, supported by two small figures who have human upper bodies and lower bodies of serpents. Their biggest questions are where was this work originally, and what is the story behind it?

The museum educator tells the group that works like this would have lined the exterior ledges of a Hindu temple. They presented what would have been familiar religious stories to those coming to or walking by this temple. She shares a version of this piece's story from her research.

According to religious texts from the Hindu tradition, the deity Vishnu takes many forms or avatars in which to come to earth. This is the third form, the Cosmic Boar. In his great compassion, Vishnu usually returns to earth to solve some dire problem facing humans. Each time, he exercises discernment and intelligence in choosing the particular form needed for each problem. At this time, the earth (represented by the earth goddess aloft on his snout) had been captured by a demon who plunged it into a dark and bottomless lake. As the Cosmic Boar, Vishnu had the superpower of smell, and he could also fly. He flew low over the dark water, and after a long time he caught the scent of something green and saw below him an open lotus gleaming on the dark water. The next instant he recognized a rich smell of wet earth. Vishnu knew that while the lotus floats on water, its roots must grow in the mud of the earth. Vishnu dove deep into the water until he pushed his snout under the earth, bringing the earth goddess and all the earth's inhabitants up and out of danger. For this and other deeds, Vishnu is called the sustainer, the preserver, the protector.

She invites each person to share one word that expresses their thoughts about the story as they look at the sculpture now. "Courage," "foresight," "power," "beauty," "strength," "trickery," and "problem solving" are all mentioned.

The museum educator shares that she chose this work thinking that the need to shape oneself to the important demands of the day, with both its rewards and stresses, might resonate with their experiences. With the powers of a superhuman being, Vishnu is able to flex and reshape himself easily, but this is not so easy for mere mortals. In order to sustain ourselves, we consider both what is needed from us, and what we need to give to ourselves. The museum educator guides the group's transition to talking more specifically about medicine: *In medicine you have encountered many different models for how to be a physician. Let's take a few minutes pause to reflect on and write about characteristics and actions that you would like to emulate, and/ or characteristics you would not like to emulate.*

Observing that most people are finished writing, the educator lets the group know they will move into their last activity, a meditation practice focused on compassion. She notes to the group that they have started with a work reflecting Western (European and Greek) traditions, that the Vishnu artwork and story are from the Hindu tradition, and that the meditation—offered as a secular practice— originates in Buddhism. She describes the context for offering this practice for her work teaching this meditation to health professionals.

As you take care of people, you may find certain experiences lingering. Sometimes these are distressing ones. Paradoxically, you may be unable to let go of the thought of something due to a lack of time during a busy day to think or feel sufficiently about it and reach some kind of closure. Or you may have felt deep concern for a patient whose suffering you were not able to fully relieve or to whom you could not promise a cure. Presence and connection can be meaningful to both caregivers and patients. At the same time the ability to accept one's own human limitations with kindness, acceptance, and self-compassion is integral to sustaining physical and mental health

There are many compassion meditation practices that do not require any particular religious belief. Today I am going to focus on a practice known as loving-kindness meditation which also addresses self-compassion.[38]

Settle into a comfortable position and when you are ready, please close your eyes or lower and soften your gaze.

Allow yourself to find an easy, relaxing pattern of breathing, using your breath coming in and going out to relax further into this moment.

I invite you to begin by focusing on someone with whom you enjoy an easy relationship—someone you care about.

While envisioning them and holding them in your mind, repeat to yourself (the educator says these words aloud throughout and adopts a slow pace and a steady, warm tone):

> *May they find ease*
> *May they be at peace*
> *May they feel safe*
> *May they know they are deeply loved.*

Let's repeat, still focusing on this same person.

The museum educator continues in this way, asking them to hold a particular person in their mind, and each time repeating the wishes of the loving-kindness meditation twice.

Now, I invite you to think about a person with whom you might have a more challenging relationship. (She repeats the wishes.)

Next, think of someone who is lingering on your mind, maybe a patient you can't forget and want to think about. (She repeats the wishes.)

And now we turn to ourselves as a loving friend might turn to us with love and kindness.

> *May I find ease*
> *May I be at peace*
> *May I feel safe*
> *May I know I am deeply loved.*
> (Repeat)

After a quiet moment, the group is invited to open their eyes. This museum experience exploring mindfulness in relationship to compassion and self-compassion comes to a close. The educator shares some final thoughts about how the loving-kindness meditation can be one resource to reset, to pay deep attention to others and to ourselves. *In this practice we hold a place in our minds and hearts for those we have cared for, but we also create an opportunity to practice grounded self-compassion—to let go of any notion of having superhuman powers. We hold our wishes for them, but not an unrealistic attachment to outcomes that are beyond any human's control.*

CONCLUSION

This chapter has offered tested designs for museum experiences exploring three dimensions of mindfulness: grounding in the body, attention and awareness, and compassion and self-compassion. Ronald Epstein writes:

Master clinicians attend to the person in front of them while attending to their own mental processes. They don't take for granted their initial impressions, or anyone else's. They attend to that which they can explicitly describe, as well as the vague impressions that influence their judgment. They use their analytic minds—knowledge, evidence, and technical skills—as well as their intuitive and imaginative minds, the sensibilities that we typically associate with the humanities.[39]

Thoughtfully chosen works of art in the museum provide unique opportunities to scan and understand it broadly, to look at details and decide which are significant, and to explore the human condition. Practicing mindfulness while looking at art provides both pleasure and practice attending to inner states (thoughts, feelings) and outer awareness (unique physical characteristics perceived through the senses), connecting participants with the richness and depth of human experiences across time and cultures.

NOTES

1. Ronald Epstein, *Attending: Medicine, Mindfulness and Humanity* (New York: Scribner, 2017), 1-14.
2. Epstein, *Attending*, 7.
3. Epstein, *Attending*, 9-10.
4. Epstein, *Attending*, 10-11.
5. Ronald Epstein, "Mindful Practice," *Journal of the American Medical Association* 282, no 9, (1999): 833-39; Michael S. Krasner, Ronald M. Epstein, Howard Beckman, et al., "Association of an Educational Program in Mindful Communication with Burnout, Empathy and Attitudes Among Primary Care Physicians," *Journal of the American Medical Association* 302, no 12 (2009): 1285-93. On this topic, see also H. B. Beckman, et al., "The Impact of a Program of Mindful Communication of Primary Care Physicians," *Academic Medicine* 87, no. 6 (2012): 1-5.
6. Jon Kabat-Zinn, *Full Catastrophe Living: Using the Wisdom of Your Body and Mind to Face Stress, Pain and Illness*, second edition (New York: Bantam Dell Publishing Group: 2013).
7. Kabat-Zinn, *Full Catastrophe Living*, lxi-lxii.
8. Kabat-Zinn, *Full Catastrophe Living*, 602-3.
9. Kabat-Zinn, *Full Catastrophe Living*, 586.
10. Epstein, *Attending*, 83-84.
11. When I came up with this idea (tracing hands), I was thinking of a common art activity: blind contour drawing. I subsequently learned that this technique is widely used in mindfulness exercises for schoolchildren.
12. Alberto Giacometti, *Standing Figure*, 1957, bronze, University of Michigan Museum of Art, https://exchange.umma.umich.edu/resources/15799.
13. Mark Bradford, *Untitled*, 2005, mixed media, University of Michigan Museum of Art, loan by Randall Kaplan, https://exchange.umma.umich.edu/resources/41466.
14. Robert Morris, *Untitled*, 1997, Sculp-metal, plaster, oil, zinc photographic plate, lead plate, and burlap on canvas, University of Michigan Museum of Art, https://exchange.umma.umich.edu/resources/40305.

15. Kehinde Wiley, *Saint Francis of Assisi,* 2008, oil wash and graphite on paper, in artist's frame, https://umma.umich.edu/exhibitions/2021/you-are-here. As of this writing, the work is also available on the website of Philips Auctioneers, LLC: https//www.phillips.com/kehinde-wiley/UK010720/128 (accessed June 13, 2022).

16. This pose is echoing that of St. Francis in the painting *St. Francis in the Desert* by Giovanni Bellini, 1476–1478, oil on panel, Frick Museum Collection, https://collec tions.frick.org/objects/39/st-francis-in-the-desert.

17. Anna Savikskaya, "'I Try to Create a Place of Disorientation'—Interview with Kehinde Wiley," *Artdependence Magazine,* February 16, 2015, https://www.artdependence .com/articles/i-try-to-create-a-place-of-disorientation-interview-with-kehinde -wiley/.

18. Laura Rice-Oeschger, personal communication (meditation), March 17, 2021. The general idea of resting in the body is not uncommon in the mindfulness community. See the work of Rhonda McGee and Rashid Hughs: https://www.mindful.org/em bracing-the-gift-of-being-alive-with-rhonda-mcgee and https://www.rashidhughs .com/r-e-s-t, accessed June 13, 2022. I (Slavin) was excited to take this idea into a museum-based activity working with artworks as "a place to rest."

19. Kabat-Zinn, *Full Catastrophe Living,* 580–81.

20. Dominique P. Lippelt, Bernhard Hommel, and Lorenza S. Colzato, "Focused Attention, Open Monitoring and Loving Kindness Meditation: Effects on Attention, Conflict Monitoring, and Creativity—A Review," *Frontiers of Psychology* 5, 1083 (September 2014): 1–5.

21. Daniel J. Siegel, "How to Gain Freedom from Your Thoughts," *Greater Good Magazine,* August 22, 2018, https://greatergood.berkeley.edu/article/item/how_to_gain_free dom_from_your_thoughts.

22. See Kabat-Zinn, *Full Catastrophe Living,* 156–65.

23. Epstein, *Attending,* 24.

24. Epstein, *Attending,* 68–73. Epstein, who trained as a musician, discusses music and concerts in connection with "presence" and also a spacious awareness.

25. Epstein, *Attending,* 30–33. Epstein's activity was inspired by a composition by his teacher, musician Ken Maue, titled "Three Days of Red."

26. Epstein, *Attending,* 24–28. I have drawn on Epstein's discussion of types of attention in interpreting the effects of this activity and physician's reactions to this activity in workshops, as well as on my own experience with participant's reactions.

27. Prompts to invoke different modes of looking and responding are part of a shared body of practice among museum educators spanning decades. However, here, I ordered them to follow Daniel J. Siegel's "SIFT" acronym in *Brainstorm: The Power and the Purpose of the Teenage Brain* (New York: Tarcher/Putnam, 2013).

28. Joan Mitchell, *White Territory,* 1970, oil on canvas, https://exchange.umma.umich .edu/resources/22573/view.

29. Carter Ratcliff, "Joan Mitchell's Envisionments," *Art in America* 62 (July/August 1974): 34–35.

30. Epstein, *Attending,* 70–73.

31. Epstein, *Attending,* 71–72; Kathy A. Zoppi, "Communications about Concerns in Well Child Visits" (PhD dissertation, University of Michigan, 1994); Epstein, *Attending,*

10-11; Mary Catherine Beach, et al., "A Multicenter Study of Physician Mindfulness and Health Care Quality," *Annals of Family Medicine* 11, no. 5 (2013): 421-28.

32. Epstein, *Attending*, 70.
33. Epstein, *Attending*, 72.
34. Epstein, *Attending*, 68.
35. Zinn, *Full Catastrophe Living*, 217; Garth W. Strohbehn, Stephanie J. K. Hoffman, Molly Tokaz, et al., "Visual Arts in the Clinical Clerkship: A Pilot Cluster-randomized, Controlled Trial" *BMC Medical Education* 20, 481 (2020). A brief, outline version of this teaching plan, for which I (Slavin) am the sole author, is a free-standing appendix to this online-only article, published under the Creative Commons License BY4 (authors retain copyright).
36. Giulio Carpioni, *The Death of Leander*, 1655, oil on canvas, University of Michigan Museum of Art, https://exchange.umma.umich.edu/resources/38955/view. Note: a version of the story of Hero and Leander is available in the University of Michigan Museum of Art object record.
37. Artist unrecorded—South Asia, Vishnu as Varaha, the Cosmic, circa tenth century, sandstone, University of Michigan Museum of Art, https://exchange.umma.umich .edu/resources/30242. Note: a version of the Vishnu as Varaha story is available in the University of Michigan Museum of Art object record.
38. The loving-kindness meditation has been adapted to this context, for a secular purpose. I have removed the traditional phrase "May you be well" due to the participants' work in a medical setting. I have learned and benefited tremendously from the work of Tara Brach, Jack Kornfield, and others on compassion. Brach's RAIN meditations for difficult emotions, as well as for compassion and spacious awareness, are excellent, short, and accessible resources.
39. Epstein, *Attending*, 33.

10

Building a Community of Practice

Thus far in this book, we have presented an elaborate, and perhaps compelling, vision for what art museums can contribute to students and clinicians in the health professions. We have offered rich descriptions of gallery teaching, detailed lesson plans with activities that build relevant skills and reflective practices, and affirming perspectives from several health professionals. We are happy to have contributed to this emerging field of collaboration across disciplines and, especially, to have worked with a seriousness of purpose to activate museum collections in ways that meet the needs of the people who are taking on the important work of caring for others.

We have worked with many visionary leaders from the health professions, leaders who have used their influence and resources to promote meaningful experiences with art for their students and colleagues. Although we have noticed a growing wave of interest in this work, even momentum, we are aware of the critical need to institutionalize some of these practices. This final chapter briefly references a handful of notable initiatives that represent growing institutional support—from both art museums and the health professions—for the sorts of collaborations for which we are advocating. It features an interview with Dr. Elizabeth Gaufberg, who introduces the first major fellowship dedicated to teaching health professionals principles of museum-based teaching and who continues to work passionately to build an extended "community of practice." It is through building such a community, individuals with shared values and understanding, that this work will continue to grow, to evolve, and to become an integral and recognized component in health professions education. Finally, we will share some recommendations for developing partnerships between art museum educators and health professions educators, based on our own experiences navigating some of the obvious disciplinary differences and developing a shared language.

EMERGING STRUCTURES

In 2016 the Edith O'Donnell Institute's University of Texas at Dallas, in collaboration with the Museum of Modern Art in New York, organized a convening of sixty museum/medical school partnerships.[1] Participants discussed individual programs, shared lesson plans, conducted interactive demonstrations of museum-based practices, and participated in panel discussions. Participants recognized that in addition to sharing emerging practices, there was an urgent need for research and evaluation in order to build institutional support for this work. In 2020, the Association of American Medical Colleges (AAMC) produced the monograph, "The Fundamental Role of the Arts and Humanities in Medical Education" (FRAHME), commissioned a research study providing an overview of arts and medical humanities programs in the United States, and developed a website offering tools to support partnerships and programs.[2] The AAMC has also initiated a grant program to support new initiatives and provide training in research and evaluation. More recently, in 2022, the Center for Visual Arts in Healthcare was established at Brigham and Women's Hospital under the leadership of Dr. Joel Katz and museum educator Brooke DiGiovanni Evans.

One highly influential project aimed at building a community of health professions educators committed to museum-based teaching was initiated in 2018. The prestigious Harvard Macy Institute (HMI) offered the Art Museum-based Health Professions Education Fellowship, the first formalized professional development program for Museum Based Education in the Health Professions.[3] The inspiration of Dr. Elizabeth Gaufberg, the fellowship is a model for interdisciplinary collaboration—it was co-created, co-designed, and is co-taught by a team of museum and medical educators. In the following interview, Dr. Gaufberg talks about the Harvard Macy Fellowship and her commitment to convening, training, and supporting an international community of people in the health professions who can integrate museum-based education strategies in a sustainable way.

INTERVIEW: A CONVERSATION WITH ELIZABETH GAUFBERG

Ruth Slavin and Corinne Zimmermann conducted an interview with Dr. Elizabeth Gaufberg on June 3, 2022. Gaufberg is an Associate Professor of Medicine and Psychiatry at Harvard Medical School; Director of the Center for Professional and Academic Development, The Cambridge Health Alliance, Cambridge, Massachusetts; and founding Co-Director of HMI Art Museum-based Health Professions Education Fellowship in Boston. The interview is presented here in an abridged and edited form for this publication.

Corinne:

You are a leader and advocate for art-museum-based health professions education, including co-authoring the important AAMC monograph "The Fundamental Role of Arts and Humanities in Medical Education" and co-founding the HMI Art Museum-based Health Professions Education Fellowship. How and why did you get started in this work? Why art?

Elizabeth:

My journey started in my own medical school training. Medical training can be profoundly gratifying and exciting, but it's deeply unsettling in a particular way because becoming a doctor involves violating deeply held social norms or taboos. There was a particular moment in one of my anatomy labs when my group was dissecting the brachial plexus, a series of nerves that run through the armpit. When you dissect them, they look like the strings of a guitar. One of my partners began to pluck them and sing a little jazz riff. Everybody laughed except one woman who stormed away from the table, saying "I can't believe you guys!" I remember quite clearly thinking: this is completely predictable. These are all good people. But you cannot thrust people into a room of dead bodies with no opportunity to reflect and *not* have something like that happen. I knew at that moment I would need to feed something humanizing back into medical culture.

I started doing that in a number of ways including creating reflective practice groups as a resident. But I can tell you, if you're sitting in a circle, and you say, "How is your life as a medical student?" people either share superficially or they close down. I discovered the value of using what educator Parker Palmer calls a "third thing." Initially, I worked with poetry and narrative: you read something aloud and it comes into the room. And pretty soon, people are sharing their own stories. The arts serve a modulating function which allows for both safety and depth; if what they reveal ever gets too personal, we can move back to the work of art.

I grew more and more passionate about using the arts in this way. I started working with Ray Williams, bringing my residents to the Harvard Art Museums (HAM), and in 2010, we organized a conference at HAM for medical and museum professionals to discuss emerging programs and possibilities. We timed it to coincide with the AAMC meeting. "A Conversation Across Disciplines" drew a capacity crowd. I remember that both of you offered gallery teaching demonstrations.

I worked closely with you (Corinne) and Judy Murray, offering an art museum elective for the HMI's educator program scholars. HMI participants wanted more! The three of us, along with Dr. Lisa Wong, founded the HMI Art Museum-based Health Professions Education Fellowships.

Becoming a doctor is practice. I always say to my clinical medical students at the end of the year that all the skills they'd learned—to greet a patient, establish rapport, take a history, try to put things together in terms of diagnosis and treatment plan—are the core skills of doctoring. But you must commit yourself to practice, practice, practice to keep getting better at it. A lot of what we do in the museum allows us to practice some of the most nuanced and challenging aspects of interacting with patients and colleagues: talking about difficult topics like suffering, loss, and racism; tolerating uncertainty; and your own emotional responses. It's really helpful to be able to practice in a safe, low-stakes environment.

Ruth:
Can you talk about the partnership between museum educators and health profession educators and the expertise each brings to this work?

Elizabeth:

Museum educators think very intentionally about curriculum development and pedagogy. They ask their medical education partners, "Who are your learners? What are they learning about now? What goals do you have for them?" Then we think together about methods of arts-based engagement to achieve specific outcomes, like the development of empathy or tolerance of ambiguity. Museum educators have a very sophisticated skill set for working with art. This can't be confused with "let's just bring a bunch of learners to a museum and stand in front of a painting and talk about it." Of course, visiting a museum can be restorative or an enjoyable diversion, but that's very different from creating something that is truly integrated into the curriculum.

We have this phrase in medicine, "See one, do one, teach one," which is said a little bit tongue in cheek. But, in fact, just because you have an MD degree, and you were taught to do something, doesn't mean that you can teach effectively.

Obviously, health professionals have the privilege and advantage of direct experience in clinical environments. They have confronted death, illness, and new life coming into the world. Because of this, faculty role-modeling is very powerful for learners. Museum-based pedagogy uses a different facilitation method than many medical educators are used to. It involves reflecting back what you hear and asking good questions, and not imposing your own viewpoints, interpretations, and stories.

Developing a successful partnership is like learning how to dance. Initially, the museum educator and the medical educator are very aware of each step (and the other person's toes!). However, over time, you gain more expertise in working together, you anticipate each other's moves, and it becomes more fluid. These partnerships evolve because you give each other feedback, always with the intention of learning and improving.

Corinne:

Can you talk about HMI's Art Museum-based Health Professions Education Fellowship as a community of practice?

Elizabeth:

As I see it, a lot of the history of this work on the medical side—maybe on the museum side too—has been dependent on individual champions who are incredibly passionate and dedicated; but if they leave their institutions, their educational offering may just die off. The HMI Museum-based Fellowship was founded in large part to create a community of practice, extending beyond individual institutions. It brings together like-minded colleagues into a validating culture to share resources and develop a common language. Each year, we select a cohort of about fifteen applicants from around the world. We introduce them to museum-based practices, followed by discussion and reflection on how to make strong connections to health professions education. Each participant designs an educational project to be implemented and evaluated at their home institution. Their projects are incredibly

Building a Community of Practice

creative and varied, but I think the thing that unites all of us is a profound belief in the power of relational learning and a commitment to reinfuse meaning into the learning and practice of medicine. We prepare participants to return to their own professional environments, supported by a growing community and, ultimately, to change culture. We are already seeing the impact with new medical school programs, new research, and several publications from our fellows. We're really building a movement.

Ruth:
Any final thoughts?

Elizabeth:
I have learned that both museum educators and physicians are differently receptive and prepared to do this work. This book will help spread the word to colleagues from both disciplines as to how powerful, important, and gratifying this work can be. A shared community of practice depends on shared belonging and identity, language and tools, goals, and evaluation. And all those aha moments when you get to collaborate with someone who has a bit different perspective from your own and creative sparks fly!

Many of the pedagogical approaches and activities described in this book are ones we have also shared through the Harvard Macy Fellowship. These include the open-ended interpretive conversations supported by "Visual Thinking Strategies"[4] developed by Housen and Yenawine and Harvard Project Zero's generative "Thinking Routines,"[5] both widely used by museum educators. Such methodologies support close looking, grounding interpretations in evidence, teamwork, and self-awareness. As fellowship participants learn to facilitate inquiry-based discussions, they hone skills of active listening and practice maintaining an open and curious stance. Ray Williams's "Personal Response Tour," developed in the mid-1990s, is also widely used in the health professions as a way to build community, honor the importance of memory and emotion, and invite personal reflection and meaning-making.[6] Creative activities—such as group poems, collaborative drawing exercises, and drama-based play—cultivate flexible thinking, stepping outside one's comfort zone, seeing in new and surprising ways. This playful engagement with others tends to reduce hierarchies, build trust, and stimulate moments of insight and delight.

It has been highly gratifying to see so many Harvard Macy Fellows go back into their professional domains and share these museum-based approaches through conference presentations, publications, and teaching in their home institutions.[7] These Fellows have benefited from being introduced to core museum-based practices and coaching on how to structure a coherent museum lesson: careful framing, interpretive conversation, activities, and time for synthesis and reflection. They are prepared to seek out collaborations with their local museum educators and show up with informed expectations about what might happen when museum collections are activated on behalf of the health professions. They are finding support from the AAMC in the form of grants that will enable the research needed for the science-oriented health professions to fully embrace the arts and humanities as integral to their work. We hope that readers of this book will also be inspired to partner, experiment, document, and spread the word. We hope that the book will become one of the useful tools that helps to build momentum for these collaborative ways of working and, ultimately, a more compassionate, holistic approach to healthcare that includes the possibility of flourishing for the caregivers themselves.

PRODUCTIVE PARTNERSHIPS

Working across disciplines requires identifying and cultivating strong partners, as well as clear communication about goals and expectations.[8] Each partner must be willing to listen carefully and respond to the opportunity to try something new. In the initial planning session, the medical educator should be prepared to articulate two to three main goals for the visit. The goals should respond to specific academic, developmental, professional, and/or social needs. A strong museum partner will ask good questions about the group and the goals for the workshop.

Check for understanding. Have you established a good rapport? Have the logistical constraints and timing been addressed? Does the museum educator seem willing and able to design a gallery experience that responds to the group's particular needs? This initial conversation gives both partners a chance to develop a shared language, as well as to begin identifying touchpoints for assessment later.

Take a quick walk through the galleries together to see which works of art might be relevant to your goals. Both partners should identify interesting works of art and practice thinking together about how the art might resonate with a medical group. Use this time in the galleries to continue developing your mutual understanding of goals and possibilities. Note areas of shared excitement.

After the planning session, the museum educator will be prepared to develop a brief outline of the workshop, identifying key works of art and related activities, and to give a sense of framing, timing, and flow. The health professions educator might share one or two relevant articles from the literature of their discipline. The readings will support the museum partner in preparing for the workshop by introducing terms and issues specific to healthcare, and they may inspire new thinking about connections to works of art. Topics might include dealing with the challenging patient, sharing bad news, mindfulness, resilience, interprofessional teamwork, cultural humility, sexuality, or spirituality. Art is grounded in the complexity of human experience, so it can provide many unexpected entry points, when our thinking is flexible!

Share plans for assessment in advance—a standard survey, perhaps, or any plans to solicit qualitative feedback from participants. The healthcare partner may want to share this information after receiving the museum educator's outline, along with any clarifying comments or suggestions. In general, it's a good idea to have

Building a Community of Practice

some back-and-forth between partners. You are building a relationship with a person who is likely juggling several priorities, and you both want to create a meaningful experience for the group. Partners should discuss what role each will play during the actual museum visit, and they should have a shared understanding of what success will look like.

Plan to follow up shortly after the visit to express appreciation, compare notes, and suggest improvements for next time. Note any moments that were particularly surprising, memorable, or relevant to your concerns. Share your own reflections on the experience and review any evaluations or reflective writing from participants. Accentuate the positive, if this is a relationship you hope to sustain. This is experimental work, and it will improve over time when partners are able to establish a mutually respectful working relationship and encourage one another's creative thinking.

CONCLUSION

The partnerships we have been describing and advocating for are timely, perhaps even urgent. The COVID-19 pandemic and other current social forces have added unprecedented levels of stress to the work of both museums and healthcare.[9] Museums are managing financial shortfalls due to lost revenues, and many have laid off large numbers of workers—including, surprisingly, the educators who have the knowledge and skills to activate these institutions on behalf of a traumatized populace. Museum workers are forming unions for the first time; some are leaving the field because of low pay. Grantmakers and communities are voicing new expectations for art museums that challenge many traditional practices and demand more equitable access for broader audiences. At the same time, physician burnout is endemic in healthcare—sometimes deadly, always costly. The United States is facing severe shortages of healthcare professionals in many regions, and this is projected to worsen just as our aging population requires more care. Healthcare administrators, always with their eye on the bottom line, would do well to consider new strategies that will motivate and encourage beleaguered staff and reverse the trend of departures. Funding required to cover clinical hours and support reflective and nourishing museum experiences is negligible when compared to the costs of replacing skilled staff

The experiences of both art and compassionate care are essential to human flourishing, and yet many of the institutions that are intended to provide these experiences are failing to change in response to current needs. In our work as educators in art museum settings, we have all found barriers to creative thinking about how traditional practices rooted in a commitment to the discipline of art history might respond to a broader imperative. This may be a time for new ways of working, new values, new partnerships. Voices of authority frame our own writing in both the foreword and afterword, and we eagerly anticipate the new work that will happen next, with the blessings of thoughtful leaders from the AAMC and the National Gallery of Art.

This book, replete with stories of human connection and meaning-making, is meant to catalyze new thinking about the potential of experiences with beauty, sorrow, spirituality, ambiguity, and diverse cultural expression inherent in encounters with works of art. If our work has been innovative, it has been informed by visionary individuals who have also worked beyond traditional boundaries. It has been motivated by the needs articulated by our partners and observed in our visitors. We are grateful to have been part of a creative community dedicated to healing in the broadest sense. We hope these ideas will be taken, discussed, adapted, expanded—and put to work in our amazing, hurting, inspiring world.

NOTES

1. This website, originally documenting the 2016 convening at the Museum of Modern Art, New York, of 135 art museum and medical school professionals, was developed by the Edith O'Donnell Institute of Art History, Center for Art in Health at the University of Texas at Dallas and now lives at the Center for Visual Arts in Healthcare @ Brigham and Women's Hospital, Boston. The website includes program descriptions, bibliographies, and syllabi, and is frequently updated with new information: https://www.artsinhealthcare.org/.
2. Lisa Howley, Elizabeth Gaufberg, and Brandy King, *The Fundamental Role of the Arts and Humanities in Medical Education* (Washington, DC: Association of American Medical Colleges, 2020), https://store.aamc.org/downloadable/download /sample/sample_id/382/.
3. For information on the Art Museum-based Health Professions Education Fellowship, please visit https://harvardmacy.org/index.php/hmi-courses/museum-fellow ship-course (accessed May 9, 2022).
4. Philip Yenawine, *Visual Thinking Strategies: Using Art to Deepen Learning Across School Disciplines* (Cambridge: Harvard Education Press, 2013)
5. Shari Tishman, *Slow Looking: The Art and Practice of Learning Through Observation* (New York: Routledge, 2018).
6. Ray Williams, "Honoring the Personal Response: A Strategy for Serving the Public Hunger for Connection," *The Journal of Museum Education* 35, no. 1 (2010): 93-102.
7. Margaret S. Chisolm, et al., "Transformative Learning in the Art Museum: A Methods Review," *Family Medicine* 52 (2020): 736-40; Ali John Zarrabi, et al., "Museum-Based Education: A Novel Educational Approach for Hospice and Palliative Medicine Training Programs," *Journal of Palliative Medicine* 23, no. 11 (2019): 1510-14.
8. Ray Williams and Corinne Zimmermann, "Twelve Tips for Starting a Collaboration with an Art Museum," *Journal of Medical Humanities* 41, no. 4 (2020): 597-601.
9. Linda Kesler, "I Quit," *Proto Magazine*, Massachusetts General Hospital.

Afterword

Museums and Our Shared Humanity

Kaywin Feldman, National Gallery of Art

When I was ten years old and living in England, my village school took a trip to the Royal Academy in London to see a Pompeii exhibition. It is the first museum exhibition I can remember visiting, and I remember it vividly. I recall the emotions I felt upon seeing the plaster casts of a dog and contorted adult bodies, the impressions of their final death struggles left in the volcanic ash of Mount Vesuvius. The other object in the exhibition I remember clearly is the 1865 painting *Faithful Unto Death* by Edward John Poynter, made about one hundred years after the sporadic excavation of Pompeii's ruins had begun.

In Poynter's painting, we see a soldier standing rigidly in a doorway, looking anxiously up at the sky but with his feet planted firmly on the ground. Behind him, balls of flame rain down as people flee in the darkness. I bought a postcard of this painting with my field trip money and pasted it into my scrapbook, which I have today. Forty-five years later, I can still see the picture in my mind's eye, the fire-red glow in the midst of blackness and the soldier's worried eyes turned upward. Even as a child, I had some feeling for what that moment must have felt like for the faithful soldier.

The cast human forms and the painting grabbed me because they helped to humanize the ancient artifacts in the exhibition which were, in comparison, lifeless artifacts from a distant past. I knew that Poynter painted *Faithful Unto Death* long after the natural disaster, but the painting helped me to understand the emotional state of terrified citizens of Pompeii. How else could I know what it felt like to experience a volcanic eruption? The expression on the soldier's face is seared into my memory, causing me to feel empathy for the people who suffered and lost their lives almost two thousand years ago.

The mission of art museums in the twenty-first century is transitioning from the twentieth century's inputs and outputs—acquire and conserve art, produce more exhibitions, programs, and building facilities—to outcomes and impacts. How do we make a difference for individuals and for our communities with the resources that we have? Our stakeholders and communities must hold us accountable for producing public benefit. Museums must be intentional about the benefits they aim to provide to their audiences. When equipped with powerful mission and vision statements and recorded institutional values, museums can be changemakers.

Institutions do not all aim to make the same societal difference, but we all must be clear about who we are and what we stand for.

I fear that the COVID pandemic, climate change, and political and societal instability will continue to confront museums, now and in the years ahead. This is the new world that we are navigating. It is time to double down on the museum's mission, vision, and values as these are the most important tools that will enable us to navigate these turbulent times.

Over the last decade, I have been thinking and writing about the experience of empathy and wonder in the context of art museums. I have come to my interest in how art inspires wonder in the viewer because I have experienced it many times and each time, feel that I have been given a gift that is so much larger than my life. As I leave the museum or place where I have been wonderstruck, I have the distinct feeling of being utterly satisfied with my life, wanting for nothing. It is a feeling of complete fulfillment and peace that I only feel when experiencing wonder.

We feel wonder when confronted with something expansive, fascinating, and beyond our daily experience, and it causes a discernible reverberation. The reaction can be emotional, intellectual, and physical; it can occur when confronted by some-thing in the natural world, by a piece of writing, or a work of art. Behavioral scientists who study wonder have shown that at the moment we feel wonder, we become less narcissistic and more curious about the world around us. We stop worrying about the minutiae in our daily lives and forget our stress. People experiencing wonder are more likely to volunteer their time and to be generous and kind. We understand that we are part of something bigger than ourselves and develop optimistic feelings about humanity and the future.

Wonder and empathy are closely aligned to each other, and both are foun-dational to the enjoyment of visual art. There are many nuanced definitions of empathy, but for my purpose here, I will define it as the act of understanding and awareness of the thoughts, feelings, and experiences of another person. Therefore, based in curiosity and a feeling of shared humanity, wonder opens us up so that we are able to feel empathy for others, even people who have lived in a distant time and place. Wonder is not necessary in order to feel empathy, but when it happens, it further readies us to experience empathy.

When art history, art education, and museology became academic disciplines and vocations, not just avocations for the wealthy, in the mid-twentieth century the nascent field was eager to emphasize that this new academic study was based on scientific research and academic expertise. It was as though we needed to eliminate the human side of the experience of looking at and studying art to justify our work as serious and professional. But art is the expression of what it is to be human. At the National Gallery of Art, you can experience love, kindness, motherhood, joy, beauty, and ecstasy, as well as poverty, war, rape, horror, destruction, and evil—all in a single visit. And that's why people come. We crave the panoply of human ex-perience observed during an art museum visit and leave knowing that we are linked to a broad swath of humanity across geography, chronology, and demographics.

In these times of increasing uncertainty, I am strongly persuaded museums must expand and justify our purpose by embracing the potential of art to find and connect with our shared humanity. This, I believe, is the future of museums. At the National Gallery, a partnership with Georgetown University Medical Center is one example of how we use art in service of human connection and need. Such partnerships between art museums, medical schools, and healthcare organizations are expanding. *Activating the Art Museum: Designing Experiences for the Health Professions* provides a compelling resource for any individual or organization embarking upon this work.

—Kaywin Feldman,
Director, National Gallery of Art

Recommended Reading

Burnham, Rika, and Elliot Kai Kee. *Teaching in the Art Museum: Interpretation as Experience*. Los Angeles: Getty Publications, 2011.

Carr, David. *The Promise of Cultural Institutions*. Walnut Creek, CA: AltaMira Press, 2003.

Charon, Rita. *Narrative Medicine: Honoring the Stories of Illness*. New York: Oxford University Press, 2006.

Cowan, Brenda, Ross Laird, and Jason McKeown. *Museum Objects, Health and Healing: The Relationship between Exhibitions and Wellness*. New York: Routledge, 2020.

D'Souza, Aruna. *Whitewalling: Art, Race & Protest in 3 Acts*. New York: Badlands Unlimited, 2018.

Edmondson, Amy C. *Teaming: How Organizations Learn, Innovate, and Compete in the Knowledge Economy*. San Francisco: John Wiley & Sons, Inc., 2012.

Epstein, Ronald. *Attending: Medicine, Mindfulness and Humanity*. New York: Scribner, 2017.

Falk, John. *The Value of Museums: Enhancing Societal Well-being*. Lanham, MD: Rowman & Littlefield, 2021.

Gokcigdem, Elif (ed.). *Fostering Empathy through Museums*. Lanham, MD: Rowman & Littlefield, 2016.

Groopman, Jerome. *How Doctors Think*. Boston: Mariner Books, 2008.

Halpern, Jodi. *From Detached Concern to Empathy: Humanizing Medical Practice*. New York: Oxford University Press, 2001.

Horton, Jillian. *We Are All Perfectly Fine*. Toronto: HarperCollins, 2021.

Hoy, Lyndsay, and Aaron Levy (eds.). *Rx/Museum: 52 Essays on Art and Medicine*. Philadelphia: The Barnes Foundation, 2022.

Kabat-Zinn, Jon. *Full Catastrophe Living: Using the Wisdom of Your Body and Mind to Face Stress, Pain and Illness*. New York: Bantam Dell Publishing Group, 2013.

Kee, Elliot Kai, Lissa Latina, and Lilit Sadoyan. *Activity-Based Teaching in the Art Museum, Movement, Embodiment, Emotion*. Los Angeles: Getty Publications, 2020.

Magee, Rhonda V. *The Inner Work of Racial Justice*. New York: TarcherPerigree, 2019.

Offri, Danielle. *What Doctors Feel, How Emotions Affect the Practice of Medicine*. Boston: Beacon Press, 2014.

Puchalski, Christina M., and Betty Ferrell. *Making Health Care Whole: Integrating Spirituality into Patient Care*. West Conshohocken, PA: Templeton Press, 2010.

Remen, Rachel Naomi. *Kitchen Table Wisdom: Stories that Heal*. New York: Riverhead Trade, 1996.

Riess, Helen, with Liz Neporent. *The Empathy Effect: Seven Neuroscience-Based Keys for Transforming the Way We Live, Love, Work and Connect Across Differences*. Boulder: Sounds True, 2018.

Tishman, Shari. *Slow Looking: The Art and Practice of Learning Through Observation*. New York: Routledge, 2018.

Tweedy, Damon. *Black Man in a White Coat: A Doctor's Reflections on Race and Medicine*. New York: Picador, 2016.

Yenawine, Philip. *Visual Thinking Strategies: Using Art to Deepen Learning Across School Disciplines*. Cambridge: Harvard Education Press, 2013.

Zaki, Jamil. *The War for Kindness: Building Empathy in a Fractured World*. New York: Crown Publishing Company, 2019.

A RESOURCE FOR ART MUSEUM AND MEDICAL SCHOOL PARTNERSHIPS

This website, originally documenting the 2016 convening at the Museum of Modern Art, New York, of 135 art museum and medical school professionals, was developed by the Edith O'Donnell Institute of Art History, Center for Art in Health at the University of Texas at Dallas and now lives at the Center for Visual Arts in Healthcare @ Brigham and Women's Hospital, Boston. The website includes program descriptions, bibliographies, and syllabi, and is frequently updated with new information: https://www.artsinhealthcare.org/.

Index

About the Authors

Ruth Slavin (bachelor of arts, history of art, University of California, Berkeley; master of arts, University of Pennsylvania's Annenberg School for Communication) has been a museum educator for thirty-five years, most recently as deputy director for education at the University of Michigan Museum of Art. At University of Michigan Museum of Art, she initiated partnerships with University of Michigan faculty in nursing, medicine, and social work. Since 2009, she has designed gallery experiences, workshops, and elective courses with and for physicians, residents, and medical students on topics including complexity and ambiguity, empathy, storytelling, and mindfulness. Since 2015, she has been the only nonphysician member of the core faculty team for the University of Michigan Medical School's Path in Medical Humanities, an elective that students participate in for all four years of medical school. This rare opportunity to work closely with medical students throughout their training has deepened her understanding of the experiences and needs of both students and clinicians.

Ray Williams (master of arts, art history, University of North Carolina, Chapel Hill; master of education, Harvard Graduate School of Education) is the Director of Education and Academic Affairs at the Blanton Museum of Art, University of Texas at Austin. He also serves as teaching faculty for the Harvard-Macy Fellowship on Art Museum-Based Health Professions Education, consults to the Kern National Network of Caring and Character in Medicine, and recently completed work with the Association of American Medical College's committee on integrating the arts and humanities in medical education. While Director of Education at the Harvard Art Museums, he initiated several partnerships with Harvard-affiliated hospitals that continue today. At the University of Texas, he teaches three museum-based workshops of small groups reaching all first-year medical students at the newly established Dell Medical School, and also works with interprofessional teams in the departments of family medicine, women's health, psychiatry, and palliative care. His work with health professionals has focused on developing curiosity, empathy, and spiritual health; improving team dynamics; and supporting young clinicians in dealing with grief and loss.

Corinne Zimmermann (master of arts, art history, Tufts University; masters of education, Harvard Graduate School of Education) has been a museum educator for thirty years. She currently works as a consultant custom designing museum-based workshops for health professions, business organizations, and museums. Areas of expertise include improving communication and team dynamics, cultivating leadership skills and empathic capacities, mitigating biases, and promoting well-being. Since 2010, she has worked with a broad range of healthcare professionals and organizations including Brigham and Women's Hospital, Mount Auburn Hospital, Cambridge Health Alliance, UMass Memorial Medical Group, Harvard Medical School, and Emory School of Medicine. Corinne is a founding co-director of the Harvard Macy Institute's Art Museum-based Health Professions Education Fellowship and co-founder of VTS@Work™, which offers interprofessional training and certification in the Visual Thinking Strategies. She has co-authored several articles in the *Journal of Museum Education* and the *Journal of Medical Humanities* on the role of museum-based education in health professions education.